JABrand

THE TRINITY—

THE TRINITY

True or False?

James H. Broughton

Peter J. Southgate

"THE DAWN" BOOK SUPPLY

First published 1995

Copyright © James H. Broughton and Peter J. Southgate

Acknowledgements

ISBN 1 874508 01 1

Published by "The Dawn" Book Supply,
66,Carlton Road, Nottingham, NG3 2AP, England

Printed and bound in Great Britain by
The Longdunn Press Ltd, Bristol.

CONTENTS

AUTHORS' FOREWORD

The importance of the subject treated in this book can hardly be overstated. It is admitted on all sides that the doctrine of the Trinity, as we have it at present, is the result of developments in thinking and expression that took place mainly in the first three centuries after Christ. Have those developments obscured the biblical teaching about God and Jesus Christ? How did the recipients of the original Christian message of salvation understand the passages about which there is now so much debate? Would a first century reader of the early Christian documents have reached the same conclusions about them as did later readers? This is what we attempt to address in these pages, using as our sole guide the teaching of the Bible, only supplemented for historical data by the well-documented views of those who lived in those formative years.

Neither of the authors lay claim to any biblical 'scholarship' as it is normally defined. This we see as an advantage because of the independence it confers. Their only qualification for this task is a lifetime's regard for and study of Scripture, and a desire that its teaching should be correctly understood. In the use and meaning of original Greek and Hebrew words we have had to rely heavily on standard works of reference and sometimes the views and comments of the 'experts'. Every effort has been made to ensure such use and meanings have been correctly interpreted; but even if an inadvertent slip may have occurred, we are confident that the main thrust of the book is in no way impaired.

As far as the division of labour is concerned, chapters 4, 5, 7 and the greater part of 3 are the work of Jim Broughton and the balance that of his co-author. Because of the input of two different minds, and especially because the subjects under consideration are so intertwined that divisions become somewhat arbitrary, we are conscious of overlap or duplication in the treatment of some aspects. The reader's indulgence is requested on the few occasions that this occurs.

The authors' preferred Bible translation for this study is the Revised Standard Version, and this is used throughout, except where otherwise indicated. This version is generally considered to be unsurpassed for accuracy—an essential factor in a detailed study such as this—even if its literary merit is surpassed by other versions.

Our thanks are due to several of our fellow Bible students to whom we showed the early drafts, and who made many helpful comments and suggestions.

Above all are we conscious of the greatness and loftiness of the subject of this book, and recognise that it is impossible to even come near to doing justice to so lofty a theme. "My thoughts are not your thoughts, neither are your ways my ways, says the Lord" (Isaiah 55.8). We pray that in attempting to study some of those divine thoughts and revelations found exclusively in His Word, we have done so to the glory of God and to the honour of His Son in whom all His fullness dwells.

P.J.S., J.H.B.

Note on abbreviations:
AV = Authorised Version of 1611 (King James Version).
Gk = Greek
Heb = Hebrew
LXX = Septuagint.
m   = margin
NEB = New English Bible of 1970.
NIV = New International Version of 1978.
NT = New Testament
OT = Old Testament
RSV = Revised Standard Version of 1946-52.
RV = Revised version of 1885.

PROLOGUE

A true story ......

The cemetery chapel was closed for repair, so the members of the small non-conformist Christian group were sitting in the adjacent church that had been made available instead. Outside, the funeral hearse was driving slowly down the road followed by the car carrying the close relatives of the deceased. At the door of the church stood their lay minister ready to receive the sad party and to escort the coffin into the church so that the service could proceed.

But as the hearse drew up at the door the local vicar appeared, and entered into earnest conversation with the minister. As a result the driver was told not to unload the coffin; the congregation in the church were ushered out again, and the whole procession proceeded directly to the cemetery, where the service was eventually conducted in a public shelter.

What was the reason for the sudden change of plan?

It was caused by one inflexible rule of the vicar. "I will not allow any to use my church who do not believe Christ to be God", he said. His conversation had established that this particular Christian group did not believe the doctrine of the Trinity, and so he applied this sanction.

Such an attitude is understandable, you might think, even if it was a little hard and uncharitable to insist on such a rule at an event like a funeral. If a belief in the Trinity is a such a basic teaching of Christianity, the vicar was justified in excluding from his church those who do not believe it.

But *should* the belief that Christ was God actually be a teaching of the Christian church at all?

That is what this book sets out to explore.

1

Chapter 1

"THY WORD IS TRUTH"[1]

The Bible the only source of true revelation

There is no doubt that despite current strivings for unity modern Christianity is a deeply divided religion. Evidence of this is to be found in almost any large city of the Western world. In the average British cathedral town the shadow cast by the towering Gothic edifice of the Church of England falls, figuratively if not literally, upon the humbler buildings of the Baptist or United Reformed Church. Down the street is an Evangelical hall and further off a simple meeting room of The Brethren. In other countries the Roman Catholic Church is dominant, or maybe the Lutheran Church is a major influence. Further east the Greek Orthodox Church takes over from the Rome-based Catholic Church. Thus everywhere the mix of different Churches and sects is apparent. All these sectors of the Christian community obviously have variations in beliefs, tradition, or ritual: otherwise the need for their separation from each other would disappear.

But among this wide spectrum of differing views and divergent practices there is a common thread that unites all these various sections of Christianity—and this is their concept of God. Whether the believer is Roman Catholic or Methodist, High Church of England or Primitive Baptist, Greek Orthodox or the television preacher from the American Bible Belt, virtually all share the view that the Godhead is a trinity composed of three persons, and that one of those persons

---

1. John 17:17

3

assumed human form and came down from heaven to earth for the salvation of mankind.

One writer[1] likens the various components of Christian belief to the parts of a motor car. Some things, such as lights or horn, could be considered non-essential as far as the actual running of the car is concerned, for it can still be driven without them. But some parts are indispensable: the car body for example. It holds all the parts together. Remove it and the car falls apart. The doctrine of the Trinity, he says, is the equivalent of the car body. It is the one basic concept that underlies and unites the whole of the Christian Church.

But the doctrine of the Trinity is usually considered to be more than just the one belief that unites the Christian world. It is also taken to *define* Christendom. God descending to earth and taking human form for man's redemption is regarded as so fundamental to Christianity that it is used as the yardstick to measure those who can appropriately claim the name of Christ. By this rule all who subscribe to the doctrine of the Trinity are classed as Christian, and all who do not believe the doctrine are considered unworthy to bear that name, despite all other criteria. Hence the understandable, even if embarrassing, scene described in the Prologue.

One of the purposes of this book is to explore the relationship between God and Jesus and so test the validity of this frequently made assertion that in order to be a Christian one must believe the doctrine of the Trinity. The authors contend that the boot is really on the other foot, and that it is only among those who *deny* the doctrine of the Trinity that the Christian tradition about God is found in its original form.

---

1. M.Green, *The Truth of God Incarnate*, Hodder and Stoughton, London

Does it matter what we believe about God?

"What does it matter?", it might be asked. "If a person has the basic belief that God exists and that mankind is saved through the work of Jesus, and tries to lead a good life, is it really necessary to understand what could be considered to be the more technical aspects of Christian belief? Let the theologians argue about the doctrines whilst we get on with practical Christianity!"

This approach superficially has a down-to-earth and common sense air to it. But is vagueness in belief altogether a good thing? Does Christianity merely consist of doing good, irrespective of what is believed? Clearly not. It would appear from the incident described in the Prologue that for some people the correct understanding of God *is* important. But, of much more relevance, this is also the teaching of the founder of Christianity himself. On the night before he died Jesus prayed to God on behalf of those who would become believers on him. He said to his Father:

"*This is eternal life*, that they might know thee the only true God, and Jesus Christ whom thou hast sent" (John 17:3).

So, on the authority of Jesus himself, a Christian's eternal life is dependent on his knowledge of God. This means that an enquiry into the nature of God is not something that can be left just to professional theologians, but is a vital exercise for all who are concerned about their salvation. The object of this book is to assist such an enquiry by reverently trying to set out a true understanding of God. This can then lead to *knowing* Him in the more personal sense of the word.

We are not writing with theological scholars in mind. They have written volumes about God, but usually such books are full of their particular jargon. Pick up a book attempting to explain the theology of the Godhead and one usually finds it full of terms such as *deism, theism, kenosis, hypostatic union, communion of the properties, Arianism, Homoiousians,* etc., which may convey something to the author's fellow scholars but leave the ordinary reader completely baffled. By contrast, the present authors' objective is wherever possible to present the true teaching about God in everyday language.

Information about God

Where can we go for information about God?

Most people look to their Church for guidance and instruction, and in seeking to learn about God there is apparently good reason for this. The Church claims that throughout its history it has been guided by the Holy Spirit into all truth. As we have seen, the Church speaks with a virtually unanimous voice about God, and furthermore does so with the authority of centuries of tradition behind it. It will point out that its views on the Godhead have continued virtually unchanged for 1650 years. Way back in the year 325 the basis of the official doctrine of the Trinity was forged out of the controversies raging at that time, and the belief has held almost undisputed sway ever since.

That year 325 saw the important council of Nicea, a town in what is now modern Turkey, at which the trinitarian formula was decided on. This was expressed as the Nicene Creed, which from that day to this has been the definitive church statement concerning the relationship between God, Jesus and the Holy Spirit.

But 325 is still nearly 300 years after the mission of Jesus and the first preaching of the apostles. Can we be sure that in formulating its final statement the church had not perpetuated wrong ideas that had gradually accumulated during those three preceding centuries? Does not the fact that the Council of Nicea was called for the very purpose of resolving *controversies* about this topic raise some legitimate doubts as to whether belief in the Trinity had also been the position of the primitive church and of the immediate disciples of Jesus?

Error predicted

One of the outstanding features of the apostles' preaching was the repeated prediction that soon after their death the original purity of the faith would become corrupted by ambitious men arising from within the Christian movement, and by wrong doctrine imported from outside. Paul's warning to the church at Ephesus is an example:

> "Take heed to yourselves, and to all the flock ... I know that after my departure fierce wolves will come in among you, not sparing the flock; and from among your own selves will arise men speaking perverse things, to draw away the disciples after them" (Acts 20:28-30).

This warning was reiterated by Peter, who said that the new Christian church would not escape the activities of false teachers any more than had the Jews in Old Testament times:

> "But false prophets also arose among the people, just as there will be false teachers among you, who will secretly bring in destructive heresies" (2 Peter 2:1).

At the end of the first century, within 70 years of the death of Christ, the Apostle John referred to some who had already corrupted at least one aspect of the original teaching about Jesus:

> "For many deceivers have gone out into the world, men who will not acknowledge the coming of Jesus Christ in the flesh: such a one is the deceiver and the antichrist" (2 John 7).

In view of this clear prediction by the Holy Spirit that the primitive faith *would be* corrupted, the modern church needs to do more than justify its belief in the Trinity by claiming uninterrupted acceptance of the doctrine back to the third or fourth century. It needs to demonstrate that the tradition went back further still, right to the days of the apostles. This it cannot do. It can only point to a gradual growth of a doctrine that reached maturity at the Council of Nicea. This introduces the possibility, which the authors sincerely believe to be the reality, that the doctrine of the Trinity was not an original Christian belief, but a prime example of the development of false teaching as predicted by the apostles.

Only one authority
Faced with this possibility the only satisfactory course is to accept as authoritative nothing but the original teaching expressed by the founders of the Christian church. In other words our knowledge of God must be obtained exclusively from the words of Jesus and the Apostles and any writings whose trustworthiness they endorse. This means that the Bible, and that alone, is the source of the information about God that is so vital for human salvation.

By the Bible we mean the whole of *both* Old and New Testaments. Most of those who claim to be Christians would accept the authority of the New Testament, but some have reservations about the Old. Such a view overlooks the fact that the Old Testament was the only Bible the first Christians possessed. They regarded it as the sole authority on divine matters, they drew their teaching largely from it, and to them a "thus saith the Scriptures" was an end to all argument.

This was particularly true of Jesus and his apostles. Christ would round on his opponents with a "Have you never read?", and then proceed to base his infallible teaching on the relevant passage from the Old Testament, quoting the words of such men as Moses, David or one of the later prophets. In fact he made acceptance of the Jewish Scriptures an essential pre-requisite for believing on himself:

"If you believed Moses, you would believe me, for he
wrote of me. But if you do not believe his writings, how
will you believe my words?" (John 5:46-47).
"If they do not hear Moses and the prophets, neither will
they be convinced if some one should rise from the dead"
(Luke 16:31).

Jesus accepted the authority of the Old Testament because he
knew that it was his Father's revelation to mankind, produced
by the Holy Spirit power of God acting upon the writers. As
the Apostle Peter was later to say:

"First of all you must understand this, that no prophecy of
Scripture is a matter of one's own interpretation, because
no prophecy ever came by the impulse of man, but men
moved by the Holy Spirit spoke from God" (2 Peter 1:20-
21).

This compulsion to speak and write the words of God is
termed in Scripture *inspiration*, and there are many examples
which show that the writers knew they were speaking God's
words, not their own. Here are some samples:

"The Spirit of the Lord speaks by me, his word is upon my
tongue" (2 Samuel 23:2).
"Hear the word of the Lord" (Isaiah 1:10).
"The word which came to Jeremiah from the Lord"
(Jeremiah 35:1)

The Jewish Scriptures, our Old Testament, are therefore an
infallible source of revelation for all time. They represent the
words of the unchanging God Himself. This is important for
our enquiry into the God of the Bible. One often hears people
contrasting the God of the Old Testament with the God of the
New Testament, as if there were two separate deities. One is
allegedly cruel and vindictive, the other loving and merciful. So
if asked the source of the following two quotations: "Our God

is a consuming fire" and "In his love and in his pity he redeemed them", many would probably instinctively locate the first in the Old Testament and the second in the New. In fact the reverse is true (Hebrews 12.29, and Isaiah 63.9), and many other examples could be given. So these stereotyped concepts of God are completely wrong. The Bible teaching about God is consistent in both the ancient Jewish Scriptures and the later Christian ones. Recognition of this essential unity of teaching throughout both Testaments is vital for a biblical understanding of God.

Turning to the origin and authority of the New Testament we are told that it was written by chosen men within the original Christian community who were also invested with the power of the Holy Spirit. Jesus spoke to them of this impending inspiration:

> "... the Holy Spirit, whom the Father will send in my name, he will teach you all things, and bring to your remembrance all that I have said to you" (John 14:26).

This inspiration, Jesus said, would give the New Testament writers the authority of Jesus and of God Himself:

> "He who hears you hears me, and he who rejects you rejects me, and he who rejects me rejects him who sent me" (Luke 10:16).

On this basis the Apostle Paul could claim:

> "What I am writing to you is a command of the Lord" (1 Corinthians 14:37).

Every genuine follower of Jesus should therefore agree wholeheartedly with Paul's assessment of the authority of Scripture as the infallible guide to Christian doctrine and behaviour:

"All scripture is inspired by God, and profitable for teaching, for reproof, for correction, and for training in righteousness, that the man of God may be complete, equipped for every good work" (2 Timothy 3:16-17).

There is no escaping the meaning of these words. The Scriptures are inspired by God, and are the source of all doctrinal information. In the spirit of this pronouncement the present authors will base their discussions and arguments relating to the doctrine of the Trinity on the Old and New Testaments.

The Authority of the Church

But some will say "Surely, this is also the position of the Church. No Christian would deny that the Bible is the ultimate source of appeal in theological questions." It is true that this is the theoretical position, but in practice the authority of the Church itself is given equal or even greater weight than that of Scripture. One of the dominant ecclesiastical figures of the nineteenth century was John Newman, an Anglican vicar who in later life switched to Rome and eventually became a Catholic Cardinal. If he is at all remembered today it is for his hymn "Lead, kindly Light", but in his day he was well known for his prolific doctrinal writings. He wrote about the doctrine of the Trinity as follows"

"It may startle those who are but acquainted with the popular writings of this day, yet, I believe, the most accurate consideration of the subject will lead us to acquiesce in the statement as a general truth, that the doctrines in question (*viz.,* the Trinity and the Incarnation) have never been learned merely from Scripture. Surely the sacred volume was never intended, and is not adapted to *teach* us our creed; however certain it is that we can *prove* our creed from it, when it has once been taught us ... From the very first, the rule has been, as a matter of fact, for the Church to teach the truth, and then appeal to Scripture in

11

vindication of its own teaching".[1]

Notice the clear implication of these words. The Church formulates the doctrines and then appeals to Scripture in an attempt to support them. This is very different from coming to the Bible with an open mind in order to learn what it teaches.[2]

Another Catholic priest, the Rev James Hughes, was even more outspoken about the real source of Church doctrine in general and the Trinity in particular:

> "My belief in the Trinity is based on the authority of the Church: no other authority is sufficient".[3]

This is a bold, even audacious claim. It alleges that the Church has greater authority in formulating its doctrines and traditions than God's own revelation to mankind. This simply cannot be right. Way back in the days of Israel's prophets God castigated those who disregarded His words:

> "Should not a people enquire of their God? ... To the law and to the testimony! If they do not speak according to this word, they have no light of dawn". (Isaiah 8:19-20 NIV)

Undoubtedly, then, if the doctrine of the Trinity cannot be reconciled with the whole tenor of Scripture, it should immediately be dismissed as spurious—no matter what the Church teaching and centuries of tradition may be.

In those comments of Newman and Hughes do we detect some uneasiness among the advocates of the doctrine of the Trinity? If the biblical evidence for the belief is unassailable

---

1. *Arians of the Fourth Century*, pp55-56

2. For a more detailed examination of this see ch. 8.

3. *Bible Christian*, quoted by White, in "The doctrine of the Trinity"

why does the Church need to justify the doctrine by invoking its own authority? Such a claim suggests that the Bible's support for the Church doctrine is, to put it mildly, not as strong as is generally supposed. A later chapter[1] will show that many theologians down the centuries have admitted that the biblical evidence for the Trinity is indeed very weak.

But not all Christians are members of an Established Church. Many non-conformists and evangelical groups claim to have by-passed the Church and to have gained their teaching directly from Scripture. And they, almost without exception, believe the doctrine of the Trinity. Yet how accurate is their claim that they are guided solely by the Bible and not by church tradition? Professor F.F. Bruce, the noted Manchester University theologian, keenly observed:

"People who adhere to *sola scriptura* (as they believe) often adhere in fact to a traditional school of interpretation of sola scriptura. Evangelical Protestants can be as much servants of tradition as Roman Catholics or Greek Orthodox Christians; only they don't realise that it is 'tradition'".[2]

The seeker after truth, then, will test every belief by Scripture, and will accept nothing that cannot be clearly demonstrated by the Word of God.

But in relying exclusively on the Bible for our understanding of God we must also recognise the fact that the Bible is an ancient book—one of the oldest in the world—and that it was originally written in languages now unfamiliar to most of us, and to a people of an entirely different culture and society. The only way that ordinary people today can understand the Bible is

---

1. Chapter 8

2. Personal communication

because it has been translated into their own language. Recognition of the fact that the English Bible is a translation —for ease of reading often a rather free translation—must always be borne in mind in our attempt to probe its teaching about God.

The Trinity a 'Mystery'

This leads us on to mention another frequent misapprehension about a word often used in relation to the Trinity. We refer to the word 'mystery'. The doctrine of the Trinity is termed a mystery, and the implication is that the relationship between God and Jesus is therefore beyond our understanding. This is based upon the conventional meaning of the word, which implies something inexplicable or unintelligible. Bishop Beverage in his *Private Thoughts on Religion* described the Trinity as the "mystery of mysteries" and went on to call it a "heart-amazing, thought devouring, inconceivable mystery". Such a view may have been prompted by a passage about the coming of Jesus in the writings of the Apostle Paul:

> "Great indeed, we confess, is the mystery of our religion: He was manifested in the flesh, vindicated in the Spirit, seen by angels, preached among the nations, believed on in the world, taken up in glory" (1 Timothy 3:16).

But by using the word translated *mystery* is Paul really saying that Christ's appearance among men is something impossible for us to understand? Not at all. His word had a slightly different meaning. Rather than describing something inexplicable it meant "what is known only to the initiated" (Young's translation). So the idea is that of *secret* information which once divulged is clearly understood by the recipient. Jesus used the word in this sense concerning his parables. The crowd could not see the underlying meaning of the stories, but Jesus explained them to his disciples with the comment:

> "To you it has been given to know the secrets (AV

mysteries) of the kingdom of God; but for others they are in parables" (Luke 8:10).

So Biblical *mysteries* are in fact Biblical *revelations* that all who read with care and understanding can readily grasp. The whole purpose of the Bible is to reveal, not to conceal. This is particularly true of this topic of the relationship between God and His son Jesus. If we allow the whole Bible to speak and if we listen to its voice to the exclusion of all others, this "mystery" becomes crystal clear.[1]

This will be our aim in the following pages.

---

1. The term 'incomprehensible' is also used to describe the Trinity, and by some it is assumed that this also refers to something unknowable. Rather the term means 'unable to be contained or confined' and is correctly used to speak of God's filling all things. "Do I not *fill* heaven and earth? says the LORD" (Jeremiah 23:24).

Chapter 2

"IS THERE A GOD BESIDE ME?"[1]

Church teaching on the relationship between God, Christ, and Holy Spirit

Before we attempt to examine the claims of Trinitarians it would be helpful to define what we are going to discuss. The need for a clear basis and starting point is shown by the fact that the Trinity often means different things to different people. For example a Christian colleague of the writer was quite definite that she thought of Jesus as a subordinate being to God. On being asked "Do you not believe in the Trinity, then?" she replied, "Of course, in theory; but in practice I always think of Jesus as a separate being, distinct from God." This viewpoint is not uncommon. Speaking of the Trinity one writer says:

> "And yet, is it really a living doctrine for the average church member? To be honest, I have a suspicion that many church people deviate from it, to one side or the other. Some are virtually 'tri-theists': the Father, Son and the Holy Spirit are regarded practically as three separate Gods. Others are virtually unitarians: in the practice of their faith the Father alone is God, while Jesus Christ is seen as a special man who reveals the Father, and the Holy Spirit is for them a power rather than a divine Person."[2]

A definition to which all can agree is obviously called for.

---

1. Isaiah 44:8

2. Klaas Runia: *Handbook of Christian Belief*, p.163. Pub Lion, 1982.

16

Developing as it did from the monotheistic Jewish faith outlined in the Old Testament, Christianity has always insisted on the unity of God. The Christian creeds however state that within that one God there are three persons, the Father, the Son and the Holy Spirit. Each of these persons shares equally with the others all the various attributes of the One God. Perhaps the best approach would be to let Trinitarians define the doctrine in their own words. Here is one example from an Anglo-Catholic Manual of Religion:

The Mystery of the Holy Trinity

There is one God in Three Persons,—the Father, the Son and the Holy Ghost. These Three Persons are co-equal in all things. "The Father is God, the Son is God, and the Holy Ghost is God, and yet they are not three Gods, but one God". This is the doctrine of the Holy Trinity, taught by the Church, and proved by the Scriptures. Whilst the Holy Scriptures teach that there is but One God, they speak of each as Divine, and thus prove to us their co-equal Godhead. The doctrine of Trinity in Unity is a great mystery. A mystery is a truth revealed by God which we are therefore bound to believe, but which we are unable fully to understand. Though the doctrine of the Trinity is above the understanding, it is not contrary to it. It is reasonable that there should be mysteries in religion, and above all that there should be mystery about the Being of God. If we could grasp the doctrine of the Trinity, we should ourselves be God....

Though a philosopher cannot explain the doctrine of the Trinity in Unity, a child can believe it. This great truth is not one about which we are to puzzle our minds. We are simply to believe it, because God has revealed it to the Church, and the Church teaches it. Reason becomes lost in wonder, and gives place to adoring faith.[1]

It is owned that this definition of the Trinity is not stated as such in Scripture, but it is claimed, as in the extract above, that it can be *derived* from Scriptural teaching. In answer to the objection that nowhere in the Bible do we find the doctrine of the trinity clearly formulated, the "Handbook of Christian Belief" says, "The Bible gives us not exposition but evidence. The theological formulation took place later, after the days of the apostles."[2]

This 'theological formulation' took place in the fourth and fifth centuries and resulted in the emergence of the Nicene and Athanasian creeds.[3] These represent the formal statement of the doctrine in its final form.

The Nicene Creed
> We believe in one God, the Father Almighty, Maker of all things and invisible.
> And in one Lord Jesus Christ, the Son of God, begotten of the Father, only begotten, that is to say, of the substance of the Father, God of God, Light of Light, very God of very God, begotten not made, being of one substance with the Father, by whom all things were made, both things in heaven and things in earth— who for us men and for our salvation came down and was made flesh, and was made man, suffered, and rose again on the third day; went up into the heavens, and is to come again to judge the quick and dead.
> And in the Holy Ghost.

1. Staley, V., *The Catholic Religion, A manual of Instruction for Members of the Anglican Church*, p.152. Pub: Mowbray

2. Op. cit. p.164

3. For a detailed examination of this development see chapter 8

The Athanasian Creed

The fullest and final statement of the doctrine of the Trinity occurs in the Athanasian Creed, probably dating from the fifth or sixth centuries, which is widely regarded as the definitive statement, at least by the Western Church. The full text of this lengthy creed is given in another chapter,[1] but the following is an extract to indicate its content and style:

'Whosoever will be saved: before all things it is necessary that he hold the Catholick Faith.

Which Faith except every one do keep whole and undefiled: without doubt he shall perish everlastingly.

And the Catholick Faith is this: That we worship one God in Trinity, and Trinity in Unity;

Neither confounding the Persons: nor dividing the Substance.

For there is one Person of the Father, another of the Son: and another of the Holy Ghost.

But the Godhead of the Father, of the Son, and of the Holy Ghost, is all one: the Glory equal, the Majesty co-eternal.

Such as the Father is, such is the Son: and such is the Holy Ghost...

... But the whole three Persons are co-eternal together: and co-equal.

So that in all things, as is aforesaid; the Unity in Trinity, and the Trinity in Unity is to be worshipped.

He therefore that will be saved: must thus think of the Trinity.

The final part of this creed makes salvation possible only to those who accept the doctrine of the Trinity. So, to complete this brief statement of the doctrine it might be asked, Why does the Church believe this doctrine of the Trinity to be so important? Why is the threefold character of God considered so

---

1. See pp. 364-366

necessary for Christian belief? We would like to quote with only the briefest comment the following extract from a more modern work:

"The Importance of the Trinity

"But why do we as Christians make so much fuss about all this? If we cannot understand it anyway, is it not wiser to drop it as a piece of sterile speculation? Does it really have any theological and religious significance? Is it important for our own personal experience? The answer is, Yes. The significance of this doctrine is so great that it is the very foundation of our Christian faith. Why?

♦ "Precisely in this doctrine it becomes clear that God is truly **the living God**, the God who has life in himself, who is literally full of life. Some of the early fathers used a remarkable expression. They said: 'God is *fertile*'. Within the three-in-one God are all the possibilities of person-to-person communication.

"God in no way needed the creation. He was not a lonely God, who had to make a projection of himself, so as to have an 'opposite'. The doctrine of the trinity is the end of all pantheism. If in the depth of his being, God is three-in-one, he does not need this world to come to his full potential. As Emil Brunner put it: 'only if, in himself, from all eternity, God is the loving One, no world is needed for him to be the loving One'.

♦ "The doctrine of the trinity is also of great importance for a proper understanding of the doctrine of **creation**. Brunner again: 'The world as a creation is the work of his love'. The idea of God does not need the world to make it complete. Athanasius told us long ago that, because God is 'fertile' and can communicate himself inwardly, he is also able to communicate himself outwardly. But this inward self-communication does not *require* the outward, since there is already communication within the Godhead.

Through his Son, God freely reached out to create a world. What he made was something other than himself, but he is its foundation and he is its aim.

♦ "This belief in the trinity is equally essential for the doctrine of **revelation**; in fact it is the basis of all revelation. In the revelation of the Father in the Son through the Spirit, we not only receive some external information about God, but we have the guarantee that God himself is speaking to us and opening his divine heart to us. Revelation is really and fully *self*-revelation.

♦ "But above all the doctrine of the trinity is of importance for our **salvation**. It is the answer to the question of whether or not our salvation is really God's work. In the final analysis this is the reason why the church is so vitally interested in the divinity of Jesus Christ and of the Holy Spirit. The vital question to ask about the nature of Jesus Christ is this: In Jesus, do we really meet with God himself?

"The same vital question is at stake in the doctrine of the Holy Spirit. Athanasius wrote: 'If the Holy Spirit were a creature, we would have no fellowship with God in him; in that case we would be alien to the divine nature, so that in no sense would we have fellowship with it.'

"None of this is bald theory. It is echoed in a Christian's personal experience. The believer knows by experience that he is a child of the Father, that he is redeemed by the Son and that the Holy Spirit is in his life. And he also knows that in all three relationships he has to do with one and the same God.

"It is, as it were, a constant moving to and fro; from the Father through the Son to the Holy Spirit in our life, and then again from the Holy Spirit in our life through the Son to the Father. True, we do not always experience this threefoldness as unity. Often the threefoldness in the relationship is more to the fore in our experience than the

21

unity. And yet there is the experience of unity too, especially as the Spirit dwells in us, for in and through the Spirit Jesus Christ himself is present with us, and through Jesus we have fellowship with the Father.

"In spite of this experience, however, it remains a fact that we cannot understand the mystery of the Trinity, let alone take it in. It is far beyond our human thinking. We can only end where we started: by worshipping God the three-in-one. In fact, this was and is the whole reason why the church tries to penetrate this mystery: that we may worship God as he really is; bring him praise, not only for what he has done for us, but above all for what he is in himself. In his worship, the believer will adore God for his incomprehensible greatness and glory."[1]

We will leave the reader to judge whether the above reasons *of themselves* necessitate belief in the Trinity, or whether a similar list could not equally be proposed to show the importance of belief in a single Supreme God who has revealed Himself by other agencies. The reader will also note a heavy reliance on the views of the 'fathers' and human reasoning, and the total lack of Scriptural references in support of such an understanding of the doctrine.

It is to such Scriptures that we now turn in our endeavour to find the true teaching about the Father, Son and Holy Spirit.

---

1. Klass Runia, op. cit. p.174-175

Chapter 3

"THE ONLY TRUE GOD"[1]

What the Bible tells us about the Father

In this chapter we will examine carefully what the Bible has to say about the One who was from the beginning, the Creator and Sustainer of this great universe in which we live, with all its marvellous manifestations of His wisdom and power. The contemplation of all these wonders took David's breath away! How puny are all human achievements by comparison!

> "When I look at thy heavens, the work of thy fingers,
> the moon and the stars which thou hast established;
> what is man that thou art mindful of him...?"
> (Psalm 8:3-4)

Truly, as he says in another Psalm:

> "The heavens are telling the glory of God;
> and the firmament proclaims his handiwork"
> (Psalm 19:1)

Many prophets drew attention to the natural wonders of both heavens and earth as potent witnesses of God's 'eternal power and deity', so that man has no excuse for ignoring the responsibility he bears to his Maker (Romans 1:20). We therefore approach this subject with all reverence, to outline what God has revealed about Himself in His Word. In this

---

1. John 17:3

23

review, whenever we use the word 'God' we refer expressly to the Father of the Lord Jesus. While it is unlikely that the Christian reader will dissent from any of the propositions about to be submitted, it will be necessary to document them in some detail, so that valid comparisons and contrasts may be recognised when we later progress to our consideration of Jesus, the Son of God, and of the Holy Spirit of God (chapters 6 and 5 respectively). In this way the trinitarian claims of the co-equality and co-eternity of the 'three persons in the Godhead' will be very carefully tested by the witness of the inspired Word.

PROPOSITION 1: GOD IS ONE—"THERE IS NO OTHER"

Among the themes that are repeated time and time again throughout the Scriptures, this proposition and declaration is one of the most emphasised. There can therefore be no possible doubt about both its importance and the outstanding need to understand its significance. Trinitarians frankly admit the strength of this emphasis but say: "Certainly, there is one God—we believe that: but in the Godhead are three persons". So often has this been reiterated by them in defence of their doctrine that one tends to forget how basically contradictory such a statement is, especially in the light of a host of Bible passages correctly understood in their context.

Let's suppose for a moment that a schoolteacher wishes to impress on his class that Britain has only one reigning monarch. What choice of words would he employ to make his point beyond any possibility of misunderstanding? "The Queen", he might say, "is the *sole* ruler of the Commonwealth. She neither knows nor recognises any other because *there isn't another*; *she alone* is the supreme ruler". With a dozen repetitions of these unambiguous statements day after day one would hope that even the thickest pupil would get the message, and not begin to wonder whether, after all, there might not be two or even three monarchs on the British throne! In view of Israel's frequent lapses into idolatry over her long history, and God's foreknowledge that His people would be subject to such weakness, it is not surprising that throughout the prophetic writings of the Old Testament He chose to use the same heavy emphasis about His unity, so that the dullest Israelite wouldn't fail to get the point. After several centuries of their national existence and many idolatrous periods this truth has indeed taken root, and now is the central dogma of orthodox Jewish belief. Indeed the pious Jew will die with the words of the 'Shema' on his lips: "Hear, O Israel: the LORD our God is one LORD" (Deuteronomy 6:4). We will not be surprised at the strength of such a conviction when we review the following Old Testament passages (which by no means exhaust the verses bearing on the matter):

"... *there is none like me* in all the earth." (Exodus 9:14)

"that you might know that the LORD is God; *there is no other besides him.*" (Deuteronomy 4:35).

"the LORD is God in heaven above and on the earth beneath; *there is no other*" (Deuteronomy 4:39).

"Hear, O Israel: *The LORD our God is one LORD*" (Deuteronomy 6:4).

"See now that I, even I, am he, and *there is no god beside me*" (Deuteronomy 32:39).

"the LORD is God; *there is no other*" (1 Kings 8:60).

"Thou art the LORD, *thou alone*" (Nehemiah 9:6).

"Let them know that *thou alone*, whose name is the LORD, *art the Most High* over all the earth" (Psalm 83:18).

".... *thou alone art God*" (Psalm 86:10).

"Before me no god was formed, nor shall there be any after me". I, I am the Lord, and *besides me there is no saviour*" (Isaiah 43:10-11).

"I am the first, and I am the last: *besides me there is no God*" (Isaiah 44:6).

> "Is there a God besides me? *There is no Rock[1]; I know not
> any*" (Isaiah 44:8).
> "I am the LORD, and *there is no other, besides me there is
> no God*" (Isaiah 45:5).
> "I am the Lord, and *there is no other*" (Isaiah 45:6, see also
> verse 14)
> "I am the Lord, and *there is no other*" (Isaiah 45:18).
> "... *there is no other god besides me*, a righteous God and a
> Saviour; *there is none besides me*" (Isaiah 45:21).
> "For I am God, and *there is no other*" (Isaiah 45:22).
> "For I am God, and *there is no other; I am God*, and *there
> is none like me*" (Isaiah 46:9).
> "... you know *no God but me*, and *besides me there is no
> Saviour*" (Hosea 13:4).

Let's be honest. Throughout these passages, is there the
slightest hint whatever that God, the great and holy one of
Israel, is in fact two, three, or for that matter thirty-three? "I,
even I, am He, and there is no god besides Me." Note the
pronouns—'I', 'He', 'Me'—is this one person speaking or
several? What other wording *could* have been selected to make
this matter clearer or more precise?

The unity of God in the New Testament
It is frankly admitted by many church leaders, Trinitarians to
a man, that the trinity is *not* taught in the Old Testament[2]. We
have to be thankful for that admission of the obvious and go on
to ask, 'Where then did the doctrine spring from?' The reply
will usually be, 'In the New Testament, for it is there that we
find the fuller revelation of the Godhead.' There is indeed a
fuller revelation there, of God's great purpose being fulfilled in
and through His only Son, but it is not, we shall find, a
revelation which in any way contradicts the Old Testament

---

1. A metaphor for God; see Deuteronomy 32:4.

2. See Chapter 8, pp. 313*ff*

teaching of the Father's unity and uniqueness. On the contrary, that teaching is re-emphasised and endorsed, as we might expect from writings inspired throughout by God. Here is a further list of passages, this time from the New Testament; we need to consider them in detail.

"Jesus answered, 'The first (commandment) is, "Hear, O Israel: *the Lord our God, the Lord is one*"' (Mark 12:29).

"You are right, Teacher; you have truly said that he is one, and *there is no other but he*" (Mark 12:32).

*"Jesus said to him: 'Why do you call me good? *No one is good but God alone*'" (Mark 10:18).

"How can you believe, who ... do not seek the glory that comes from the *only God*?" (John 5:44).

*"And this is eternal life, that they know thee *the only true God*, and Jesus Christ whom thou hast sent" (John 17:3).

*"... to *the only wise God* be glory for evermore through Jesus Christ! Amen" (Romans 16:27).

"To the King of ages, immortal, invisible, *the only God*, be honour and glory for ever and ever. Amen" (1 Timothy 1:17).

*"... the blessed and only Sovereign, the King of kings and Lord of lords, *who alone has immortality* and dwells in unapproachable light, *whom no man has ever seen or can see*" (1 Timothy 6:15-16).

*"To the *only God, our Saviour* through Jesus Christ our Lord, be glory, majesty, dominion and authority, before all time and now and for ever. Amen" (Jude 25).

"... O King of the ages! Who shall not fear and glorify thy name, O Lord? *For thou alone art holy*" (Revelation 15:4).

"... we know ... that *there is no God but one*" (I Corinthians 8:4).

*"yet for us *there is one God, the Father*, from whom are all things" (I Corinthians 8:6).

*"*there is ... one God and Father of us all*, who is above all and through all and in all" (Ephesians 4:6).

27

* *"For there is one God*, and there is one mediator between God and men, the man Christ Jesus" (1 Timothy 2:5).

Christ's endorsement of the Old Testament

The very first quotation listed above shows Christ's firm endorsement of Old Testament teaching. A scribe had asked Jesus which was the first commandment of all, and Jesus replied with the passage from Deuteronomy 6:4 quoted above: "Hear, O Israel: the Lord our God, the Lord is one." The scribe was discerning and responded with approval and added, "You are right, Teacher; you have truly said that He is one and that there is no other than He"—for which, as we have seen, he had plenty of Old Testament backing. Did Jesus take this splendid opportunity to correct the scribe's statement on the basis of trinitarian teaching? Far from it! When he 'saw that the scribe had answered wisely', he told him, 'You are not far from the kingdom of God'. Perhaps the scribe had overheard Christ's earlier reply to the rich young man who had addressed him as 'Good Teacher': 'Why do you call me good? No one is good but God alone.' This is the first of no less than eight passages (marked *) in the above list in which God's unity and uniqueness are proclaimed *in clear distinction to Jesus'position*. Study them one by one. Do they in any way 'confound the persons'? Do they not, each in turn, acknowledge the Father as 'the only God' (especially the first ten), and then add, as quite distinct, some role or position of the Lord Jesus? It will not do to fall back on the excuse that Jesus had temporarily 'relinquished' his godhead status in order to 'become man' and thus spoke as he did. Most of these passages refer to the *post-*resurrectional era when, according to Trinitarians, the Lord had resumed his full honour and glory, and we must take this into account when evaluating the import of these verses. And even those spoken during Christ's earthly ministry exhibit his full support for Old Testament teaching, a support he showed on every occasion and whatever the subject under discussion.

John 17:3 is extremely important in that the gift of eternal life is predicated on a believer's sound knowledge of the Father as 'the only true God', *and* of the Son whom He sent into the world.[1] We are not therefore arguing fine debatable details but the very fundamentals of belief and salvation. C.K. Barrett in his celebrated commentary on John comments on this verse: "The God whom to know is to have eternal life is the only being who may properly be so described; he and, it must be added, *he alone is truly 'theos' (God).*[2] Note too here the order of precedence, repeatedly stated in this Gospel (over 20 times): it is the *Father* who *sent* the Son—a clear indication of the greater directing the subordinate (see further in chapter 6).

The Apostle Paul's testimony

The Apostle Paul, God's chosen vessel to make His name known to the Gentiles, has several of these important passages in his writings. His concluding words to the Romans read: "*to the only wise God* be glory for evermore *through* Jesus Christ." Why make this distinction if the two are 'co-equal'? And why use only for the Father the description 'the *only* wise God'? When discussing with the Corinthians food offered to idols he distinguishes 'one God, the Father' from 'one Lord Jesus Christ' (1 Corinthians 8:6): all things are '*from*' the former but '*through*' the latter— the difference between primary source and vehicle. To the Ephesians he cites seven entities in the 'unity of the Spirit', amongst which are 'one Lord' (clearly Jesus, see 3:11), 'one faith, one baptism, *one God and Father of us all, who is above all* and through all and in all' (Ephesians 4:5-6). He tells Timothy '*there is one God*, and there is one mediator between God and men, *the man* Christ Jesus ...' (1 Timothy 2:5). So Jesus—in his exalted state still styled 'man'— acts as intermediary between God and men—a faithful High Priest for God's household of believers, but clearly not equal in

---

1. Incidentally, this statement may also be understood in reverse, viz. that those granted eternal life will by then have attained a full knowledge of the Father and Son.

2. p.420.

status to his Father, for otherwise there would be little point in this mediatorial role being assigned to him. In chapter 6:15-16 of this same letter it must be perfectly clear that the description "the blessed and *only* Sovereign" applies to the Father, for the sentence concludes, "whom no man has ever seen or can see". Plenty of people saw Jesus in his earthly life; Stephen and Paul saw him in his exalted state (Acts 7:55; 9:17,27), but "no one has ever seen God" (John 1:18; 1 John 4:12). The Apostle Jude's concluding doxology also distinguished between "*the only God*, our Saviour" and "Jesus Christ our Lord" (Jude 25).

"I and the Father are one"

We have listed above fourteen direct New Testament statements reinforcing the Old Testament doctrine of the Father's uniqueness, and half of these making a clear distinction between the role and status of 'the only wise, true and holy God' and that of the Lord Jesus who, as exalted man, is the divinely-appointed mediator between God and man. It is no answer to cite a couple or so of verses *apparently* teaching otherwise, in view of this preponderant testimony. But we will anticipate such a response and look at the verses usually quoted to see whether in fact they really teach the opposite to the above. Most often quoted are Jesus' words in John 10:30: "I and the Father are one", in the context of the Good Shepherd caring for his sheep. The Jews managed, as usual, to misinterpret his statement and they accused him of making himself God (verse 33)—but only because he claimed to be *the Son* of God (verse 36). What then did Jesus mean in verse 30? It is important to recognise that there can be *unity without equality*—a unity of aim, purpose, enterprise. In John 17:22-23, just before his arrest and condemnation, Jesus prayed that all whom God had given him might become one, even as he and his Father were one: "*I in them and thou in me*, that they may become perfectly *one* ..."

Here is a unity, *many* in one, based on identity of conviction and holy living, but clearly not an equality of status. Similarly, a husband and wife become 'one', but scripturally they are certainly not accounted as equal! (see Ephesians 5:22-24; Titus 2:4). Referring to John 10:30, the sense of the Greek might fairly be brought out by rendering the passage "I and the Father *have one purpose*" (viz. the care of the sheep); exactly the same Greek construction is so translated by the New International Version in 1 Corinthians 3:8 "The man who plants and the man who waters *have one purpose*", (literally 'are one', as in John 10:30).[1]

A similar false charge by the Jews appears in John 5:17-18:

> "... Jesus answered them, 'My Father is working still, and I am working.' This was why the Jews sought all the more to kill him, because he not only broke the sabbath but also called God his Father, *making himself equal with God.*"

But Jesus refutes this charge immediately by replying (verse 19): "Truly, truly, I say to you, *the Son can do nothing of his own accord*, but only what he sees the Father doing ..." In fact the charge was palpably false and merely the Jews' own wrong conclusion—*just as the other charge here was equally false*: "he ... broke the Sabbath." Jesus was altogether without sin (John 8:46,29) so there is no question that he transgressed any of the ten commandments. Verse 18 echoes *what the Jews themselves said*, and the sense would be better brought out here by using quotation marks in the appropriate places:

> "This was why the Jews sought all the more to kill him, because 'he not only broke the Sabbath' but also called God his Father, 'making himself equal with God'."[2]

---

1. See also pp. 215*ff*

2. For other examples of this type of implicit quotation, see Corinthians 8:1,4; 10:23 in the RSV.

The only other New Testament passage which comes to mind as apparently teaching the trinitarian kind of unity is found in the Authorised Version text of 1 John 5:7:

> "For there are three that bear record in heaven, the Father, the Word, and the Holy Ghost: and *these three are one.*"

The short answer to this is that these words are known to be spurious, and have been omitted by virtually every subsequent translation (see also p.198). More details of how they came to be included in the AV are recounted by Prof. F.F. Bruce in his "The Books and the Parchments" (1963, p210). He states that the words "first appeared in the work of a Spanish Latin writer named Priscillian who died in 385, then in a few Old Latin authorities, from which they were later imported into the Vulgate text. Erasmus rightly omitted them from his first two printed editions of the Greek New Testament (1516 and 1519)." He only reluctantly included them in the third edition because *one* late Greek manuscript was found to contain them (albeit in a form which betrayed their Latin origin).

To sum up. We have in the *Old Testament* the unity and uniqueness of God repeatedly affirmed in the clearest possible way; the *New Testament* fully confirms this teaching and makes perfectly clear that the birth of God's Son into the world in no way undermined this cardinal doctrine of the Father's supremacy.

PROPOSITION 2: GOD IS ETERNAL—"FROM EVERLASTING TO EVERLASTING"

There is overwhelming testimony to the fact that God is without beginning or end. Abraham "called on the name of the LORD, *the Everlasting God*" (Genesis 21:33). Moses' blessing of Israel concluded with the comforting assurance: "*The eternal God* is your dwelling place, and underneath are *the everlasting arms*"

(Deuteronomy 33:27)—words which are taken up in Psalm 90:

"Lord, thou hast been our dwelling place in all generations. Before the mountains were brought forth, or ever thou hadst formed the earth and the world, *from everlasting to everlasting thou art God"* (Psalm 90:1-2).

Other Psalms conform (93:2; 102:24,27; 106:48), as do the prophets (Isaiah 40:28; Jeremiah 10:10; Habakkuk 1:12), notably Isaiah 57:15: "the high and lofty One *who inhabits eternity*, whose name is Holy"; so too the apostles (Romans 1:20; 16:26; 1 Timothy 1:17; Revelation 4:9; 10:6; 15:3 RV). Needless to say, our finite minds cannot comprehend an eternal existence, nevertheless a study of astronomy compels the recognition of boundless time and space. If we attempt to set limits to these, the question comes immediately—what is beyond those limits? Similarly we cannot imagine anyone or anything bringing God into existence or, in view of His nature (see below), terminating it. The simple testimony of the Word, illustrated in the passages cited, is wholly adequate and satisfying to the enquiring mind. Through the prophet Isaiah God has said it explicitly: "Before me no god was formed, nor shall there be any after me" (43:10), and again, "I am the first and I am the last ..." (44:6). Thus He is literally "from everlasting to everlasting".

PROPOSITION 3:—GOD IS INCORRUPTIBLE

This proposition follows logically on the previous one, especially in the sense of His nature being immortal (i.e. not subject to decay), but it includes *moral* incorruption too—God cannot tolerate sin or wickedness in any form (although He is merciful and forgiving to repentant sinners). Consider the following passages:

"... and changed the glory of *the incorruptible God* for the likeness of an image of corruptible man ..." (Romans 1:23, RV).
"Now unto the King eternal, *incorruptible*, invisible, the only God, be honour and glory for ever and ever" (1 Timothy 1:17,RV).

The moral aspect of God's incorruptibility is frequently referred to in Scripture, as we might expect. Abraham's plea to the Almighty: "Shall not the Judge of all the earth do right?" (Genesis 18:25), is expanded in Moses' farewell song to Israel:

"He is the Rock, his work is perfect, for all his ways are judgment: a God of truth and without iniquity, just and right is he" (Deuteronomy 32:4 AV).

Elihu had similar comments:

"Yea, surely God will not do wickedly, neither will the Almighty pervert judgment" (Job 34:12 AV).

The words of Habakkuk to God are very much to the point:

"Thou who art of purer eyes than to behold evil, and canst not look on wrong ..." (Habakkuk 1:13).
This saying echoes the tribute of the Psalmist:

"Thou art not a God who delights in wickedness; evil may not sojourn with thee" (Psalm 5:4).

Closely related to this theme is God's justice and impartiality (see under Proposition 7, part ii).

The other aspect of incorruptibility concerns *spirit nature*, a Bible theme of which the average reader seems to know very little, yet which leads to certain firm conclusions when the relevant passages are collated, as follows. Jesus said of his

Father: "God is spirit" (John 4:24) and in this he was reflecting God's words in Isaiah 31.3:

> "The Egyptians are men, and *not God*:
> and their horses are flesh, and *not spirit*."

Likewise the angels are "ministering spirits" (Hebrews 1:14, quoting Psalm 104:4). Further, Jesus himself after his resurrection is styled "the Lord the Spirit" and "a life giving Spirit" (1 Corinthians 15:45; 2 Corinthians 3:17-18 RV). What is common to these affirmations, in addition to the term 'spirit', is the fact that all these persons are immortal, as the following table illustrates:

SPIRIT NATURE		IMMORTALITY/ INCORRUPTIBILITY
"God is spirit" (John 4.24)	**GOD**	"The King of ages, *immortal*, invisible (1 Timothy 1:17)
"The Lord the spirit" (2 Cor. 3:17-18,RV)	**JESUS**	"has become a priest ... by the power of an indestructible life (Heb.7:16)
"Ministering spirits" (Hebrews 1:14)	**ANGELS**	
"it is not the spiritual which is first but the physical, and then the spiritual"(1 Cor.15:46)	**BELIEVERS AFTER RESURRECTION**	"they cannot die any more, because they are equal to angels" (Luke 20:36)

Similarly, God's great and precious promises to faithful men and women are that they too will be made partakers of "the divine nature", having escaped the corruption that is in the whole world because of passion (lust) (2 Peter 1:4). The Apostle Paul puts it this way:

> "Now this I say, brethren, that flesh and blood cannot inherit the kingdom of God, *neither doth corruption inherit incorruption*. Behold, I show you a mystery (i.e. a secret).

> We shall not all sleep, but we shall all be changed ... *For this corruptible must put on incorruption, and this mortal must put on immortality.*" (1 Corinthians 15:50-53, AV).

It is not difficult to deduce from these references that spirit nature is the divine nature, immortal and sinless; it is the nature possessed by God and the angels, and by the Lord Jesus after his resurrection—and it is also promised to all who in faith overcome the flesh (i.e. the debased *human* mind) by their allegiance to God's law, for such will be made "like him" (Jesus), their lowly bodies changed to be "like his glorious body" (1 John 3:2; Philippians 3:21).

PROPOSITION 4—GOD IS OMNIPOTENT

There is no lack of Scripture testifying to this proposition that God is all-powerful. God's own title 'the Almighty' is witness to this (see further under 'Titles of Deity').[1] The basic Hebrew word for God, 'el', appears to be closely related to the concept of power, and is sometimes so translated, e.g. in Laban's anger with Jacob when he says "It is in my *power* to do you harm (Genesis 31:29), and again when Jacob named an altar he had built 'El-elohe-Israel' (Genesis 33:20), which the N.I.V. translates as "mighty is the God of Israel". Of more general testimonies we may cite Genesis 18:14: "Is anything too hard for the LORD?"; also Job 42:2 "I know that thou canst do all things, and that no purpose of thine can be thwarted"; also Jeremiah 32:17: "Nothing is too hard for thee ..." From the New Testament we have Jesus' words "With God all things are possible" (Matthew 19:26), as well as the record in Revelation: "We give thanks to thee, Lord God Almighty" (11:17) and "the Lord our God the Almighty reigns" (19:6). The only 'limits' to God's power are those in which He would act inconsistently

---

1. p. 63

with His own principles. Thus we have Paul, in affirming God's faithfulness, declaring that He "cannot lie" (Titus 1:2; see also Numbers 23:19). No sane person is going to charge the Almighty with inconstancy or vacillation in such circumstances.

PROPOSITION 5—GOD IS OMNISCIENT

Again the Bible is replete with proof passages demonstrating that God knows all things. Psalm 147:5: "His understanding is beyond measure"; Isaiah 40:28: "... his understanding is unsearchable." The story of Job illustrates the breadth of God's knowledge and wisdom as well as His power. Indeed all the works of creation manifest that wisdom and knowledge, and David among others marvels at them (Psalm 8:3-5), as we noted at the beginning of this chapter. When summing up the divine purpose to save eventually both Jews and Gentiles, Paul breaks into a paean of praise to God (Romans 11:33):

"O the depth of the riches and wisdom and knowledge of God! How unsearchable are his judgments and how inscrutable his ways!"

A special aspect of God's omniscience is his *foreknowledge*, "... declaring the end from the beginning and from ancient times *things not yet done* ..." (Isaiah 46:10). His great plan to establish His Kingdom on earth, with all its stages (and apparent setbacks), was foreseen and controlled from the beginning, indeed "*before* the foundation of the world" (John 17:24; Ephesians 1:4; 1 Peter 1:20; Revelation 17:8). The lives and characters of men and women are known beforehand, and even their very thoughts are read before they themselves can formulate them. Psalm 139 is specific on this:

"O LORD, thou hast searched and known me ...
thou discernest my thoughts from afar ...
Even before a word is on my tongue,

37

lo, O LORD, thou knowest it altogether" (Verses 1-4).[1]

PROPOSITION 6—GOD IS OMNIPRESENT

Here the Scriptures present us with an apparent paradox, viz. that on the one hand God has a definite location or 'dwelling place', and yet He is said to be present *everywhere* and at all times. Solomon's prayer at the dedication of the temple repeatedly uses the expression: "Hear thou *in heaven thy dwelling place* (1 Kings 8:30,39,43,49), which fact the Lord Jesus endorses in his model prayer: "Our Father who art in heaven ..." (Matthew 6:9). Similarly Hebrews 9:24 speaks of Jesus entering "heaven itself, now to appear in the presence of God on our behalf" (see also Luke 1:19). But Solomon also included in his prayer the rhetorical question:

> "But will God indeed dwell on the earth? Behold, heaven and the highest heaven cannot contain thee: how much less this house which I have built" (1 Kings 8:27).

How then can God at one and the same time be located in a specific place (which the Bible simply calls 'heaven') and yet be present *everywhere*? The most detailed answer is afforded us in Psalm 139:7-12; the passage begins:

> "Whither shall I go *from thy Spirit*?
> Or whither shall I flee *from thy presence*?"

The remaining verses plainly state that nowhere can one be beyond God's sight and control (Jonah discovered this when he attempted to flee from 'the presence of the LORD'). The verse just quoted from Psalm 139:7 is a Hebrew 'parallelism', where 'Spirit' is the equivalent of 'presence' (i.e. of God Himself), so

---

1. See also verses 15-16 of this psalm; Acts 15:18; Romans 9:10-13.

we may say that God is everywhere present *by His Spirit*, i.e. by His power. This power is not a separate 'person' in a trinitarian sense, but God's own mind and disposition (see chapter 5). Through Jeremiah God confirms what we have read in Psalm 139:

> "Am I a God at hand, says the LORD, and not a God afar off? Can a man hide himself in secret places so that I cannot see him? says the LORD. *Do not I fill heaven and earth*? says the Lord" (Jeremiah 23:23-24).

We just mention here (fuller consideration is reserved for chapter 4) "the Angel of the Presence" that God appointed to lead Israel through the wilderness (Exodus 23:20-22). This is an extension of the concept of God's omnipresence, clearly exercised in part through His servants the angels. The Psalmist describes these agents in glowing terms. After a reference to *God's worldwide dominion*, he proceeds to address them:

> "Bless the LORD, O you his angels, you mighty ones who do his word, hearkening to the voice of his word!
> Bless the LORD, all his hosts, his ministers that do his will" (Psalm 103:20-21).

Thus God sees fit to delegate authority to His heavenly servants, who are guiding human affairs towards the establishment of His Kingdom. As God's 'authorised agents' they are an extension of His 'presence'. The subsequent application of this principle to the Lord Jesus is a marvellous feature of the divine revelation and will be the subject of chapter 6, Section 3.

PROPOSITION 7—GOD IS INVISIBLE

The Scriptures teach that God veils Himself from human sight in order that mortal men should not perish instantly in the dazzling and blinding glory of His presence:

> "Who among us can dwell with *the devouring fire*?
> Who among us can dwell with *everlasting burnings*?"
> (Isaiah 33:14)

The first line here is a specific allusion to God's presence on Mount Sinai (Exodus 24:17). Even Moses, who was permitted to draw near to God, was not allowed to see His glory. As it was, the radiance he did receive was sufficient to persist in his face for some time afterwards (Exodus 34:29*ff*).

> "... you cannot see my face; *for man shall not see me and live.*" (Exodus 33:20).
> "No man has ever seen God ..." (John 1:18; 1 John 4:12).
> "Ever since the creation of the world *his invisible nature*, namely, his eternal power and deity, has been clearly perceived in the things that have been made ..." (Romans 1:20).
> "He (Jesus) is the image of *the invisible God ...*" (Colossian 1:15).
> "To the King of ages, immortal, *invisible*, the only God, be honour and glory for ever and ever. Amen." (1 Timothy 1:17).
> "The blessed and only Sovereign, the King of kings and Lord of lords, who alone has immortality and dwells in unapproachable light, *whom no man has ever seen or can see.*" (1 Timothy 6:15-16).
> "... for he (Moses) endured *as seeing him who is invisible*' (Hebrews 11:27).

The combined force of these testimonies, and notably 1 Timothy 6:15-16, leaves no alternative but to conclude that our Creator has a literal brilliance and energy so great that mortal man would not survive an instant in His presence. The reader should note the contrast between this unapproachableness and the access by which people drew near to Jesus, even touching him with their hands (Luke 5:13; 24:39) and vice versa, as well as seeing and handling him (1 John 1:1). Stephen and Saul saw him after his ascension (note the blinding glory in the latter case). At his return too, "every eye will see him, every one who pierced him" (Revelation 1:7).

Jesus himself claimed to have seen the Father (John 6:46). The implications of this will be explored in chapter 6.

PROPOSITION 8—GOD'S MORAL ATTRIBUTES

These include holiness, jealousy for His Name, impartiality, love, compassion, mercy and forgiveness. All these are well known and recognised by those enlightened by the Scriptures, so that for the most part only a few illustrations and confirmatory passages will be quoted. These attributes are of the greatest importance because apart from them there would be no salvation for the human race. Further, they are traits which must also be developed in the characters of all who wish to be included in God's spiritual family, as indeed they were supremely developed in the character of Jesus. Let's review each in turn.

i. God is holy and jealous for His Name
The term 'holy' has a very clear and precise meaning in the Bible. The Hebrew word comes from a root signifying 'to be set apart, consecrated for a particular purpose, dedicated.[1] God describes himself as 'the Holy One of Israel' some forty times in the Old Testament, most of these in the prophecies of Isaiah. The perfection and completeness of God's character *distinguishes* Him altogether from the gods of the nations (as any comparison with the pantheons of Babylon, Greece and Rome will quickly reveal), and He is *jealous* of the honour of

1. Brown, Briggs, and Driver: *A Hebrew and English Lexicon of the Old Testament* p.872, O.U.P.

His Name. He will not tolerate idol worship or any rival of man's invention. Is not this why there is repeated emphasis on the necessity to *know* Him?. Isaiah is particularly scathing against the simpleton who, having chosen a tree out of the forest, uses half to fuel his cooking fire, then sets up the other half as an idol and bows down to it, invoking a mere block of wood to save him! (Isaiah 44:9-20).

Under the Law of Moses God required that His people Israel were to be holy too, distinct and separate from the surrounding nations. Especially were they to shun the abominable practices of the Canaanites whom God was to drive out of the land by Joshua's victorious campaigns (see Leviticus 20:22-26). They were strictly forbidden to indulge in Baal worship and its immoral cult practices, and they were not to tolerate mediums or wizards.

The same principle of separation, in its basic, moral aspects, has also been made binding on Christian believers (see 2 Corinthians 6:14-7:1; 1 Peter 1:14-16). Hence the use of the term 'saints' (i.e. holy, separate ones) applied in the New Testament letters to *all* believers, not to just a select few 'canonised' by the orthodox churches.

ii. God is just and impartial
As God is "Judge of all the earth" (Genesis 18:25) it is right and fitting that He Himself should be the exemplar of justice, and 'no respecter of persons'. Again the Scriptures speak with unanimous voice:

"For the LORD your God is God of gods and Lord of lords, the great, the mighty, and the terrible God, *who is not partial and takes no bribe*" (Deuteronomy 10:17).
"... take heed what you do, for there is no perversion of justice with the LORD our God, or partiality, or taking of bribes" (2 Chronicles 19:7).
"... who shows no partiality to princes, nor regards the rich

more than the poor ..." (Job 34:19).

Peter ... said "Truly I perceive that God shows no partiality, but in every nation anyone who fears him and does what is right is acceptable to Him" (Acts 10:34-35).

"Masters ... forbear threatening, knowing that he who is both their Master and yours is in heaven, and that there is no partiality with him" (Ephesians 6:9).

"and if you invoke as Father him who judges each one impartially according to his deeds, conduct yourselves with fear ..." (1 Peter 1:17).[1]

But God's justice is very much tempered with mercy and forgiveness, as we now proceed to consider with gratitude.

iii. God is merciful and forgiving

After Israel had made the golden calf, Moses successfully interceded with God to forgive them and asked to see God's glory. In response he was favoured with a revelation of God's *character*—His *moral* glory—the beauty of which runs like a golden thread throughout the rest of Scripture:

"The LORD passed before him, and proclaimed, 'The LORD, the LORD, a God *merciful* and *gracious*, slow to anger, and *abounding in steadfast love and faithfulness*, keeping *steadfast love* for thousands, *forgiving* iniquity and transgression and sin, but who will by no means clear the guilty, visiting the iniquity of the fathers upon the children, to the third and the fourth generation" (Exodus 34:6-7).

The mercy and forgiveness of God, both towards individuals and nations, are repeatedly shown in His relationship with Israel, first in the events of the Exodus and the forty years wandering in the desert, and subsequently in their chequered

---

1. See also Deuteronomy 32:4; Psalm 119:137; Nehemiah 9:33; Ezekiel 18:25; Daniel 4:37; 9:14; Romans 2:9-11; Galatians 2:6; Colossians 3:25; Revelation 19:1-2.

history in the land of promise. Psalm 78 summarises their behaviour up to the days of David, and how God repeatedly bore with their backslidings:

> "He restrained his anger often, and did not stir up all his wrath. He remembered that they were but flesh, a wind that passes and comes not again" (Psalm 78:38-39).

After listing Israel's many transgression, the leaders of the returned exiles repeatedly referred to the Exodus declaration—Nehemiah 9:17,19,31; see also Daniel 9:9. The *individual* aspects of forgiveness, shown even to such wicked men as Ahab and Manasseh at the slightest sign of their repentance, will surely give the greatest encouragement to the humble believer of every age, distressed at his own repeated failings. How well it is expressed by the Psalmist!;

> "If thou, O LORD, shouldst mark iniquities, Lord, who could stand? But there is forgiveness with thee, that thou mayest be feared" (Psalm 130:3-4).

These two characteristics of God's character, mercy and grace, form the basis of the proclamation of the divine name YAHWEH (usually rendered JEHOVAH), concerning which we will have much to say in subsequent pages.

iv. God shows steadfastness and faithfulness

These fundamental traits, also included in the Exodus declaration reproduced in the previous section, speak for themselves. There is no vacillation with the Almighty towards those who love Him and keep His commandments. Repeatedly these twin aspects appear together, especially in guaranteeing the eventual fulfilment of the "covenants of promise" made to the Jewish patriarchs.[1]

---

1. See for example Psalm 89:1,2,14,28,33; 92:2; 98:3; 100:5; Micah 7:20;
2 Timothy 2:13; Hebrews 6:13-18 etc.

It is time now to expound these moral characteristics together under a general consideration of God's name YAHWEH, and also relate them to the main titles by which He has made Himself known.

THE NAME AND TITLES OF GOD

Because of its importance in Scripture, whole books have been written on this subject. We propose to examine first the one and only *name* of God (hence the singular 'name' in our heading), and then list in tabular form the meaning and usage of the principal *titles* by which He has been pleased to reveal Himself. (Note the distinction between a 'name', specific to a person or place— e.g. 'Jesus'— and a 'title'—e.g. 'king of Israel'— which at different times could apply to various persons).

GOD'S GREAT NAME: 'YAHWEH'[1]

This, the sole name of the God of Israel, occurs nearly 7000 times in the Hebrew Old Testament, far more often than the title next to it in frequency, viz. ELOHIM (2570 times). It is therefore of prime importance to ascertain its meaning, which was first revealed to Moses at the burning bush in Midian, although this name had already been frequently used in patriarchal times and earlier (see. Exodus 6:3, where "made known" must mean, as elsewhere, 'caused to be understood').

When Moses asked to know God's name (to tell Israel in due course) he was given this cryptic reply (according to the translation in most English versions):

"God said to Moses, "I AM WHO I AM".[a] And he said,

---

1. For adopting this form rather than the commoner 'Jehovah' see Appendix to this chapter, p.61.

45

"Say this to the people of Israel, 'I AM has sent me to you.'" God also said to Moses, "Say this to the people of Israel, 'The LORD,[b] the God of your fathers, the God of Abraham, the God of Isaac, and the God of Jacob, has sent me to you:' this is my name for ever, and thus I am to be remembered throughout all generations ..." (Exodus 3:14-15).

RSV footnotes to this verse:
a. Or I AM WHAT I AM or I WILL BE WHAT I WILL BE.
b. The word LORD when spelled with capital letters stands for the divine name, *YHWH*, which is here connected with the verb *hayah*, to be.

In these verses the words in capitals represent the following Hebrew words respectively: EHYEH ASHER EHYEH, EHYEH and YAHWEH. There can be no doubt that EHYEH normally means 'I will be' rather than 'I am', and is so translated elsewhere, usually in God's affirmation about Himself, such as in verse 12 of this same chapter: "But *I will be* with you ..." However it also occurs with the same future significance in the ordinary conversation of Israelites, e.g.:

"If you bring me home again to fight with the Ammonites, and the LORD gives them over to me, *I will be* your head" (Judges 11:9).
"... you shall be king over Israel, and *I shall be* next to you" (1 Samuel 23:17).
"*I will be* your servant, O king ..." (2 Samuel 15:34).
(other examples will be found in 1 Samuel 18:18; 2 Samuel 16:18-19; Isaiah 3:7; 47:7)

The fuller expression 'EHYEH ASHER EHYEH', when literally translated, will therefore read '*I will be who* (or *what*— ASHER can mean either) *I will be*'. But what does this *mean*? What is the significance of the repetition? J.B.Rotherham, in the introduction to his 'Emphasised Bible', demonstrates that the repetition of the verb either side of ASHER is a common Hebrew idiomatic construction. Here are some examples (his translation):

> "And *they went* whithersoever *they could go*" (1 Samuel 23:13).
> "Seeing *I go* whither *I may go*" (2 Samuel 15:20).
> "And *sojourn* wheresoever *thou canst sojourn*" (2 Kings 8:1).

It will be seen that in English we can omit part of the repetition and still retain the sense. Similarly, in Exodus 3:14, EHYEH ASHER EHYEH means "I will be (or, become) whatever I will (or, please, choose)". The related name YAHWEH is the causative form of HAYAH, 'to be' (Illustrated Bible Dictionary, pp571-572); in its context here it may be translated "He Who causes to be (or, become) what He chooses." The relevance of this is seen when we find that the same construction appears in the preface to *the declaration of the divine Name* in Exodus 34. Moses had asked to see God's glory. God replied:

> "I will make all my goodness pass before you
>   and will proclaim before you my name 'The LORD';
> And *I will be gracious* to whom *I will be gracious*
>   and *will show mercy* on whom *I will show mercy*".
> (Exodus 33:19).

Here again we have ASHER (with the accusative particle ETH) translated 'to whom' and 'on whom', bracketed either side with the relevant verb. In Romans 9:15 the Apostle Paul quotes this verse, and after a reference to Pharaoh's rôle in causing God's name to be proclaimed in all the earth he adds:

> "So then *he has mercy* upon whomever *he wills*" (Romans 9:18),

47

which is clear New Testament confirmation of the correct interpretation of the idiom, viz. "He who becomes what he chooses".

What then *does* God choose to be or become, in fulfilment of the name YAHWEH—'He will cause to be (become) what He chooses'? The answer in Exodus 34:6-7 is this: He chooses to reveal himself as a merciful and gracious God, One who is

> "slow to anger, and abounding in steadfast love and faithfulness, keeping steadfast love for thousands, forgiving iniquity and transgression and sin, but who will by no means clear the guilty ..."

These are the traits of character which God has chosen to associate with His name YAHWEH, the LORD. These attributes are repeated as a golden thread throughout the Old Testament in the many quotations or allusions to this Exodus passage.[1] There is also frequent reference to 'the *memorial name*'—Hebrew 'zikkaron'—i.e. Yahweh—by which God is to be remembered throughout all generations.[2]

It is important to recognise that there are both *past* and *future* aspects of God *making a name* for Himself. The past aspect refers to the fame and honour He gained in the outstanding events of the Exodus of Israel from Egypt—the plagues on the Egyptians and the subsequent miracles during the desert journeys. As He warned Pharaoh through Moses:

> "... for this purpose have I let you live, to show you my power, so that *my name may be declared throughout all the earth*" (Exodus 9:16).

---

1. E.g. Numbers 14:18; 2 Chronicles 30:9; Nehemiah 9:19; Psalm 86:15; 103:8; 111:4; 112:4; 116:5; 145:8; Jeremiah 32:18; Daniel 9:4; Jonah 4:2; cp John 1:14-17.

2. Psalm 30:4; 97:12; 102:12; 111:4; 135:13; Isaiah 26:8; Hosea 12:5.

This purpose was magnificently fulfilled, as Isaiah records:

> "Where is he ... who divided the waters before them, to make for himself an everlasting name? ... *So thou didst lead thy people, to make for thyself a glorious name*" (Isaiah 63:11- 14).[1]

YAHWEH's intervention on His people's behalf had a powerful and devastating effect on the morale of Israel's neighbours and potential enemies, as various incidental references bear witness—see, for example, Joshua 2:8-11; 9:9-10,24; 1 Samuel 4:8— all in fulfilment of God's express promise in Deuteronomy:

> "This day I will begin to put the dread and fear of you upon the peoples that are under the whole heaven, who shall hear the report of you and shall tremble and be in anguish because of you." (Deuteronomy 2:25).

All this is now history. We are told, however, that the main events of the Exodus deliverance of Israel are to be *re-enacted* on a much larger scale in the near future (Isaiah 11:11-16; Micah 7:18-20). God will, at Christ's return to the earth, *again* be manifested, this time by making a new name for Himself—a 'name' embodying all the true believers *in Christ*, His dear Son. Through this 'name' He will declare His glory among all nations (Isaiah 60:9; 66:15-19) and fill the earth "with the knowledge of the glory of the LORD, as the waters cover the sea" (Habakkuk 2:14). The agency for this transformation in world affairs is God manifested in Spirit, i.e., in the servants of Christ raised from the dead and transformed into Spirit nature, to live and reign with him for the millennial age and beyond (more on this in chapter 4, p.78*ff*).

---

1. See also 2 Samuel 7:23; 1 Chronicles 17:21; Nehemiah 9:10; Jeremiah 32:20.

THE CONCEPT OF 'NAME' IN BIBLICAL USAGE

Consider the following definitions of the word 'name' from various sources:

> **'shem'** (= name)—"reputation ... making oneself a name", also: "fame, glory".[1]
>
> **'onoma'** (= name)—"By a usage similar to that with reference to Hebrew 'shem' ... of all that the name implies, of rank, authority, character etc., ... especially the name of God as expressing the divine attributes; ... similarly, of the name of Christ".[2]
>
> **'The Name':** the revelation of God, especially His power and glory."[3]

The 'name' may be used a) for the person himself, or b) for the person's representative or agent, acting with his authority. For the former usage, compare the following verses:

> "Behold, *the name of the LORD* comes from far, burning with his anger, and in thick rising smoke;
> His lips are full of indignation, and his tongue like a devouring fire" (Isaiah 30:27).

> "For behold, *the LORD* will come in fire, and his chariots like the storm-wind,
> to render his anger in fury, and his rebuke with flames of fire" (Isaiah 66:15).

It is clear from this example that the name of the LORD stands for the LORD Himself, or His representative.

---

1. Brown, Driver, Briggs: *Hebrew and English Lexicon of the Old Testament*, p.1028

2. Abbot-Smith: *Manual Greek Lexicon of the New Testament*, p.319

3. NIV Study Bible: footnote to Isaiah 30:27 (quoted below).

As an example of the latter usage, (b), consider the following parallels:

> "I have *manifested thy name* to the men whom thou gavest me ..." (John 17:6).
> "No-one has ever seen God; the only Son, who is in the bosom of the Father, he has *made him known*" (John 1:18).

Elsewhere we have noted Exodus 23:21, where God says concerning the Angel of His Presence "My Name is in him". i.e. the angel has the authority to act for and on behalf of YAHWEH Himself (see next chapter on 'God-manifestation').

In the New Testament we are expressly told that Jesus obtained *by inheritance* a 'name' excelling that of the angels, viz., that he is God's *Son* (Hebrews 1:4). To the Philippians Paul writes:

> "*Therefore*" [because of Jesus' obedience, even to death on a cross] "God has highly exalted him and bestowed on him *the name which is above every name*, that at the name of Jesus every knee should bow, in heaven and on earth and under the earth, and every tongue confess that Jesus is Lord, *to the glory of God the Father*' (Philippians 2:9-11).

When we appreciate that Jesus is the Greek form of 'Joshua', meaning 'Yahweh *saves*', we can see the relevance of these words to the declaration in Isaiah 45:

> "Turn to me and *be saved*, all the ends of the earth! For I am God and there is no other.
> By myself I have sworn, from my mouth has gone forth in righteousness a word that shall not return (i.e. 'be revoked'):
> To me every knee shall bow, every tongue shall swear.
> Only in the LORD, it shall be said of me, are righteousness and strength" (Isaiah 45:22-24).

51

Thus the exalted Jesus has been 'freely given' (charizomai, as in Romans 8:32) by his Father, God's own name YAHWEH which, as God's Son, he has inherited, and with that name all the honour and glory which go with it. The doxology of Revelation 5:13 confirms this favour of the Father towards His Son:

> "To him who sits upon the throne (i.e. God Himself—Revelation 7:15) *and to the Lamb* be blessing and honour and glory and might for ever and ever."

Note again here that the Father is the giver, the Son is the beneficiary; further, as the Philippians quotation says, this is "to the glory of God the Father." Scripture consistently maintains the Father's supremacy over the Son.

The wonderful thing is that the honour and blessing of sharing in the name of YAHWEH is not restricted to the Son, but is offered to all who are willing to submit to God's law. When men and women hear and believe the gospel message, they are invited—indeed commanded—by God to become united with Christ by being *baptised* (i.e. by total immersion in water) *into* (Greek 'eis') *the name of Jesus* (Romans 6:3-5; Acts 8:16; 19:5). By their faith they are kept (guarded) within that name (John 17:12) and, as a seal of ownership, have the name of both Father and Son written on their foreheads (Revelation 14:1).

If the idea of sharing a name seems strange at first sight, think of two well known human institutions: that of *marriage* where, in Britain at least, the bride takes her husband's family name (similarly in Israel—see Isaiah 4:1 and compare Jeremiah 23:6 with 33:16 RV); also the custom of *adoption*, in which children become members of the adopting family and henceforward take their name. Both these arrangements have their Scriptural parallels in the divine plan. Those who are baptised into Christ are collectively *his bride* (2 Corinthians

11:2; Revelation 19:7-8); they are also by that same institution of baptism *adopted sons and daughters* of the Almighty and brothers and sisters of Jesus (Romans 8:14-17,29; Galatians 4:4-7).

These sons (and daughters) are the prospective 'kings and princes' of the coming Kingdom of God on earth (Psalm 45:16-17; Revelation 5:9-10; 2 Timothy 2:12). At Jesus' return he and they will constitute 'the name of YAHWEH', exercising all the power of the Spirit to subject the nations to the laws of God issuing from Jerusalem (Psalm 2:7-11; Isaiah 2:2-4). This 'plurality in unity' or 'many in one' is 'memorialised' in the compound name of God so frequently used in the Hebrew Scriptures: YAHWEH ELOHIM (translated LORD God in most English versions but, from considerations already outlined, to be interpreted as 'He who will be(come) *mighty ones*' (see ELOHIM in the subjoined table). The same concept is implied in Isaiah 41:4:

"I, the LORD, *the first* (singular), and with *the last* (plural); I am He."

In anticipation of this future work, Jesus says of all his faithful followers:

"The glory which thou hast given me I have given to them, *that they may be one even as we are one*, I in them and thou in me, that they may become perfectly one." (John 17:22-23).

The purpose of God in having the gospel preached to the Gentiles is that out of these may be taken '*a people for His name*', as James declared (Acts 15:14), to share with faithful Israel the promises made to the Jewish forefathers.

From this consideration we can see that the 'Name' of God tells us that He chooses to become:

1. A merciful and gracious redeemer.
2. Manifested in His Son.
3. Manifested in the multitude of the redeemed.

These three aspects will be elaborated in the next chapter. Meanwhile it will be useful to consider how the Name and titles of God have been rendered in our English Bibles.

THE ENGLISH TRANSLATIONS OF THE NAME AND TITLES OF GOD

To the English reader there are two main Biblical terms for the Deity, *God* and *Lord,* and these are often regarded as synonymous. But the original readers were presented with a wide range of Hebrew or Greek words to denote God, each with its own meaning. The recognition of this is particularly relevant to our study of the Old Testament, where the original Hebrew text contains different shades of meaning that are easily lost on translation into English. For example, to us the word 'God' conveys the idea of the Supreme Being Himself, and we generally attach this meaning to the word when we read it in the Bible. Yet 'God' or 'god' in the Old Testament is used as a translation of *six* different words in the original Hebrew, some of which clearly do not even refer to God Himself at all. The English word 'Lord' presents even more difficulties—it is used to translate no less than *eleven* completely distinct original words in the Old Testament, and *five* in the New Testament. So when we find the word 'God' or 'Lord' in our Bibles we must remember that whilst usually it is a reference to God Himself *it is not necessarily so in every case*. To appreciate this is obviously vital to our study, and it will be worth while spending a little time explaining the meaning of some of the original words used to describe God.

The situation is not as confusing as might appear at first sight because the AV translators have in most cases used a sort of code to indicate the different original words. This code is easy to miss at first reading, but becomes obvious once it is pointed out. The code consists of the differing use of capital and small letters in the English translations of the original. If you look carefully you will see that in the Old Testament the words describing God are sometimes printed in small (lower case) letters and sometimes in capitals, and sometimes in a mixture of both. The various alternatives are:

God	god	GOD
Lord	lord	LORD
Lord God	LORD God	Lord GOD

In the Greek and Hebrew in which the Bible was originally written some of these words define titles, offices or attributes. In such cases 'God' in our conventional sense is not always intended. For example the word 'Lord' in the English Bible could apply to a human ruler rather than a divine one.

But as well as being titles these words translated 'God' or 'Lord' often contain the personal name of God that we have already considered[1], YAHWEH, sometimes spelled 'JEHOVAH'. In such cases the whole word is always printed in capital letters: as 'LORD' and 'GOD' in the examples above.

It would be useful at this point to look at Scriptural examples of this use of the titles and names. This information is summarised on the table on p.63

Lord. As already mentioned, this is the translation of no fewer than eleven Hebrew words. One of the most frequent is *adon* and its plural *adonim*. The meaning of *adon* conveys the idea of 'master', and is used in this way as a title of both men and God as these examples show:

---

1. p. 45*ff*

"Do not slander a servant to his master (*adon*)"
(Proverbs 30:10).
"Tell my lord (*adoni*) the king" (1 Kings 20:9).
"The Lord (*adon*) of all the earth" (Psalm 97:5)
"And if I am a master (*adonim*), where is my fear, says the
LORD of hosts ...   (Malachi 1.6).

In the first two examples the 'lord' is obviously human, whilst in the third and fourth the same word is clearly used of God Himself.

Adonai is another plural form of *adon*, preferred by the traditional scribes in place of *adonai* when God Himself is being referred to:

"I will give thanks to thee, O Lord (*adonai*) my God"
(Psalm 86:12).
"For the Lord (*adonai*) will not cast off for ever"
(Lamentations 3:31).

These examples show that *adon* can be used of human masters or the divine one. When used of God the word 'Lord' indicates God's supremacy and rulership over all, recognising that He is King and that man is subordinate to Him. This is its fundamental meaning, and no other is implied when the word is used.

The New Testament equivalent of the Hebrew *adon* is *kurios* and has exactly the same meaning of 'master'. Thus in the gospels when the disciples referred to Jesus as 'Lord' they were in general acknowledging him as their master, not attributing any divine status to him.

LORD. As soon as they are printed in capital letters these same four letters take on a different meaning. They are now the translation of the *personal name* of God rather than one of His titles. In the Hebrew this name of God consists of four letters, the English equivalents of which are YHWH. With added vowels this becomes YAHWEH, sometimes rendered JEHOVAH: pious Jews do not dare to pronounce the actual name of God.[1] This is God's personal Name and is generally used only of Him, although there are notable occasions when it is also used of God's agents who carry out His work, the angels for example.

> "I am the LORD (*Yahweh*), that is my name; my glory I give to no other" (Isaiah 42:8).

In the Authorised Version this word is occasionally transferred untranslated, as in this example:

> "That men may know that thou, whose name alone is JEHOVAH, art the most high over all the earth" (Psalm 83:18).

So 'LORD' is a translation of God's name (as distinct from His titles) and is used exclusively of either God Himself, or of those who personally represent Him. An example of such representatives are the angels. As Bishop Burnet observed:

> "Angels carry the name of God when they went on special deputations from Him, the angels being called Jehovah"[2].

An example of this is when God once said:

---

1. Scholars generally accept that because YHWH was not to be pronounced in any form by pious Jews, the vowel 'pointing' belonging to one of the *titles* of God was placed underneath the name. In the combination ADONAI YHWH the vowel points of the word 'Elohim' were inserted under YHWH as a signal to the synagogue reader to use 'Elohim' instead of YHWH, and the combination read as 'Adonai Elohim'. The Gentile translators were ignorant of this device and so put the vowels of 'ADONAI' *into* YHWH, making an inaccurate mixture of the two - JEHOVAH. (See Appendix to this chapter for further details).

2. *Exposition of Thirty-nine Articles,* p.43

"Behold, I send an angel before you ... give heed to him ... do not rebel against him .... for *my name* is in him" (Exodus 23:20-21).

So when such a 'name-bearing' angel appeared to Abraham in company with two 'ordinary' angels he was quite appropriately given God's name of Yahweh. Although the angel was obviously not God Himself, as God's messenger he was empowered to assume God's name:

"The LORD (*Yahweh*) appeared to him .... and behold, three men stood in front of him" (Genesis 18:1-2).

In the description of the conversation that followed, the angel is again given God's name:

"The LORD (*Yahweh*) said to Abraham ...." (v13)

Thus early on in this study the principle is established that whilst 'LORD' is a translation of the personal name of God, it is also used of those whom He has commissioned to work on His behalf.

The other Hebrew and Greek words translated 'Lord' are used fairly infrequently and need not be considered here.

God or **god.** In the Old Testament this is the translation of a variety of words, most of which derive from the Hebrew word *el*, meaning 'a mighty one' (plural: *elim*). These derivations are *elah*, and *eloah* with its plural *elohim*. The terms are used variously to describe the idols of the heathen, the true God of the Bible, angels, or even powerful human figures or rulers.

Some examples will show the range of meaning attached to the words:

To describe *God Himself:*

> "The heavens are telling the glory of God (*el*)" (Psalm 19:1)
> "Hear, O Israel: The LORD (*Yahweh*) our God (*Elohim*) is one LORD (*Yahweh*)" (Deuteronomy 6:4).

To describe *angels:*

> "Thou hast made him (man) a little lower than the angels (*elohim*)" (Psalm 8:5, AV).
> "Who among the heavenly beings (*elim*) is like the LORD (*Yahweh*)" (Psalm 89:6).

To describe *false gods and idols:*

> "Who is like thee, O LORD, among the gods? (*elim*) (Exodus 15:11).
> "You shall have no other gods (*elohim*) before me" (Exodus 20:3).
> "Chemosh the god (*elohim*) of Moab" (1 Kings 11:33).

To describe *human* 'mighty ones', that is, judges and rulers:

> "God has taken his place in the divine council (lit: council of *el*); in the midst of the gods (*elohim*) he holds judgment: How long will you judge unjustly and show partiality to the wicked? .... I say "You are gods (*elohim*)...."(Psalm 82:1-2,6). (Note: Jesus in John 10:34 quotes this in a way that confirms that the reference here is to mortal men.)

To describe the coming *Messiah:*

> "The Mighty God (*el*)" (Isaiah 9:6).

This range of instances of the original words translated 'God' shows that whilst in the majority of cases God Himself is meant, lesser beings are frequently intended. Thus no trinitarian argument can be advanced from the mere occurrence of the Hebrew words translated 'God'.

In the original of the New Testament no distinction is made by the use of different words for God; the Greek word *theos* is used to embrace all the aspects mentioned above.

GOD. As with the word 'Lord' the use of capital letters is here reserved for occasions when the personal name of God is found in the original. Thus:

> "The spirit of the Lord GOD (*Yahweh*) is upon me" (Isaiah 61:1).

LORD God, and **Lord GOD.** In many instances the personal name of God is combined with His titles *adon* (Lord or Master) or *Elohim* (Mighty One). Thus the original of the first example above is *Yahweh Elohim*, meaning 'Yahweh the Mighty One', and in the case of the second *Adonai Yahweh*, 'The Lord Yahweh'.

Although the study of these original terms for God may have seemed tedious or even unnecessary, it will be most useful when in later chapters we come to consider the various references to the relationship that exists between Jesus and his Father. Some knowledge of the original meaning might prevent our jumping to conclusions about this relationship solely on the basis of words used in the English translation.

APPENDIX: The Spelling of God's Name: YAHWEH

According to the Old Testament, the Jews frequently used God's name YAHWEH in everyday conversation, but later generations (on the basis of Exodus 20.7) abstained from pronouncing the word at all. What happened, then, when the Hebrew Scriptures were to be read aloud in temple or synagogue services? They adopted the simple expedient of substituting a title of God, usually ADONAI, in place of YAHWEH, whenever the latter appeared in the sacred text, whether it stood alone or in combination (as in YAHWEH ELOHIM). However, the combination ADONAI YAHWEH also occurs quite frequently, so to avoid a repetition of ADONAI here the title ELOHIM was substituted for YAHWEH; thus both combinations were read out as ADONAI ELOHIM. The Authorised Version distinguishes between these two original combinations by printing the translations as "LORD God" and Lord GOD" respectively (i.e. full capitals represent YAHWEH in the Hebrew text).[1]

In a 'pointed' Hebrew text, i.e. one which supplies the vowels as small dots and dashes *under* the Hebrew letters (which are all consonants), the reader was always reminded of these substitutions by the following expedient:

> the vowel points of the substitute title *replaced* the vowels which would have belonged to the name YAHWEH.

Unfortunately, early translators did not appreciate that this replacement signalled to the reader that he should pronounce the substitute title (either ADONAI or ELOHIM) when reading

---

1. On just seven occasions the A.V. itself uses JEHOVAH instead of LORD or God. The form 'YAH' (A.V. 'JAH' in Psa.68.4) is an abbreviation of Yahweh; it occurs frequently as a component of Hebrew personal names, and 24 times in the compound 'Hallelu-Yah' (plus 4 times in the N.T.)

the text out loud. Instead they proceeded to *incorporate* the substitute vowels into the original consonants. From this misunderstanding arose the form 'JEHOVAH' (more strictly 'Y'H*OV*A*H*), which has the *consonants* YHWH (strictly YHVH) with the *vowels* of AD*ON*A*I*!

The true vowels of YHWH are a matter of debate amongst scholars, but the general consensus is that they were A and E, producing the form 'YAHWEH'. [1]

---

1. See F.F. Bruce: *The Books and the Parchments*, London 1950, pp. 119-120

TITLES OF THE DEITY

Hebrew O.T.	Greek LXX & N.T.	AV	Everyday usage	Basic meaning	Notes and references
ELYON (53)* (of God x31)	Hupsistos (10) (x7 in Luke, Acts)	Most High	upper (town, gate, room) highest (basket, room) (Gen 40.17; Ezek 41.7)	Most High (N.B. *not* connected with EL)	Cp. Isa 6.1;57.15 - "the High and Lofty one; Ex 15.2 "My father's Elohim & I will exalt him". Ps 97.9; 99.2;53.2 etc. (Also x4 in Aramaic, Dan.7)
SHADDAI (48) (x31 in Job)	Pantokrator (10)	Almighty		Beneficent (?)	From 'SHADAD'. *deal violently*, or 'SHADAH', *moisten*, whence SHAD, *breast*. As EL SHADDAI (x7), God of Abraham, I & J, to bless. See Gen 17.1;28.3;35.11;48.3 & note 49.25.
ADON (ca350)	Kurios	Lord	lord, master, owner (e.g. 1 Kings 16.24)	Lord, Owner	Often occurs as Adoni - *My Lord*. Adonim, une plural (often with verb in singular) applied to men 100+ times, e.g. Gen 24.9; Mal 1.6., & must be understood as singular, (so SHADDAI above).
ADONAI (ca.300)	Kurios	Lord		My Lord(s)	Same Heb. consonants as for 'Adoni' (my Lord), but vocalised 'Adonai' whenever applying to God.
EL (217)	Theos	God	power (e.g. Gen 31.29)	Strong One	Applied to men, e.g. Nebuchadnezzar (Ezek. 31.11) as also the plural Elim (but vocalised as *elim* = rams, i.e. mighty men). Applied to angels - lit. 'sons of Elim'. Ps 29.1;89.6. Plural used of gods of nations (x16) & their idols. Note - El Elim (Dan 11.36); 'The God' (x12), 'My God' (x12), 'A jealous God' (x7), 'A living God' (x4)
ELOAH (57)	Theos	God		Strong One	Apparently the same as 'EL'. - cp Neh 9.17 (Eloah) citing Ex 34.6 (El). Used of true God, x52, of which 42 occur in Job.
ELAH (94)	Theos	God		Strong One	Aramaic equivalent of Eloah. Used in Ezra 4.26; Dan. chaps. 2-7. Main word for God in Aramaic, - cp. 'Eloah' in Job, and Muslim/Arabic 'Allah'.
ELOHIM (2570)	Theos	God	God; also 'judges' (e.g. Ex 21.6;22.7-9)	Strong One(s) (pl. of Eloah)	Used with verb in singular when applied to God, also of individual gods of nations. 'Intensive plural of rank', e.g. 2 Kings 11.33 - of Astarte, a goddess! Used of Moses, Ex 4.16;7.1; of Christ, Ps 45.6 (Heb 1.8); of angels, Ps 8.5; 97.7 (Heb 1.6); of gods of nations (over x200), also of idols, images, 'strange', 'false' gods. Yahweh is (the) Elohim (10-8x). Note titles; E. of Jacob (x12); of Abraham (x8); of Abr, Is & Jac (x4); of Abr, Is and Israel (x3); E. of Israel (x200); of Hebrews (x5); E. of David (x4); E. of our father(s) (x57).

---

*The number in parenthesis is the frequency of occurrence

Chapter 4

"MY NAME IS IN HIM"[1]

The Bible teaching of God-manifestation

In the final section of our outline of God's attributes in chapter 3 we cited several passages expressly stating that He is invisible, veiled from mortal sight—"whom no man has ever seen or can see" (1 Timothy 6:16). Yet a number of times in the Old Testament we read of men and women seeing God. For example, after Jacob had wrestled with 'a man' until daybreak, he called the name of the place Peniel (i.e. 'face of God') saying, "*For I have seen God face to face*, and my life is preserved" (Genesis 32:30). Again, after the covenant between God and Israel had been confirmed:

> "Then Moses and Aaron, Nadab and Abihu, and seventy of the elders of Israel went up, and *they saw the God of Israel*: and there was under his feet a pavement of sapphire stone, like the very heaven for clearness. And he did not lay his hand on the chief men of the people of Israel; *they beheld God*, and ate and drank" (Exodus 24:9-11).

Further similar statements include:

> "Manoah said to his wife, 'We shall surely die, *for we have seen God*'" (Judges 13:22).

> "In the year that King Uzziah died *I saw the Lord* (Adonai)

---

1. Exodus 23.21

64

sitting upon a throne, high and lifted up; ... And I said: "Woe is me ... for *my eyes have seen the King*, the LORD (YAHWEH) of hosts!" (Isaiah 6:1,5).

How are we to reconcile these apparently quite contradictory statements? If God is invisible to man how could He be seen on such occasions? Whilst obviously in the vast majority of cases 'God' or 'Lord' means the Creator himself, if we come to the Scriptures with the preconception that the term 'God' *always* means the Creator, the Father of the Lord Jesus, we are going to be in serious difficulties! But preconceptions are just what we must not bring, but rather a humble enquiring mind to ascertain what the Bible itself means by 'God' (and for that matter, any other expression or description it employs). Only a careful examination of its use *in its contextual setting* will provide a legitimate explanation of the term 'God' consistent with the basic teaching of Scripture, as we now hope to demonstrate. We will show that when they were engaged on His work God sometimes permitted other beings to speak as if they were God Himself, indeed even to use His personal Name. This principle we term 'God Manifestation'. Clearly if this is understood it will have far-reaching implications when we consider those passages that speak of Christ as God.

GOD-MANIFESTATION THROUGH ANGELS
The context of the above-quoted passage in Judges 13 shows clearly that it was 'the angel of the LORD' who appeared to Manoah and his wife. "Manoah knew that he was the angel of the Lord" (v21), and it was he, consequently, whom they styled 'God'. Similarly the prophet Hosea, when recalling the incident of Jacob's wrestling to which we have previously alluded, writes of him:

"... in his manhood he strove *with God*.
He strove *with the angel* and prevailed ...
He met God at Bethel, and there *God* spoke with him—

65

the LORD the God of hosts, the LORD is his name"
(Hosea 12:3-5).

In the latter part of this passage Hosea also refers to the God of
Bethel—the place where Jacob made a vow to serve *'the
LORD, the God* of Abraham ... and the *God* of Isaac' (Genesis
28:13*ff*), but in Genesis 31:11, however, this same personage is
styled *'the angel of God'*. Thus in these quotations we have a
clear Scriptural clue which will enable us to solve the apparent
contradiction about whether God has been seen by men or not.

Is there further support for the proposition that in every case
it is 'the angel of the LORD' (remember, when 'LORD' occurs
in capital letters it always denotes the personal Name of God,
Yahweh) who appears on behalf of God and is called 'God'?
There certainly is, as the following testimonies prove:

1. WHEN AN
ANGEL MET
HAGAR
Genesis 16

"*The angel of the Lord* found her by a
spring of water in the wilderness...And
he said 'Hagar, maid of Sarai, where
have you come from' ..." (verses 7-8).
She called the name of *the LORD who
spoke to her,* 'Thou art a God of
seeing'; for she said, 'Have I really
seen God and remained alive after
seeing him?' Therefore the well was
called Beer-lahai-roi (= the well of
one who sees and lives)" (vv. 13-14).

2. WHEN
ABRAHAM
ENTERTAINED
ANGELS
UNAWARES
Genesis 18-19

"*The LORD* appeared to him by the
oaks of Mamre ... *three men* stood in
front of him" (18:1-2)... "*The LORD*
said to Abraham (v13) ... Then the
men set out from there ... The LORD
said 'Shall I hide from Abraham what I
am about to do? (vv16-17) ... I will go
down to see whether they [Sodom and

Gomorrah] have done altogether according to the outcry which has come to me' ... So the men went toward Sodom; but Abraham still stood before the LORD"—[to intercede on behalf of his nephew Lot] (vv21-22). *"And the LORD went his way, when he had finished speaking to Abraham (v33) ... The two angels* came to Sodom in the evening (19:1) ... [*the men* urge Lot to leave] (v12) ... *the angels* urged Lot, saying 'Arise, take your wife ...'"* (v15).

Comment— Much can be learned from this account. The three visitors obviously looked like men and were at first taken to be so (cf. Hebrews 13:2; "some have entertained angels unawares"). The narrative gradually makes it clear that at least two of the three were angels, who went on to Sodom, while the third, as spokesman, was superior and is expressly called 'the LORD'. Abraham clearly recognises his superior status and appeals to him to spare Sodom—even if only ten righteous men can be found there. This 'first of the three' may have been an archangel (only one, Michael, is named in Scripture); in view of the passages about God's invisibility referred to at the beginning of this chapter he certainly was not God Himself. We can therefore dismiss as totally untenable any suggestion that these three were 'the Trinity' or that the name-bearer was Jesus. In the following examples it is clear that **'God'**, **'the LORD'**, and **'angel'** are used almost interchangeably.

3. JACOB
ADMITS
GOD'S CARE
IN HIS LIFE

"And he (Jacob) blessed Joseph, and said,'*The God* before whom my fathers Abraham and Isaac walked, *the God* who has led me all my life long to this day, *the angel* who has redeemed me from all evil, bless the lads...'(Genesis 48:15-16).

4. WHEN AN ANGEL MET MOSES

"*The angel of the LORD* appeared to him [Moses] in a flame of fire out of the midst of the bush ... *God* called to him out of the bush ... '*I am the God of your father, the God* of Abraham, *the God* of Isaac, and *the God* of Jacob.' And Moses hid his face, for *he was afraid to look at God..*'Go and gather the elders of Israel together, and say to them, *The LORD, the God of your fathers, the God of* Abraham,of Isaac, and of Jacob, **has appeared to me**'" (Exodus 3:2,6,16).

5. THE TEN COMMANDMENTS AT SINAI

In Acts 7:38 Stephen, speaking of Moses says: "This is he who was in the congregation in the wilderness *with the angel who spoke to him at Mount Sinai*, and *with our fathers.*" The last phrase must be a reference to the giving of the law, when Moses "brought the people out of the camp *to meet God* ... And *the LORD* came down upon Mount Sinai ..." (Exodus 19:17,20)."And *God* spake all these words, saying, 'I am the LORD your God, who brought you out of the land of Egypt'" (Exodus 20:1-2).

6. ISRAEL'S GUIDE AT THE EXODUS

But who did in fact lead Israel out of Egypt? In Exodus 20:1-2 just quoted it was '*the LORD your God*'—but now consider these passages:
"But *God* led the people round by the way of the wilderness toward the Red Sea" (Exodus 13:18).
"*And the LORD went before them* by

day in a pillar of cloud to lead them along the way, and by night in a pillar of fire .." (Exodus 13:21).

"Then the *angel of God who went before the host of Israel moved* and went behind them" (Exodus 14:19).

"And in the morning watch *the LORD* in the pillar of fire and of cloud looked down upon the host of the Egyptians ..." (Exodus 14:24).

"Now the *angel of the LORD* went up from Gilgal to Bochim. And he said, '*I* brought you up from Egypt, and brought you into the land which I swore to give to your fathers" (Judges 2:1).

"In all their affliction he was afflicted, and *the angel of his presence saved them* ... But they rebelled and grieved his holy spirit ... Like cattle that go down into the valley, the Spirit of the LORD gave them rest. So *thou* didst lead thy people, to make for thyself a glorious name" (Isaiah 63:9-10,14).

Comment—Note that only *one* personage is mentioned at any one time; it is the style of address that varies, sometimes 'the LORD', sometimes 'God', sometimes 'the angel of the LORD' (or of 'God'). In the incidents just considered, it was evidently the LORD who led them but who was *manifested* as the *'angel of his presence'* (as Isaiah calls him), vested with full divine authority, as this further passage shows:

7. PROMISE OF A GUARDIAN ANGEL TO ISRAEL	"Behold, I send *an angel* before you, to guard you on the way and to bring to the place which I have prepared. Give heed to him and hearken to his

voice; do not rebel against him, for he will not pardon your transgression: *for my name is in him*. But if you hearken to *his voice* and do all that *I say*, then I will be an enemy to your enemies, and an adversary to your adversaries. When *my angel* goes before you, and brings you in to the Amorites ..." (Exodus 23:20-23).

Note here the equivalence: when Israel heard this *angel's* voice, they heard *God* speaking! Evidently the angel was a divine messenger with full power (a 'plenipotentiary') both to speak and to act on God's behalf, for he spoke in God's name, and that name he *bore*. Perhaps it was the same angel who appeared to Joshua on the eve of operations to capture Jericho (the chapter division here interrupts the story):

8. JOSHUA AND THE COMMANDER OF THE LORD'S ARMY

"When Joshua was by Jericho, he lifted up his eyes and looked, and behold, *a man* stood before him with his drawn sword in his hand ... *'as commander of the army of the LORD* I have now come ... Put off your shoes from your feet: for the place where you stand is holy' ... And *the LORD* said to Joshua, 'See, I have given into your hand Jericho ... '" (Joshua 5:13-6:2).

9. GIDEON IS COMMISSIONED TO FIGHT MIDIAN

"And *the angel of the LORD* appeared to him and said to him, 'The LORD is with you ...' and Gideon said to him, ... 'why has all this befallen us?' ... And *the LORD turned to him* and said, 'Go in this might of yours ...' And *the LORD* said to him, 'I will be with

> you ...' Then Gideon perceived that he
> was *the angel of the LORD*, and
> Gideon said, 'Alas, O Lord GOD! For
> now I *have seen the angel of the LORD*
> face to face'" (Judges 6:12,13,16,22).

It must therefore be apparent to the discerning reader that whenever we read that 'God' or 'the LORD' appeared to men, it was by *angelic agency* that He was manifested, all necessary authority and power being invested in these heavenly beings, so that they became the mouthpiece of God Himself. Even trinitarian writers, convinced of the pre-existence of Jesus, incline to the interpretation of the facts submitted here.[1]

One might think that such an exalted role would be reserved for the angels alone, as God's immortal messengers (the Hebrew for angel simply means 'messenger'), seeing that they are "all ministering spirits sent forth to serve, for the sake of those who are to obtain salvation" (Hebrews 1:14). On the contrary, God has seen fit, in certain circumstances, to entrust chosen *men* with a comparable status, as we shall now show.

GOD MANIFESTATION THROUGH MEN
But God was not only manifested through angels. 'The book of the Covenant' given through Moses (Exodus 21-23) has an interesting comment about the judges in Israel. As God's representatives they were admonished to hear cases impartially, acquitting the innocent but condemning the guilty. Being 'rulers instituted by God' (Romans 13:1-2) it should not be considered inappropriate that they are called 'God' (i.e. 'elohim'). As a comment in the NIV Study Bible notes (on Exodus 22:11): "the judges were God's representatives in court cases". Consider the following passages:

---

1. See for example *The New Bible Commentary Revised* p.134, and the footnote to Genesis 16:7 in the *NIV Study Bible*.

"But if the slave plainly says,' I love my master, my wife, and my children; I will not go out free', then his master shall bring him *to God* ..." (Hebrew 'elohim', [Exodus 21:5-6]). RV agrees here with RSV but RVm, AV and NIV read *'the judges'*; similarly in the next two passages.

"... the owner of the house shall come near *to God*, to show whether or not he has put his hand to his neighbour's goods".
"For every breach of trust ... the case of both parties shall come *before God*; he whom *God* shall condemn ['condemn' is plural here, to agree with 'elohim'][1] shall pay double" (Exodus 22:8-9).

"You shall not revile *God*, nor curse *a ruler* of your people" (Exodus 22:28). AVm and NIVm have 'the judges' instead of 'God'; the parallelism supports this alternative.

N.B. Girdlestone in his *Synonyms of the Old Testament* (1871) pp 40-42 confirms and amplifies these conclusions.

A special case of the above, which could be easily overlooked, is that of Moses himself. If rulers of thousands and hundreds were appointed to judge smaller matters, while he adjudicated in the more difficult cases (as was agreed following Jethro's suggestion—Exodus 18:24*ff*), Moses was unquestionable 'Lord Chief Justice' in Israel, as well as God's prophet and therefore supreme among Israel's 'elohim'. This was true both as regards Moses' relationship with his people and with Pharaoh. In view of Moses' extreme reluctance to shoulder this burdensome responsibility, God had earlier assigned to Aaron the *public* role of proclaiming His words, but Moses himself was the channel of communication:

---

1. 'Elohim', although a plural, regularly takes the single form of the verb, as is fitting for the 'One God', unless the reference is to pagan 'gods' or, as here, to men deputising for the true God.

"He [Aaron] shall speak for you to the people; and he shall be a mouth for you, and *you shall be to him as God"* (ELOHIM, Exodus 4:16).

"And the LORD said to Moses, 'See, *I make you as God* (elohim) to Pharaoh; and Aaron your brother shall be your prophet ..." (Exodus 7:1).

Moses' special position is further illustrated in certain passages where he makes statements about himself which fundamentally belong to God alone:

"*The LORD* will send upon you curses, confusion and frustration ... because you have forsaken *me* (Deuteronomy 28:20, cp 31:16).

"And Moses summoned all Israel and said to them ...'*I have led you* forty years in the wilderness; your clothes have not worn out upon you ... that you may know that *I am the LORD your God'*" (Deuteronomy 29:2-6).

"And if you will obey my commandments which I command you this day .. *I* will *give the rain for your land* ... And *I* will give grass in your fields for your cattle ... Take heed lest your heart be deceived ... and the anger of the LORD be kindled against you, and *he shut up the heavens, so that there be no rain,* and the land yield no fruit ..." (Deuteronomy 11:13-17, RSV footnote).

The 'I' in verses 14 and 15 of the last passage is a correct translation of the Hebrew text. But sensitive to the apparent 'anomaly' of attributing to Moses power over rain and crop yields, the ancient versions (Samaritan, Greek and Latin) have altered this to 'he' (i.e. God) and the RSV text follows suit, but with the principle of God-manifestation clearly understood, no difficulty need be felt about the verses here cited literally.

The identification of Israel's judges as 'elohim' received full endorsement from the lips of Jesus, when he condemned the rulers of his own day for sitting in judgment on him and coming to an unjust verdict. He quoted a line from Psalm 82, and in so doing illustrated the principle outlined above:

> "The Jews answered him, 'We stone you for no good work but for blasphemy; because you, being a man, make yourself God!' Jesus answered them, 'Is it not written in your law (i.e. Psalm 82:6), "I said, you are gods"? If he called them 'gods' to whom the word of God came (and Scripture cannot be broken), do you say of him whom the Father consecrated and sent into the world, "You are blaspheming", because I said, 'I am the Son of God'?" (John 10:33-36).

So, unarguably, the Scripture called some men 'gods'. Perusal of this psalm reveals a graphic picture of these wicked 'gods', i.e. the judges of Israel, being reproved for their neglect of the poor and needy (see Matthew 23:4,23 and Mark 12:40 as illustration of this neglect). The reprover is also styled 'elohim' (verse1) and in the final verse is bidden to "arise and judge the earth" because he will "inherit all nations". From many other passages we know that this judge and heir is Jesus himself (e.g. Psalm 2:7-8; 72:1-8; Isaiah 9:6-7, 11:1-4; Revelation 19:11-16). This consideration leads us to the next phase in which we can recognise a crucial further stage in the development of God's great purpose with the earth and man.

GOD MANIFESTATION IN JESUS[1]
No-one acquainted with the New Testament Scriptures will dispute the fact that they present Jesus of Nazareth as the greatest manifestation of the God of Israel. Here are some relevant passages:

---

1. See also chapter 6, section 4 'The Word of God'. (pp.218-254)

"And the Word became flesh and dwelt [Greek 'tabernacled'] among us, full of grace and truth: we have beheld his glory, glory as of the only Son from the Father" (John 1:14).

"No-one has ever seen God; the only Son, who is in the bosom of the Father, *he has made him known*" (John 1:18).

"... He who believes in me, believes not in me but in him who sent me. *And he who sees me sees him who sent me*" (John 12:44-45).

"Philip said to him, 'Lord, show us the Father, and we shall be satisfied'. Jesus said to him, 'Have I been with you so long, and yet you do not know me, Philip? *He who has seen me has seen the Father*; how can you say, "Show us the Father"? Do you not believe that I am in the Father and the Father in me? The words that I say to you I do not speak on my own authority, *but the Father who dwells in me does his works*'" (John 14:8-10).

"All this is from God, who through Christ reconciled us unto himself and gave us the ministry of reconciliation; that is, *God was in Christ* reconciling the world to himself ..." (2 Corinthians 5:18-19).

"*He* [margin: Greek 'Who'; other ancient authorities read 'God'; others 'which'] *was manifested in the flesh*, vindicated in the Spirit, seen by angels, preached among the nations, believed on in the world, taken up in glory" (1 Timothy 3:16).

"- the life was made manifest, and we saw it, and testify to it, and proclaim to you the eternal life which was with the Father and was made manifest to us -" (1 John 1:2).

The passage from John 14:8-10 quoted above is particularly enlightening. Clearly we must not *confuse* Father with Son, otherwise we should, in the words of the creed, be 'confounding the persons'! It is a simple fact of life that in most sons we can see the image of their fathers, and this is equally true of the Son of God, as the following verses demonstrate:

"... the glory of Christ, who is the *likeness* of God" (2 Corinthians 4:4).

"He is the *image* of the invisible God, the first-born of all creation" (Colossians 1:15).

"He reflects the glory of God and bears *the very stamp of his nature*" (Hebrews 1:3).

What was this 'glory' that Christ reflected? Apart from the literal brilliance of Jesus during his transfiguration (Matthew 17:2), Jesus did not appear 'glorious' in a physical sense.[1] What in fact the disciples witnessed was the *normal* appearance of Jesus while on earth, but at the same time he was in some way an exhibition of the glory of the Father (John 1:14, 2:11). Clearly Jesus was a perfect manifestation of all the *attributes* of God.

The latter part of John 14:8-10 (quoted above) shows the close parallel between this and previous manifestations of God that we have already considered, viz. that in each case it was *the Father's words* being spoken by the agent of *His* choice, and *the Father's deeds* being done through that same agent. Time and again Jesus makes his own *subordinate* role perfectly clear:

---

1. Although a light from heaven, brighter than the sun, temporarily blinded Saul of Tarsus when Jesus appeared to him on the road to Damascus (Acts 9:3-9, 26:12-13).

"Jesus said to them, 'Truly, truly, I say to you, *the Son can do nothing of his own accord*, but only what he sees the Father doing"
"I can do nothing on my own authority ..."
"... the testimony which I have is greater than that of John; for the works which *the Father* has *granted me* to accomplish ... bear me witness that *the Father has sent me*" (John 5:19,30,36).

"Jesus answered them, *'My teaching is not mine, but his who sent me*: if any man's will is to do his will, he shall know whether the teaching is from God or whether I am speaking on my own authority'" (John 7:16-17).

"I have not spoken on my own authority: the Father who sent me has himself given me commandment what to say and what to speak ... What I say, therefore, I say as the Father has bidden me" (John 12:49-50, see also 14:10 and 17:8).

In Jesus, then, we have not a fresh and different phenomenon of God manifestation, but an *extension* of what God had done previously by angels. He was applying the same principle through a special man, son of the virgin Mary, who was also and uniquely 'Son of God' (although made temporarily 'lower than the angels'—Hebrews 2:5-9). When we 'hear' Christ's words (or, as it is now, read them in the inspired pages of the Bible), we are hearing *God's* words; when we obey Christ's commands, they are *God's* commands given through Christ that we are following. The pattern of Old Testament revelation is logically developed; we should no more confuse the agent with the source in Jesus' case than we would when noting how the angel of the LORD fulfilled what God had commissioned him to do. Nor are we to assume from these simple facts an *equality* of Father and Son, any more than we would infer it in relation to an *angelic* manifestation of the Deity.

But the process does not end here; God's purpose is to bring into being not just one but a *multitude* of sons, to be glorified together with His first-born.

GOD-MANIFESTATION IN BELIEVERS

We have examined some of the numerous Scriptural references to God-manifestation through angels and through the judges of Israel. To these examples one should add the Old Testament *prophets*, whose word was with power to effect whatever God had decreed. They too were His spokesmen and representatives on earth. We have seen also that the greatest manifestation of God's power and authority has been (and always now will be) vested in His dear Son. But Jesus is the firstborn among many sons and daughters of God,[1] who are all to bear His likeness, being heirs with him of the coming kingdom of God on earth.[2]. Because they are to be kings and priests in the age to come, we might reasonably expect that they also will, with Jesus, manifest God's great Name and power in their coming exaltation. This is exactly what we do find quite clearly taught in Scripture. Two phases of this manifestation can be noted. The first was in the apostolic age, and is partly anticipatory of the second. This was when Jesus' apostles were granted miraculous power to perform signs and wonders, explicitly to confirm the truth and authenticity of their preaching.[3] At that time they (like some others, whose fidelity was open to question) had "*tasted* the heavenly gift and the *powers of the age to come*".[4] Clearly the *fuller* use of these same powers is reserved for the second and greater phase— the future kingdom of God. Here are some key passages for each period. Note

---

1. Heb. 2:10; 2 Cor. 6:17-18

2. 1 Jo. 3:2; Eph. 3.6; 2 Tim. 2:11-12

3. Mark 16:20, AV

4. Heb. 6:4-5

particularly that because Jesus has now been given "all authority in heaven and on earth",[1] and because "all the fulness of God" was pleased to dwell in him,[2] the words and deeds of his apostles and prophets are therefore *his* words and deeds, just as his words and deeds were those of his Father.

Phase 1: the Apostolic Age

"*He who hears you hears me*, and he who rejects you rejects me, and he who rejects me rejects him who sent me" (Luke 10:16).

"So *we are ambassadors for Christ*, God making his appeal through us. We beseech you *on behalf of Christ*, be reconciled to God" (2 Corinthians 5:20).

"I am *an ambassador* in chains" (Ephesians 6:20).

Phase 2: the Age to Come

"...in the new world, when the Son of man shall sit on his glorious throne, you who have followed me will also *sit on twelve thrones, judging* the twelve tribes of Israel" (Matthew 19:28).

"Well done, good servant! Because you have been faithful in a very little, *you shall have authority over ten cities*" (Luke 19:17, similarly in verse 19).

"... those who are accounted worthy to attain to that age and to the resurrection from the dead ... cannot die any more, because *they are equal to angels* and *are sons of God*, being sons of the resurrection" (Luke 20:35-36).

"Do you not know that *the saints will judge the world*? ...

---

1. Mat. 28:18; Phil. 2:10

2. Col. 1:19

Do you not know that *we are to judge angels*?" (1 Corinthians 6:2-3).

"... if we endure,*we shall also reign with him*" (2 Timothy 2:12— thus obtaining "the salvation which is in Christ Jesus with eternal glory"—verse 10).

"For it was *not to angels* that God subjected *the world to come* .. As it is, we do not *yet* see everything in subjection to him. But we see Jesus ... crowned with glory and honour ... it was fitting that he, for whom and by whom all things exist, *in bringing many sons to glory*, should make the *pioneer* of their salvation perfect though suffering" (Hebrews 2:5,8-10).

It will be apparent from the foregoing that, in the coming kingdom of God on earth,[1] the glorious reward of those judged worthy of everlasting life will be to share with Jesus not only his throne and personal companionship,[2] but also the honour of ruling the world *in place of* the present (and mainly unseen) control of the angels. Their noble task will be to teach the nations God's law, guiding them into all religious truth and righteous conduct, and in every way manifesting themselves as God's appointed rulers, shepherds and teachers. With all necessary wisdom and power of God bestowed on them (of which the first century miracles were but a foretaste) they will, under Christ's supervision, bring the whole world into subjection to God, ready for "the end". Then the Son of God himself "will also be subjected to him who put all things under him, that God may be everything to everyone".[3] In this way God's great purpose in creating the world, the purpose we

---

1. For a fuller treatment of this important Bible theme see P.J.Southgate: "Thine is the Kingdom", published by Light Bible Publications, Dartford, Kent.

2. Rev. 2:26-27, 3:21.

3. 2 Cor. 15:24,28

understand to be expressed in His name YAHWEH ELOHIM ("He who shall become mighty ones") will be brought to fruition.

In conclusion, we can apply this principle of God-manifest-ation to our present study. We have seen that God in the past invested His agents, be they angels or men, with His own Name. Thus they were able without impropriety to use the personal Name of God when conveying the divine message, although they clearly were not the Almighty Himself. This principle particularly applies to Jesus, who pre-eminently was the manifestation of the Father: "For in him all the fulness of God was pleased to dwell" (Colossians 1:19). But this does not mean that Jesus was therefore God, any more than the previous agents of manifestation had been God.

Chapter 5

"THE POWER OF THE MOST HIGH"[1]

The Nature and Role of the Holy Spirit

Proposition: The Holy Spirit is the Father's mind and power, and not a separate person.

With the sobering words of Jesus very much in mind: "... whoever speaks against the Holy Spirit will not be forgiven, either in this age or in the age to come" (Matthew 12:32), we approach this subject with all reverence. We are nevertheless confident that a humble and honest searching of God's Word to ascertain what it does say on this very important matter will receive commendation and not disapproval.

We will consider this topic within four main sections:

Section 1. The Trinitarian position.
Section 2. Scriptural use of "Spirit" and "Holy Spirit". (p.83)
Section 3. Is the Holy Spirit a person? (p.100)
Section 4. Spirit gifts—Past and present. (p.118)

SECTION 1. THE TRINITARIAN POSITION
By the fourth century A.D. most of Christendom had reached the conclusion that the Holy Spirit was the "third person" of a trinity. The Athanasian Creed sets out this concept in laborious detail (see chapter 8 for an historical sketch of the development

---

1. Luke 1:35

of trinitarian doctrine). For our present purpose it will be sufficient to quote item five of the Church of England's "Articles of Religion", first adopted in 1562:

> "The Holy Ghost, proceeding from the Father and the Son, is of one substance, majesty, and glory, with the Father and the Son, very and eternal God."

Other definitions are considerably more complicated, but even this brief one poses several problems of comprehension to anyone not familiar with the theological terms "Ghost", "proceeding", "substance" and "very". We have shown in chapter 1 (p.14) that it is not valid to claim that the whole subject is a "mystery"; the Scriptures themselves present a simple and straightforward concept, as the proposition at the head of this chapter indicates.

SECTION 2. SCRIPTURAL USE OF "SPIRIT" AND "HOLY SPIRIT"

a) The wide scope of "spirit" in the Old Testament

We need to examine first the various uses of the term "spirit" in the Old Testament, for this is the inspired "background" for a proper understanding of its usage in the New Testament. Incidentally, whether or not to employ an initial capital to the word depends upon the translators' judgment—the original texts do not make this distinction.

'RUACH' is the Hebrew word translated 'spirit' in the O.T. The Oxford *Hebrew & English Lexicon of the Old Testament* (pp 924-926) gives the following basic meanings for RUACH: "*breath, wind, spirit* ("spirit" here signifying temper or disposition). Further, "the spirit of God" is described as impelling the prophets to utter instruction or warning, also imparting warlike energy and executive and administrative power to judges and rulers, especially to the Messianic king, also endowing men with various gifts, e.g. of wisdom and skill." Similarly, in *Young's Analytical Concordance*, the introductory "Hints & Helps to Bible Interpretation", item 66, reads: "SPIRIT—is used of God himself, or the Divine Mind, His energy, influence, gifts; of the vital principle of animals, and of breath, wind, or air in motion, etc. Gen. 1.1; 3.8; 6.3,17; 8.1; 26.35 etc." A few examples of each of these uses will be helpful in laying a foundation for exposition; in each case the references could be greatly multiplied.

In the following examples the italicised word indicates the English translation of the original word under consideration.

RUACH as breath, animating both man and animals (and synonymous with NESHEMAH):
   ".. I will bring a flood of waters upon the earth, to destroy all flesh in which is the *breath* of life from under heaven; everything that is on the earth shall die" (Genesis 6:17).
   "If he [God] should take back his *spirit* to himself, and gather to himself his breath [neshemah], all flesh would perish together, and man would return to dust" (Job 34:14-15).
   ".. when thou takest away their *breath* , they die and return to their dust. When thou sendest forth thy *Spirit* , they are created; and thou renewest the face of the ground" (Psalm 104:29-30).
   "When his *breath* departs he returns to his earth; on that very day his plans perish" (Psalm 146:4).

   See also Ecclesiastes 3:21; 12:7; Isaiah 11:4; Ezekiel 37:9.

RUACH as wind:
   "..And God made a *wind* blow over the earth, and the waters subsided ... ;" (Genesis 8:1).
   "But the LORD hurled a great *wind* upon the sea, and there was a mighty tempest on the sea, so that the ship threatened to break up" (Jonah 1:4).

RUACH as mind, spirit, disposition—
(1) as part of man's natural make-up:

"..[Esau's wives] made life bitter [lit: "they were bitterness of *spirit"]* for Isaac and Rebekah" (Genesis 26:35).

"..[the people] did not listen to Moses, because of their broken *spirit* .." (Exodus 6:9).

"and if the *spirit* of jealousy comes upon him, and he is jealous of his wife who has defiled herself ..." (Numbers 5:14).

"And as soon as we heard it, our hearts melted, and there was no *courage* left in any man, because of you;" (Joshua 2:11).

See also Genesis 41:8; Numbers 14:24; Deuteronomy 2:30; 1 Samuel 1:15; 1 Kings 21:5 and very frequently; cf. God's sending an evil spirit upon Saul (1 Samuel 18:10) and a spirit of confusion upon the Egyptians (Isaiah 19:14).

(2) Imparted by God to man:

"Create in me a clean heart, O God, and put a new and right *spirit* within me"(Psalm 51:10).

"... get yourselves a new heart and a new *spirit*! Why will you die, O house of Israel"? (Ezekiel 18:31).

"A new heart I will give you, and a new *spirit* I will put within you; and I will take out of your flesh the heart of stone and give you a heart of flesh. And I will put my *spirit* within you, and cause you to walk in my statutes ..." (Ezekiel 36:26-27).

"And I will pour out on the house of David and the inhabitants of Jerusalem a *spirit* of compassion and supplication ..." (Zechariah 12:10).

RUACH as God's power, word, mind:
(1) in creation:

"The *spirit* of God has made me, and the breath [neshemah] of the Almighty gives me life" (Job 33:4).

"By the word of the LORD the heavens were made, and all their host by the *breath* of his mouth ... For he spoke, and it came to be; he commanded, and it stood forth" (Psalm 33:6-9).

"Thus says God, the LORD, ... who spread forth the earth and what comes from it, who gives breath [neshemah] to the people upon it and *spirit* to those who walk in it" (Isaiah 42:5).

(Note the parallelism in each of these quotations).

(2) conferring various gifts ...:

"See, I have called by name Bezalel ... and I have filled him with the *Spirit* of God, with ability and intelligence, with knowledge and all craftsmanship ... " (Exodus 31:2-3).

"Thou gavest thy good *Spirit* to instruct them, [i.e. Israel in the desert] ..." (Nehemiah 9:20).

"Then the *Spirit* of the LORD came upon Jephthah, and he ... crossed over to the Ammonites to fight against them;..." (Judges 11:29-32).

"... and the *Spirit* of the LORD came mightily upon David from that day forward" (1 Samuel 16:13).

"And the *Spirit* of the LORD shall rest upon him, (i.e. the Messiah)

the *spirit* of wisdom and understanding,

the *spirit* of counsel and might,

the *spirit* of knowledge and the fear of the LORD.

And his delight shall be in the fear of the LORD" (Isaiah 11:2-3).

"Behold my servant, whom I uphold, my chosen, in whom my soul delights; I have put my *spirit* upon him, he will bring forth justice to the nations" (Isaiah 42:1).

Note these last two quotations, unarguably Messianic in their application. As referring to God's power bestowed on His Son they are clear; but not if taken as referring to a third divine *person* bestowed on a second person.

(3) ... especially to speak God's word:

"...and when the *spirit* rested upon them, they prophesied. ... 'Would that all the LORD's people were prophets, that the LORD would put his *spirit* upon them!" (Numbers 11:25-29).

"The *Spirit* of the LORD speaks by me, his word is upon my tongue. The God of Israel has spoken, the Rock of Israel has said to me ..." (2 Samuel 23:2-3).

"The *spirit* of God came upon Azariah ... When Asa heard ... the prophecy of Azariah ... he took courage .." (2 Chronicles 15:1,   8).

"Then the *Spirit* of God took possession of Zechariah ... and he said to them: 'Thus says God, "Why do you transgress the commandments of the LORD ...?"'" (2 Chronicles 24:20).

"..thou .. didst warn them by thy *Spirit* through thy prophets .." (Nehemiah 9:30).

RUACH as God's omnipresence —please refer back to chapter 3, proposition 6 (page 38).

It will be apparent from a study of the citations made so far (and a concordance will supply many more) that **RUACH** has a wide and varied usage in the Old Testament, but in every case there is the underlying idea of invisible and intangible mind or power.

USE OF THE TERM "HOLY" IN CONNECTION WITH "SPIRIT"

In chapter 3, proposition 8 (p.41), it was explained that "holy", in its Scriptural usage, signifies "set apart for a particular purpose". What then is the special significance of the term *Holy Spirit*? Surely *every* aspect of the Spirit of God (as distinct from man's spirit) is holy, "set apart"? This is so, but particularly when speaking of God's intervention to save men and women through their faith in His promises, and in the redemption through Jesus, the New Testament often uses the phrase "Holy Spirit" rather than simply "the Spirit". Nevertheless very frequently the latter term must, in its context, also mean "Holy Spirit".[1] Apart from this distinction of *purpose* (roughly, either in creation or redemption), it should be clearly recognised that on the divine side there is only *one* Spirit (Ephesians 4:4), *one* mind and power, but in a wide variety of manifestations (c.f. "Gifts of the Spirit" p.118*ff*).[2]

OLD TESTAMENT USE OF "HOLY SPIRIT"

There are only three occurrences in the Old Testament:

> "Cast me not away from thy presence, and take not thy *holy Spirit* from me" (Psalm 51:11).

Here David, deeply repentant over his great transgression with Bathsheba (see psalm title), prays that God would not expel him from His presence, nor withdraw from him the spirit of prophecy with which he had been endowed at his anointing (1 Samuel 16:13; 2 Samuel 23:2; Acts 2:30)—expressly a Holy Spirit gift (2 Peter 1:21). The other two occurrences are:

> "In all their affliction he was afflicted, and the angel of his presence saved them;... But they rebelled and grieved his *holy Spirit*; therefore he turned to be their enemy, and himself fought against them. Then he remembered the days of old, of Moses his servant. Where is he who brought up out of the sea the shepherds of his flock? Where is he who put in the midst of them his *holy Spirit*, who caused his glorious arm to go at the right hand of Moses, who divided the waters before them to make for himself an everlasting name, who led them through the depths? ... Like cattle that

---

1. E.g. Acts 2:4,17,33; 6:5,10; 8:17,18; 11:28 with 2 Peter 1:21 etc.

2. The idea of "free spirit" as a separate entity is based upon a misunderstanding of Psalm 51:12 in the AV. Both the RSV and NIV make it clear that what David was praying for there was a *willing* spirit to be restored to him.

go down into the valley, the Spirit of the LORD gave them rest. So *thou* didst lead thy people, to make for thyself a glorious name" (Isaiah 63:9-14).

This graphic description of God's care of Israel in the wilderness, after redeeming them from Egyptian bondage, refers in verse 9 to the angel of God's presence (Exodus 23:20 *ff*) as the guardian and guide of the people. The references to "his Holy Spirit" might well refer to this angel (the angels are elsewhere described as "ministering *spirits* sent forth to serve, for the sake of those who are to obtain salvation"—Hebrews 1:14). Alternatively, "grieved his holy Spirit" could refer to the sorrow felt by the Almighty Himself over Israel's rebelliousness. In support of this we have Psalm 78:40-41: "How often they ... *grieved him* in the desert! They .. *provoked the Holy One of Israel.*" This thought is picked up by Paul in Ephesians 4:30: "Do not grieve the Holy Spirit of God, in whom you were sealed for the day of redemption." There is no good reason here to divorce "the Spirit of the LORD" from "the LORD" Himself—it was *His* grieving over His people's waywardness, just as it was also His leading them, as verse 14 of the Isaiah passage states.

b) NEW TESTAMENT USE OF "SPIRIT" AND "HOLY SPIRIT"[1]

When we examine the large number of New Testament passages in which "spirit" (or "Spirit") is featured we find many parallels with Old Testament usage. Generally speaking in the N.T. the Greek *pneuma* is used as the equivalent of the O.T. Hebrew *ruach*. In view of the New Testament emphasis on God's great purpose to save both Jew and Gentile through the new covenant in Christ Jesus it is not surprising that the

---

1. AV "Holy *Ghost*" - "derived from Old English **'gastlic'** ghost-like, where 'ghost' = spirit, soul, breath, the breath of God". (E Partridge: "Origins" London: Routledge & Kegan Paul 4th edn 1966). RV puts "Holy Spirit" in margin, subsequent translations consistently use it in the text.

majority of verses refer to God's *Holy* Spirit, either expressly so-named or simply as "the Spirit" where the context implies "the Holy Spirit" (c.f. footnote references on page 5.7). Nevertheless the foundation ideas of breath, wind or disposition are very much in evidence, with a remarkable number of passages presenting the Holy Spirit as an invisible fluid medium, able to be "poured out". The following list repeats the sequence of themes already exemplified from the Old Testament; in nearly every case the Greek word is "pneuma", with "hagion" (holy) where added:

PNEUMA as breath:

"For as the body apart from the *spirit* is dead, so faith apart from works is dead" (James 2:26).

"And when he had said this, he breathed [enephusesen[1]] on them, and said to them, 'Receive the Holy *Spirit*'" (John 20:22).

"... the Lord Jesus will slay him with the *breath of his mouth* ..." (2 Thessalonians 2:8).

"All scripture is *inspired by God* .." (2 Timothy 3:16; Greek: theopneustos—God-breathed).

"But after the three and a half days a *breath* of life from God entered them, and they stood up on their feet .." (Revelation 11:11).

PNEUMA as wind:

"The *wind* blows where it wills, and you hear the sound of it, but you do not know whence it comes or whither it goes .." (John 3:8).

"..a sound came from heaven like the rush of a mighty wind [pnoe] .. And they were all filled with the Holy Spirit .." (Acts 2:2,4).

"Of the angels he says, 'Who makes his angels *winds* ..'" (Hebrews 1:7).

---

1. Similarly in the LXX of Genesis 2:7 and Ezekiel 37:9

PNEUMA as mind, disposition:

".. My soul magnifies the Lord, and my *spirit* rejoices in God my Saviour" (Luke 1:46-47).

"Blessed are the poor in *spirit*, for theirs is the kingdom of heaven" (Matthew 5:3).

"And the child grew and became strong in *spirit*..." (Luke 1:80).

".. and being fervent in *spirit*, he (Apollos) spoke and taught accurately the things concerning Jesus .." (Acts 18:25).

"for God did not give us a *spirit* of timidity .." (2 Timothy 1:7).

PNEUMA as God's power:

"The *Holy Spirit* will come upon you, and the *power of the Most High* will overshadow you; therefore the child to be born will be called holy, the Son of God" (Luke 1:35).

"And behold, I send the promise of my Father upon you; but stay in the city, until you are clothed with *power* from on high" (Luke 24:49).

"But you shall receive power when the *Holy Spirit* has come upon you;" (Acts 1:8; literally: ... power, the Holy Spirit coming upon you").

"...how God anointed Jesus of Nazareth with the *Holy Spirit* and [or: "even"] with power; .." (Acts 10:38).

"May the God of hope fill you with all joy and peace in believing, so that by the power of the *Holy Spirit* you may abound in hope" (Romans 15:13).

".. what Christ has wrought through me .. by the power of the Holy Spirit .." (Romans 15:18-19).

".. my speech and my message were .. in demonstration of the *Spirit* and [or: "even"] power, that your faith might .. rest .. in the power of God" (1 Corinthians 2:4-5).

Even a cursory glance through this last set of passages will demonstrate the close connection between the Holy Spirit and power. But several of them go further than this. They require us to recognise that the two are identical. Luke 1:35 is a typical example of this, where Hebrew parallelism—the same thought repeated in different words—requires us to equate "the Holy Spirit" *with* "the power of the Most High": i.e. the two are one and the same. Similarly, the literal translation (in parentheses) of Acts 1:8 shows "power" and "the Holy Spirit" grammatically parallel with one another.[1] Christ's promise of the *Holy Spirit* as the Counsellor in John 14-16 (see pages 5.23-31) was repeated in Luke 24:49, where it is described as being *"clothed with power* from on high". Again the two terms are seen as interchangeable. The last four references in the above list fall readily into the same category. It could also be said that in harmony with the foregoing, in Acts 10:38 and 1 Corinthians 2:4-5, the "and" could legitimately be translated as "the Spirit *even* power" by the figure of "epexegesis"[2].

PNEUMA as God's mind

In the Old Testament the prophet Isaiah, extolling God's uniqueness and His majesty and power in creation, wrote (Isaiah 40:13):

"Who has directed the *Spirit* of the LORD, or as his counsellor has instructed him?"

But when the inspired apostle Paul quotes this passage (using the Greek Septuagint translation), he twice renders the phrase as "*mind* of the Lord":

"For who has known the *mind* of the Lord, or who has

---

1. The same association is exhibited in Gabriel's prophecy about Zechariah's son John, the Baptist: "He will go before him [the Lord] *in the spirit and power of Elijah* ..." (Luke 1:17). Unlike Elijah, "John did no sign" (John 10:41), so by the figure of hendiadys (i.e. 'one through two') this passage should read: "in the *powerful spirit* of Elijah."

2. I.e. "added words to clarify the meaning;" Winer's "Grammar of New Testament Greek" pp 545-546 lists a number of examples of this figure of speech.

been his counsellor?" (Romans 11:34).
"For who has known the *mind* of the Lord so as to instruct him? But we have the mind of Christ" (1 Corinthians 2:16).

Thus *spirit* and *mind* are equivalent terms. But the Corinthians quotation has a very instructive context which brings out an important point about the relationship of God to His spirit. The apostle refers to the human mind in a simple analogy:

"For what person knows a man's thoughts except the spirit of the man which is in him? So also no one comprehends the thoughts of God except the Spirit of God" (v.11).

Clearly "the spirit of the man" referred to here *is the man's own mind, part of him* . It is certainly not a separate person. We use *spirit* in this sense in everyday speech when we speak of someone being happy or sorrowful or bitter *in spirit*. And Paul uses a similar analogy to describe the relationship of God and His spirit. *God's* Spirit is part of *Him*, His *mind* in fact, just as the spirit of man is *his* mind, as the verse so clearly shows. Thus the *mind* or *spirit,* is *not* to be interpreted as a separate entity from the person.

The importance and implications of this necessary conclusion can scarcely be over-stated and may well be described as an axe laid to the root of the trinitarian tree! The Spirit of God is *His* mind, His agent, not a separate person.

And the *mind* of God has been revealed to mankind by the process of "inspiration" (literally "in-breathing"). Inspiration has made possible the enlightenment of those who seek Him by expounding and interpreting His purpose in creating our world. It "came mightily"[1] upon the men and women whom God

---

1. cp. Judges 14:6

selected to further His plan of salvation. And in particular, "men moved by the Holy Spirit"[1] spoke and wrote the Holy Scriptures, the Word of God. Hence Paul's statement, already quoted: "All scripture is inspired by God".[2]

PNEUMA and God's word of command and power
We have seen that in the O.T. *spirit* is used to describe the word of God in action. This was illustrated in the passages quoted in connection with creation, notably Psalm 33:6,9, which follows the repeated Genesis 1 pattern: "And God said .. *and it was so*". Similarly in the N.T. *spirit* and God's spoken commands are often regarded as synonymous. Thus Paul exhorts the Ephesians to

"take ... the sword of the *Spirit,* which is the *word of God"* (Ephesians 6:17).

In this reference the English reader is likely to understand the "word of God" as referring to "the sword", but the original makes it clear that the word "which" belongs to "Spirit" and not to "sword".[3] Thus it is unambiguously "the sword of *the Spirit word of God"*.[4] In the same vein the writer to the Hebrews speaks of Christ "upholding all things by the *word of his power* (Hebrews 1:3).

Such passages illustrate that "the word of power"—whether it be from the mouth of God or Jesus, or the prophets and

---

1. 2 Peter 1:21

2. 2 Timothy 3:16

3. Marshall's Interlinear Translation footnote, in loc.

4. Note in passing that this association of "sword" and "Spirit word" graphically explains one item in the figurative description of one who is named "the *Word of God"* in the book of Revelation: "... *from his mouth* issues a sharp *sword* .. " with which he will make war against both individuals and nations (Rev. 19:15).

apostles who likewise performed miracles of healing and raising the dead—is describing the effect of the spirit of God at work.

PNEUMA as Christ's mind and power

The observant reader will have noticed that the references just quoted apply to Jesus as well as to his Father. This should occasion no difficulty once the previously examined implications of 1 Corinthians 2:11 are followed through:

> "For what person knows a man's thoughts except the spirit of the man which is in him? So also no one comprehends the thoughts of God except the Spirit of God" (v.11).

Applying this to Jesus it means that the Spirit of Christ is *his* (i.e. Christ's) mind, part of him and again not a separate person. During his earthly ministry Jesus totally dedicated himself to fulfilling his Father's will, doing nothing of his own accord, but only what he saw the Father doing [1]; as he also said: "The words that I say to you I do not speak on my own authority; but the Father who dwells in me does his works. Believe me that I am in the Father and the Father in me ..."[2]. In short, Jesus was completely of *one mind* with his Father.[3] With his victory over sin and death, and all authority given him in heaven and on earth, Jesus has become God's "chief executive" and plenipotentiary, to watch over the household of believers and "bring many sons to glory".[4] Thus, Spirit power has been fully vested in Jesus by his Father, and is the central aspect of "the work of the Spirit" in the field of salvation. In

---

1.John 5:19

2. John 14:10-11

3. On very similar lines "the spirit of Elijah" rested on Elisha (2 Kings 2:15) and much later on John the Baptist (Luke 1:17). Was this spirit a separate *person* from these prophets?

4. Matthew 28:18; Hebrews 2:10 - see Marshall's comment on this in his introduction, p.xvii.

confirmation of this we find "the Holy Spirit", "the Spirit of your Father", "the Spirit of Christ" and "the mind of Christ" used interchangeably. This is demonstrated in the following passages:

1. "for it is not you who speak, but the *Spirit of your Father* speaking through you" (Matthew 10:20).

2. "... for it is not you who speak, but the *Holy Spirit*" (Mark 13:11).

3. "... *I* [Jesus] will give you a mouth and wisdom, which none of your adversaries will be able to withstand or contradict" (Luke 21:15).

4. "But they could not withstand the wisdom and the *Spirit* with which he [Stephen] spoke" (Acts 6:10).

5. "... having been forbidden by *the Holy Spirit* to speak the word in Asia ... they attempted to go into Bithynia, but the *Spirit of Jesus* did not allow them" (Acts 16:6-7).

6. "... because the *Spirit intercedes* for the saints according to the will of God ... (Romans 8:27). Who shall bring any charge against God's elect? ... who is to condemn? Is it *Christ Jesus ... who indeed intercedes* for us?" (v33-34).

7. "... because you are sons, God has sent the *Spirit of his Son into our hearts*, crying, 'Abba, Father!'" (Galatians 4:6).
8. "My little children, with whom I am again in travail until *Christ be formed in you*!" (Galatians 4:19).

9. "... For I know that through your prayers *and the help of the Spirit of Jesus Christ* this will turn out for my deliverance" (Philippians 1:19)

10. "Now the *Lord [Jesus* c.f. 4:5-6] *is the Spirit* ... for this

comes from the *Lord* who is *the Spirit"* (2 Corinthians 3:17-18).

Reviewing these passages in order of citation, note first the gospel parallels in (1), (2), and (3), where "the Spirit of your Father" = "the Holy Spirit" = "I" (Jesus); and where (4) records a fulfilment of this promise. Passages (5), (7) and (8) each use the various terms in such close context as to be virtually synonymous. Similarly, unless we are to infer the existence of *two* quite distinct intercessors with the Father, we must assume in (6) that "the Spirit" v27 is the same as "Christ Jesus" in v34—i.e. *one* faithful high priest acting on behalf of his flock. As Paul writes elsewhere: "For there is one God, and *there is **one** mediator* between God and men, the man Christ Jesus .."[1]—"since he always lives *to make intercession* for them".[2] The reference in Philippians (9) neatly and decisively confirms our assumptions and (10) *identifies* Jesus with "the Spirit".

In no case have we here a separate agent with its own volition. The *Spirit* is clearly the mind or power of God or Jesus at work on behalf of the believers.

There is one other aspect under this heading which needs consideration. It is the apostle Peter's description of the Old Testament prophets puzzling over statements they made by the Spirit, the significance of which was hidden from them:

> "The prophets ... inquired what person or time was indicated by the *Spirit of Christ* within them when predicting the sufferings of Christ and the subsequent glory" (1 Peter 1:10-11).

---

1. 1 Timothy 2:5

2. Hebrews 7:25

Does this mean that Christ was already alive ("pre-existed") in Old Testament times? No, for in this same chapter Peter writes of Jesus(verse 20 RV): "... who was *foreknown* indeed *before the foundation of the world*, but was *manifested at the end of the times* for your sake." In many and various ways God spoke by the prophets of the coming Messiah; the testimony they bore to Jesus is "the spirit of prophecy".[1]

SUMMARY SO FAR

Our argument so far (and this will be expanded in Section 3) is, simply, that the Holy Spirit is not itself a person. Instead it is the manifestation of the mind and/or power of another person already clearly defined in Scripture—in the Old Testament this means God Himself (directly or through His agents); and in the New Testament, it defines the word and/or power of the Father or the Son. This spirit power operated either directly or through selected agents, including both angels and "holy men".

Let us test this by a typical example. When Paul and Barnabas were called to undertake missionary work amongst the Gentiles we read:

> "While they [in the Antiochan church] were worshipping the Lord and fasting, the *Holy Spirit* said, "Set apart for me Barnabas and Saul for the work to which I have called them"" (Acts 13:2).

This is clearly the *Spirit of Jesus* speaking, in fulfilment of the very purpose for which Jesus himself had appeared to Saul of

---

1. Revelation 19:10. However, the statement is ambiguous; translators and commentators are broadly divided between rendering the (literal) words "the testimony of Jesus" as either "the testimony borne *by* Jesus" or " ... *to* Jesus". Alford's Greek Testament, in loc, comes down strongly in favour of the latter interpretation for contextual reasons, and is supported by J B Phillips, Weymouth, Schonfield, the Translator's New Testament and the New American Bible; the construction (simple genitive) is the same as that of John 2:17: "the zeal of (= concerning) your house", and is adopted here.

Tarsus on the road to Damascus.[1]

Similarly, Paul told the Ephesian elders at Miletus that the Holy Spirit had forewarned him of imprisonment and afflictions awaiting him in every city (a warning repeated by the prophet Agabus when Paul reached Caesarea[2]). Again, this will be recognised as the intimation of Jesus himself or his Father. There are indeed plenty of examples in Acts where Jesus, simply styled "the Lord",[3] intervenes to guide his servants.[4]

Sometimes the (Holy) Spirit seems to be used as an alternative for the angel of the Lord. Thus an *angel* instructed Philip the Evangelist to approach the Ethiopian eunuch, but later in the narrative "*the Spirit* said to Philip 'Go up and join this chariot'".[5]

Personal pronouns applied to the Spirit

Once the "person" is understood as the one *manifesting* these Holy Spirit powers, not the power itself, it will be seen that there is no problem about the employment of personal pronouns such as "he", "who", etc., in connection with the Holy Spirit. They refer back to Jesus, his Father or an angel, as the context and parallelism so often demonstrates. The widespread popular view of "a *third* person" is the result of faulty thinking, based on a long history of erroneous indoctrination. Our own conclusion, reached from a careful analysis of Scriptural usage, receives powerful support from the following further considerations which do not seem to have occurred to most Trinitarians.

---

1. See Acts 9:4-6,15-16; 20:24; 22:17-21; and notably 26:15-18.

2. Acts 20:23; 21:11.

3. Acts 2:36

4. E.g. Acts 7:55-56; 9:5, 10*ff*; 18:9; 23:11.

5. Acts 8:26,29

SECTION 3. IS THE HOLY SPIRIT A PERSON?

The trinitarian claim is that there are three 'persons' in the Godhead, one of whom is God the Holy Spirit. Is this understanding borne out by Scriptural references and allusions?

(1) INTRODUCTORY SALUTATIONS IN PAUL'S LETTERS

Every one of Paul's epistles contains an introductory salutation that includes reference to God and Jesus:

> "Grace to you and peace from God our Father and the Lord Jesus Christ" (Romans 1:7; 1 Corinthians 1:3; 2 Corinthians 1:2).
> "Grace to you and peace from God the Father and our Lord Jesus Christ" (Galatians 1:3).
> "Grace to you and peace from God our Father and the Lord Jesus Christ" (Ephesians 1:2; Philippians 1:2).
> "Grace to you and peace from God our Father" (Colossians 1:2).
> "To the church of the Thessalonians in God the Father and the Lord Jesus Christ: grace to you and peace" (1 Thessalonians 1:1).
> "Grace to you and peace from God the Father and the Lord Jesus Christ" (2 Thessalonians 1:2).
> "Grace, mercy, and peace from God the Father and Christ Jesus our Lord" (1 Timothy 1:2; 2 Timothy 1:2, also see 4:1).
> "Grace and peace from God the Father and Christ Jesus our Saviour" (Titus 1:4).
> "Grace to you and peace from God our Father and the Lord Jesus Christ" (Philemon 3).

Is it not an extraordinary thing that if Paul, *the* apostle to the Gentiles, were convinced of trinitarian doctrine, he should exclude this third "equal and eternal person" from all his greetings! And more strangely still, where in the body of one letter he *does* include a further name, it is *not* the Holy Spirit:

"In the presence of God and of Christ Jesus *and of the elect angels* I charge you to keep these rules without favour ..." (1 Timothy 5:21)

If the Holy Spirit was a third member of the Trinity why was it omitted in favour of the angels, who indisputably are of lower status? Here, to add weight to this argument, are two comparable passages where reference to the Holy Spirit is lacking and one to the angels included. Would a 'God the Holy Spirit' be absent from the scenes described here?:

"For whoever is ashamed of me and of my words, of him will the Son of man be ashamed when he comes in his glory and the glory of the Father and *of the holy angels*" (Luke 9:26).
"I [Jesus] will confess his name before my Father and *before his angels*" (Revelation 3:5).

What a contrast this makes to the endless repetition of the trinitarian doxology in church liturgy throughout Christendom! If the Holy Spirit exists as a separate person, why this repeated omission?

(2) NO WORSHIP OF THE HOLY SPIRIT

Careful students of the Scriptures have also noted that although there are innumerable verses describing worship offered to God the Father, many also to His Son, and at least a few to men,[1] there is *no place* where the Holy Spirit is said to be worshipped, or a command to do so is given! Again, what a contrast with church practice.

---

1. e.g. 1 Chronicles 29:20; Matthew 18:26; Revelation 3:9

(3) THE FATHER OF JESUS

There is an inherent contradiction in trinitarian doctrine over the identity of the father of Jesus. All Scripture and reason recognises God the Father (in trinitarian parlance "the first person") as the begetter of Jesus. Do Trinitarians ever ask themselves how it is that the Father is the father of Jesus, when actually he is described as being begotten of the Holy Spirit? The angel Gabriel told Mary:

> "'The Holy Spirit will come upon you, and the power of the Most High will overshadow you; therefore the child to be born will be called holy, the Son of God"' (Luke 1:35).

And in Matthew's record we read:

> "Now the birth of Jesus Christ took place in this way. When his mother Mary had been betrothed to Joseph, before they came together she was found *to be with child of the Holy Spirit*" (Matthew 1:18).

The begetter here is expressly stated to be the Holy Spirit, who, according to trinitarian teaching, was "the third person" and not "the first"! Where is Jesus ever called the Son of the Holy Spirit?. What are we to believe—this false teaching or the straightforward declaration that Jesus was begotten by *"the power of the Most High"*, as Luke's parallelism makes perfectly clear?

(4) IS A "PERSON" DIVISIBLE INTO FRACTIONS?

If the Holy Spirit is a person, yet another serious objection involves the *partial* bestowal of one person upon another:

> "And in the last days it shall be, God declares, that I will pour out my Spirit upon all flesh .. yea, and on my menservants and my maidservants ... I will pour out my Spirit; and they shall prophesy" (Acts 2:17-18).

The Authorised and Revised Versions have here the literal rendering (in both places) *"of* my Spirit", meaning *"some* of my Spirit". The same Greek preposition (apo) is used in Mark:

> "When the time came, he sent a servant to the tenants, to get from them *some of* [apo] the fruit of the vineyard" (Mark 12:2).[1]

On the Acts 2:17-18 passage Weymouth's translation has a footnote: "literally 'of' or 'from' My Spirit—a *share* or *portion.*" In the sense of sharing a power there is no difficulty, but how possibly can one receive a fraction of a *person*?

Nor is this the only occurrence of this concept; we have also:

> "By this we know that we abide in him and he in us, because he has given us *of his own Spirit*" (1 John 4:13).

Here a different preposition (ek—"out of") is used, but the import is the same. Schonfield's "Authentic New Testament" reads: "Has given us *some of* his own Spirit;" the "Translator's New Testament" and "Today's New Testament" read: "a *share* of his Spirit", and Weymouth "a *portion* of ..."[2] A *person* cannot be portioned out in this way, but a *power* easily can be.

(5) IS A "PERSON" A "FLUID"?

The Acts passage just considered (2:17) poses a further problem to Trinitarians, viz. how a "person" can be "poured out" on others. This expression is to be found in not a few biblical texts besides that quoted by Peter from Joel 2:28-29 (see also Proverbs 1:23; Isaiah 32:15; 44:3; Ezekiel 39:29;

---

1. For further examples see Luke 6:13; John 21:10; Acts 5:2.

2. Parallel examples using "ek" will be found in Luke 8:3; 1 Corinthians 9:7; 10:17; Galatians 4:19; Ephesians 4:13.

Zechariah 12:10; Acts 10:44-45; Romans 5:5; Titus 3:6). In most of these passages, if not in all, the analogy of anointing with oil is being used (with Acts 10:38 compare 1 John 2:27). The likeness of Spirit to a fluid (either liquid or, in the case of wind and breath, a vapour) underlies many diverse New Testament references. For example, the Spirit is likened to "rivers of living water" (John 7:38-39): the Corinthians were a letter from Christ "... written not with ink but with the Spirit of the living God" (2 Corinthians 3:3), and they had been "made to drink of one Spirit" (1 Corinthians 12:13). The Ephesian believers were exhorted not to drink wine but to be filled with the Spirit (Ephesians 5:18). These analogies are consistent with an invisible motivating or controlling *power,* but are they fitting—even compatible—with a *person?*

(6) THE WITNESS OF "ACTS"

Yet another serious problem for the trinitarian believer is the "deafening silence" of the record in "Acts of the Apostles" about the alleged "three persons of the Godhead". Over half this book is concerned with the Jewish scene, mainly in Jerusalem but also in Judea and Samaria, and in synagogues abroad. There can be no shadow of doubt that the strong monotheism of Jews and Samaritans would have flared up instantly and vehemently, had the apostles preached anything remotely savouring of trinitarian doctrine. But on this subject Luke is silent throughout; not a hint, not a whisper of such contention does he mention, and the only reasonable and fair conclusion is that such novel teaching was totally absent from "the words of salvation" proclaimed in the earliest decades of the Christian era. False doctrine on this subject first appears in the writing of the sub-apostolic church fathers, after the entry of "fierce wolves" into the flock as Paul had warned (Acts 20:29)—many of them only half-converted Greek philosophers, whose speculations are known to have included concepts of a triune godhead. This historical trend is described in chapter 8.

"THE COUNSELLOR, THE HOLY SPIRIT"

The conclusions we have come to from our analysis of many Scriptural references to the Holy Spirit (see pp.83*ff*) may now be applied to the series of passages on "the Comforter" in John 14-16. Trinitarians consider these to be some of the strongest evidence for believing in the existence of a "third person" in the Godhead. It will be helpful at the outset to reproduce the passages in full and then examine the detailed statements of each:

"If you love me, you will keep my commandments. [16]And I will pray the Father, and he will give you another Counsellor, to be with you for ever, [17]even the Spirit of truth, whom the world cannot receive, because it neither sees him nor knows him; you know him, for he dwells with you, and will be in you. [18]I will not leave you desolate; I will come to you" (John 14:15-18).

"These things I have spoken to you, while I am still with you. [26]But the Counsellor, the Holy Spirit, whom the Father will send in my name, he will teach you all things, and bring to your remembrance all that I have said to you" (John 14:25-26).

"But when the Counsellor comes, whom I shall send to you from the Father, even the Spirit of truth, who proceeds from the Father, he will bear witness to me; [27]and you also are witnesses .." (John 15:26-27).

"Nevertheless I tell you the truth: it is to your advantage that I go away, for if I do not go away, the Counsellor will not come to you; but if I go, I will send him to you. [8]And when he comes, he will convince the world of sin and of righteousness and of judgment: [9]of sin, because they do not believe in me; [10]of righteousness, because I go to the Father, and you will see me no more; [11]of judgment, because the ruler of this world is judged. [12]I have yet many things to say to you, but you cannot bear them now. [13]When the Spirit of truth comes, he will guide you into all the truth; for he will not speak on his own authority, but whatever he hears he will speak, and he will declare to you the things that are to come. [14]He will glorify me, for he will take what is mine and declare it to you. [15]All that the Father has is mine; therefore I said that he will take what is mine and declare it to you" (John 16:7-15).

First, some facts which should be borne in mind in approaching these verses:

(1)   The subject of the Counsellor is introduced in John 14:16. There is no mystery about the Greek word "parakletos"; it means literally "called to one's side", i.e. to one's aid. It was used in a court of justice to denote a legal assistant, a counsel for the defence, an advocate; then, generally, one who pleads another's cause, an intercessor, advocate.[1] The AV "Comforter" is based on the related verb and noun, both of which are frequently translated as "comfort", "console" or "consolation", but this rendering fails to evoke the court-room flavour of the term, hence the choice of "Counsellor" by both RSV and NIV. This aspect is well brought out in the only occurrence of the word outside John's gospel:

"... but if any one does sin, we have an *advocate* with the Father, Jesus Christ the righteous" (1 John 2:1).

(2)   "*Another* Counsellor" (Greek "allos"—another of the same kind) is a promise of someone (or something) of comparable status other than the personal presence of Jesus.

(3)   The other names here for the Counsellor are "the Holy

---

1. Vine: "Expository Dictionary of New Testament Words".

Spirit" (14:26) and, three times, "the Spirit of truth" (14:17; 15:26; 16:13). This latter phrase reappears in John's first epistle:

> "By this we know the spirit of truth and the spirit of error" (1 John 4:6).[1]

The context, from 1 John 4:1 onwards, explains these two contrasting "spirits":

> "Beloved, do not believe every spirit, but test the spirits to see whether they are of God; for many *false prophets* have gone out into the world. By this you know the Spirit of God: *every spirit* which confesses that Jesus Christ has come in the flesh is of God, and *every spirit* which does not confess Jesus is not of God. This is the spirit of antichrist, of which you heard that it was coming, and now it is in the world already" (1 John 4:1-3).

It is evident that these "spirits" are themselves real people—John is referring to *true* and *false* prophets in Christian assemblies. In the mouths of the former is *"the spirit* [or "Spirit"] *of truth"* but from the mouths of the latter proceeds *"the spirit of error"*, or falsehood. A splendid Old Testament illustration of this conflict between truth and falsehood is to be found in Micaiah's confrontation with the prophets of Baal in Ahab's reign, when the LORD put a *lying spirit* into the mouths of all the king's prophets (1 Kings 22:21-23). But, like a later namesake, the true prophet here was "filled with power, with *the Spirit of the LORD* ... to declare to Jacob his transgression and to Israel his sin" (Micah 3:8).

---

1. Note that the RSV does not capitalise "spirit" here; the NIV capitalises the first occurrence only, but with a footnote offering "spirit" with a small "s" as alternative.

Towards the end of his epistle John says explicitly: "the Spirit *is* the truth".[1]

(4) The sending of the Counsellor from the Father by Christ's request was contingent upon Jesus "going away" from the disciples, i.e. his ascension to the Father's right hand (see John 16:7 and 7:37-39). Yet Jesus expressly said: "I will not leave you desolate [literally: "orphans"]; *I will come to you*" (14:18).

(5) This promise was given to "the Twelve",[2] and it is more than possible that the Pentecostal outpouring of the Spirit was only upon these (see below on "Spirit gifts" pp. 118*ff*).

(6) According to these chapters the role of the Counsellor was
(a) to teach the twelve all things
(b) to bring to their remembrance all that Jesus had told them (John 14:26).
(c) to bear witness to Christ (John 15:26)
(d) to convince the world of sin, righteousness and judgment (John 16:8)
(e) to guide the twelve into all the truth
(f) to declare the things that were to come (John 16:13)

(7) The impression made by these passages on the reader looking for proof of the existence of the Trinity is that another *person* is being described (i.e. other than Jesus

---

1. This statement is explored in some detail in chapter 7 (page 299).

2. Judas' place being taken by Matthias, Acts 1:26.

or his Father)—both by the frequent personal pronouns[1]
and also the various functions assigned to the Counsellor:
indeed the very title "Counsellor" strongly suggests this.

COMMENT

We propose that the key to the problem is to be found in the
circumstances in which Jesus made this promise. The occasion
was, of course, "the last supper", when Jesus' arrest, trial and
crucifixion were but hours ahead. For three years he had been
the close companion, guide and protector of the twelve. Now
he was about to be taken from them, no longer to be *physically*
with them (except for the forty days before his final
ascension—Acts 1:3). There had, however, been at least one
occasion during his earthly ministry when the Twelve, and later
the Seventy, were sent out in pairs, on a mission to preach the
gospel and heal the sick—and for the latter work they were
given Spirit power, about which they rejoiced on their return to
Jesus (Luke 9:1*ff*; 10:1*ff* and 10.17*ff*). The promise of
Pentecost was that, in the absence of Christ's *physical*
presence, his Spirit power was to be poured out upon them in
much fuller measure than previously—to perform even greater
works than he himself had accomplished (John 14:12). Nevertheless it was *as if* he were still bodily with them, hence he said
categorically: "I will not leave you desolate; *I* will come to
you" (John 14:18). The record in Acts shows how "the Spirit"
of Jesus taught, guided and stimulated the memories of the
Twelve of all Jesus had said and done during their three-year
discipleship. By this Spirit they became effective and fruitful
witnesses to his sacrificial death, resurrection and glorification

---

1. It should be borne in mind, however, that the personal pronouns used here
are not decisive. The Greek original uses "he" and "him" etc in connection
with "Counsellor" because "parakletos" is grammatically of masculine
gender, while with "Spirit" (being neuter gender), "it" and "which" appear.
Thus 14:7 is literally "... even the Spirit of truth, *which* the world cannot
receive, because it neither sees *it* or knows *it*". In short, the choice of
pronouns does not necessarily decide between personal and impersonal
subjects. See also Ch. 6 Sect. 4 (p.248).

at his Father's side.[1]

The identification of the Counsellor with the Spirit of Jesus has strong confirmation from a number of other passages, notably the reference (already quoted) in John's first epistle (this epistle is indubitably an inspired commentary on his gospel): "but if any one does sin, we have an *advocate* [parakletos] with the Father, Jesus Christ the righteous" (1 John 2:1). We may well ask, are there really *two* separate advocates? Does not such an idea call into question the adequacy of Christ's own omnipresence and power with his followers? We are plainly told that there is only *one* mediator between God and men, the man Christ Jesus (1 Timothy 2:5). So Jesus would appear to have a two-fold role, viz.: as our advocate in heaven with the Father, and on earth by his Spirit guiding and directing the witness of his Apostles. As for the Spirit of Christ in action—and in a law court too!—what better example could we have than that described by Paul?:

> "At my first defence no one took my part; all deserted me ... But *the Lord stood by me* and *gave me strength to proclaim the word fully,* that all the Gentiles might hear it. So I was rescued from the lion's mouth" (2 Timothy 4:16-17).

This identification receives further support from some Old Testament references to the promised Messiah:

> "And the *Spirit of the LORD* shall rest upon him, the spirit of wisdom and understanding, the *spirit of counsel* and might, the spirit of knowledge and the fear of the LORD" (Isaiah 11:2).
> "For to us a child is born .. and his *name will be called Wonderful Counsellor*, Mighty God, Everlasting Father,

---

1. See Appendix at the end of this chapter (p.146-7) for further details.

Prince of Peace" (Isaiah 9:6).

For those who prefer the title "the Comforter" we have:

> "The *Spirit of the Lord GOD* is upon me, because the
> LORD has *anointed* me ... to *comfort* all who mourn; to
> grant to those who mourn in Zion—to give them ... the *oil
> of gladness* instead of mourning ..." (Isaiah 61:1-3).

Thus the prophet Isaiah looked forward to a messianic ruler
who would be both Counsellor and Comforter, especially to
Israel.

Further points of coincidence are found:

> "... the *anointing* which you received from him *abides
> in you*, and you have no need that any one should teach
> you; as *his anointing teaches you about everything*, and is
> true, and is no lie, just as *it has taught you*, abide in him"
> (1 John 2:27).

This anointing, says John in verse 20, was by "the Holy
One"—almost certainly Jesus himself, for so Scripture
describes Jesus in the quotation made by Peter on the Day of
Pentecost (Acts 2:27—"thou wilt not ... let *thy Holy One* see
corruption"). The anointing "*abides* in you," says John,
confirming what Jesus had said in John 14:17: "he *dwells* with
you" (same word). And again in this context Jesus says:
"Abide in me, and I in you ..." (John 15:4*ff*). Note particularly
in both passages, that this Spirit anointing *would teach them all
things*.[1]

---

1. This teaching role has many Old Testament precedents e.g.: Nehemiah
9:20 "Thou [YAHWEH, the covenant God - verse 17 and Exodus 34:6]
gavest thy good Spirit [the angel of the presence?] *to instruct them*, and
didst not withhold thy manna from their mouth ..." Psalm 143:7,10 "Make
haste to answer me, O LORD! *My* spirit fails! ... *Teach me* to do thy will, for
thou art my God! Let *thy* good spirit lead me on a level path!"

Finally, the Counsellor would be *with the apostles for ever* (John 14:16). This agrees with Jesus' own promise: "*I am with you always*, to the close of the age" (Matthew 28:20). In sum, there are so many points of contact between what is revealed about the nature and work of "the Spirit of truth" and of "the Spirit of Jesus" that the two phrases may be taken as synonymous. However, a variant on this has been proposed, viz. that just as in the Exodus from Egypt God appointed the angel of His presence to lead His people through the desert to the promised land (Exodus 23:20*ff*), so the corresponding *angel of Christ's presence* oversees and directs the lives of his saints—the *guiding* role of the Spirit of promise (John 16:13) corresponds exactly to that of the Exodus angel (Isaiah 63:14 LXX).

For references to Christ's angel see Acts 12:11, where he rescued Peter from prison, and Revelation 1:1; 22:16—two verses particularly appropriate to John 16:13: "... he will declare to you *the things that are to come*"—the context of Jesus' last message in a nutshell! Maybe some of the outworking of Christ's promise is along these lines.

For completeness, mention should be made of the proposal of some that the Counsellor is purely a personification of the power of God. While it is true that personification is often used in both Testaments e.g. Wisdom and Folly in Proverbs 9, and Sin as a master in Romans 6, the details of Jesus' promise are, in the authors' opinion, much more satisfactorily understood on the lines expounded above. But in neither case is separate personality ever ascribed to the Spirit in Scripture.

REVIEW OF OTHER PASSAGES ALLEGED TO SUPPORT A "THIRD PERSON" IN THE GODHEAD[1]

We have examined in some detail "the Counsellor" verses in

---

1. See also Chapter 6, Section 3, p.190*ff*)

John 14-16, and have demonstrated how the Scriptural concept of the Spirit as the mind and power of both Father and Son disposes of any need to postulate a "third person". Attention to the precise wording of Jesus' promise in the light of parallel testimonies reveals clearly enough the teaching and guiding role *he* played in the apostolic age. We wish now to look at some other verses often quoted to support a trinitarian viewpoint, largely, it seems, because each refers to Jesus and his Father together with the Spirit. In fact it would be surprising if these three were *not* associated, in view of the very close connection between them, as defined above. It is quite another matter, however, to infer from this association that the Spirit is a person; we are persuaded that this inference is nearly always drawn because people come to these verses already strongly indoctrinated with trinitarian ideas. What is needed is an open-minded approach to such passages to interpret them in the light of their immediate context and the wider framework of biblical teaching as a whole. This we will now attempt to do, reviewing passages often quoted in standard Bible dictionaries and other reference works as proofs of a trinity. In the following quotations we must remember that the capital letter 'S' at the beginning of the word *spirit* has been included at the discretion of the translators: there is no such indication in the original.

(1) "And because you are sons, God has sent the Spirit of his Son into our hearts, crying, 'Abba! Father!'" (Galatians 4:6).

Is this a reference to the indwelling of a personal spirit-being in the heart of a believer? There are other comparable "Abba, Father" verses which ought to be considered before we answer:

> "... When we cry, 'Abba! Father!' it is the Spirit himself [Greek auto, "itself"] bearing witness with our spirit that we are children of God" (Romans 8:15-16).

The context of this passage in Romans 8 includes these words:

113

> "For all who are led by the Spirit of God are sons of God" (Romans 8:14).
>
> "But you are not in the flesh, you are in the Spirit, if the Spirit of God really dwells in you. Any one who does not have the spirit of Christ does not belong to him. But if Christ is in you ..." (Romans 8:9-10).

And what was this spirit of Christ that has to be received? It was demonstrated at the time when he too cried *Abba, Father*:

> "And he said, 'Abba, Father, all things are possible to thee; remove this cup from me; yet not what I will, but what thou wilt'" (Mark 14:36).

This last passage makes it clear that "the Spirit of Christ" is the spirit of the Son's *obedience* and submission to God—obeying the Father's will and not his own. The others indicate that all believers are *required* to have this motivating spirit—it is the characteristic attitude of a true son (or daughter) of God and a "sine qua non" of his (her) thought and behaviour if he (she) is to attain to salvation. We must be led, in humility and trust, by this spirit and attitude so perfectly exemplified by Christ. Only in such a spirit can we acceptably approach the Father in prayer, as Paul elsewhere writes:

> ".. for through *him* [i.e. Christ Jesus—verse 13*ff*] we both [Jews and Gentiles] *have access in one Spirit* to the Father" (Ephesians 2:18).

Not one of all these passages requires, or even favours, a separate "third person".

(2) "The grace of the Lord Jesus Christ and the love of God, and *the fellowship* [Greek: koinonia] *of the Holy Spirit* be with you all" (2 Corinthians 13:14).

Is this a passage that demands the personality of the Holy

Spirit? The only close parallel to the italicised phrase is in Philippians 2:1-2

> "So if there is any *encouragement* [Greek: paraklesis "comfort", hence "the Comforter"!] *in Christ*, any incentive of love, any *participation* [Greek: koinonia] *in the Spirit*, any affection and sympathy, complete my joy by *being of the same mind*, having the same love, being in full accord and *of one mind*."

What does the apostle Paul mean by "the fellowship (koinonia) of the Holy Spirit" in these verses? He is plainly appealing to the Philippians to be wholly of "one mind" with each other, not in any worldly way but with the true Christian virtue of *love*—the spirit shown above all by Jesus in the sacrifice he offered in order to become the Saviour of the world. We must *share with Jesus* this mind and motivation, for *fellowship* [Greek: koinonia] means sharing, participation, having things in common. Our will must be subordinated to his, as his was to his Father's. Again there is no good ground whatever to invoke a "third person". Let anyone still minded to do so on the basis of this verse ponder the apostle John's words:

> "that which we have seen and heard we proclaim also to you, so that you may have fellowship with us; *and our fellowship is with the Father and with his Son Jesus Christ*" (1 John 1:3).

Has "the beloved disciple" *forgotten* to include "the third person" in the scope of his fellowship?! Or should we not rather accept his inspired statement that the *body of faithful believers*, who are led by the Spirit (mind) of Jesus within them, completes the true divine family? This theme will be explored in chapter 7.

(3) "chosen ... by God the Father and *sanctified by the Spirit*

115

for obedience to Jesus Christ and for sprinkling with his blood ..." (1 Peter 1:2).

How are believers "sanctified by the Spirit"? The identical statement appears also in 2 Thessalonians 2:13 and in both cases the original Greek *could* simply mean "sanctification of [the believer's] spirit" as in fact the RSV margin proposes for the latter reference. In this case clearly no personal Holy Spirit is intended. Romans 15:16 is different: ".. sanctified by the Holy Spirit", pointing to God's or Christ's power as the *agent* of sanctification. And this of course is the sense of the RSV and NIV in 1 Peter and 2 Thessalonians. But it must be noted that elsewhere the power of sanctification is attributed not to a personal being but to the *Word of God*. Jesus prayed: "Sanctify them by the truth: your word is truth" (John 17:17 NIV). Jesus had said earlier (John 6:63): "*the words* that I have spoken to you *are spirit* and life." Thus it is the *Spirit Word of God* (Ephesians 6.17) spoken by Christ, humbly accepted by the believer and allowed to rule his mind and actions, that purifies, separates and sanctifies his life, not an indwelling member of the Trinity. We may add that there is a demonstrably close connection between the biblical concepts of "spirit", "word" and "truth", and this also is explored in chapter 7.

(4) "... Grace to you and peace from him who is and who was and who is to come, and from the seven spirits who [Greek: "which"] are before his throne, and from Jesus Christ the faithful witness ..." (Revelation 1:4-5).

The One "who is and who was and who is to come" is identified in verse 8 and 4:8 as "the Lord God, the Almighty". Jesus himself, as stated, is "the faithful witness ...", but who (or "what"—the pronoun is neuter in Greek) are "the seven spirits before the throne"? Again the book tells us—they are "seven torches of fire" burning before the throne (4:5), while 5:6 identifies them as the seven horns and seven eyes of the slain Lamb, evidently symbolic of the Lamb's divine power and penetrating insight, given him by his Father. Taken as symbols these seven spirits present no problem (see Isaiah 11:2 already quoted on page 110), but are there seven "Holy Ghosts"? The NIV, perhaps sensing the anomaly, offers as an alternative translation "the sevenfold Spirit", but the Greek is plural and reads: "from the seven spirit*s*" (apo tön hepta pneumatön).

(5) "...'All authority in heaven and on earth has been given to me. Go therefore and make disciples of all nations, baptizing them in [Greek: eis "into"] the name of the Father and of the Son and of the Holy Spirit, teaching them to observe all that I have commanded you; and lo, I am with you always, to the close of the age'" (Matthew 28:18-20).

In the authors' opinion this is the *only* biblical passage which might reasonably be adduced by Trinitarians in favour of "three persons" sharing one name.[1] But on what principle are we to allow *one* verse, apparently teaching a certain doctrine, to rule out the testimony of a *hundred* verses teaching the opposite? The faithful expositor's duty is to ascertain the *consensus* of scriptural teaching, and construe the obscure or *apparently* non-conforming passage in the light of the many clear testimonies on any particular subject. This is the principle we have been conscientiously pursuing throughout this book, and we propose to do so for the passage now under review.

Matthew 28:19 is the only record of Jesus specifically *commanding* baptism, but the necessity of this rite may also be seen in his words in Mark 16:16 and John 3:5. The baptismal formula given here is unique as such in its naming of Father, Son and Holy Spirit. In the "Acts of the Apostles" and Paul's letters the corresponding formula is simply "baptised *into* (the name of) the Lord Jesus" (with some slight variants)—see Acts 8:16; 19:5; Romans 6:3; Galatians 3:27. As with our

---

1. Ignoring 1 John 5:7 in the AV, recognised by all scholars as spurious—see page 32.

Matthew passage, all these references use the Greek preposition "eis", i.e. "into" rather than "in", but translators have not always been consistent in their English rendering.

We can infer that this apostolic formula is "shorthand" for the fuller one in Matthew's account, and that therefore Jesus is, as it were, the focus of "the Name"—YAHWEH.[1] God has given this name to His dear Son also (Philippians 2:9-11), for "Jesus" is the Greek form of "Joshua", whose name means *"YAH[WEH] is Salvation"*. The Holy Spirit is "the Spirit of YAHWEH" with which Jesus was anointed, and which as "the Word of Truth" begets every son and daughter of God (James 1:18) as they rise to "newness of life" from the baptismal waters.[2] Thus the "one Name" covers all three entities, without recourse to "the personality of the Holy Spirit" as taught by Trinitarians.

There is also the possibility that the words "in the name of the Father and of the Son and of the Holy Spirit" were a later addition. This is supported by the fact that they were never included in quotations of Matthew 28:19 by the "early fathers". For example, Eusebius, who died about the year 340, quotes the verse at least 18 times, but always in the form "Go ye into and make disciples of all the nations *in my name*, teaching them to observe all things, whatsoever I commanded you".

SECTION 4. SPIRIT GIFTS—PAST AND PRESENT

We have already cited several passages which state that the Spirit of God was given to men and women in order to endow them with supernatural abilities (see pages 86-87, 105*ff*). We

---

1. See p. 51*ff*.

2. For the biblical principles pertaining to baptism see "Thine is the Kingdom", pp 154-156.

propose now to examine in more detail what the Bible reveals on this subject. We need to do this because similar gifts have been claimed in the post-apostolic era by various disparate sects and denominations, and indeed by followers of non-Christian religions. We believe such claims are inadmissible, whether in the 4th century or the 20th. As always, we need to lay first an Old Testament foundation. The chief gifts described in the Old Testament record appear to be these:

1. the gift of prophecy, i.e. acting as God's spokesman (see Exodus 7:1-2), whether it be to guide, or reprove human conduct, or to predict future events (e.g. Enoch, Noah, Abraham, Moses, Balaam, Samuel, Saul, David and many others);

2. wisdom and skill, either
(i) for a specific task, such as the construction of the tabernacle or temple (Bezalel and Oholiab—Exodus 31:2*ff*; 35:30*ff*; David—1 Chronicles 28:11-19); or
(ii) more generally, in the government and administration of a nation (Joseph—Genesis 39:2,23; 41:38; Moses—Numbers 11:17; so too Joshua, Solomon, Daniel etc.);

3. physical strength and valour in war (e.g. Othniel, Gideon, Samson and David);

4. working miracles of healing or of punishment, or of special signs of power to confirm the possession of divine authority (Moses, Elijah, Elisha). Very often, however, these miracles have been God's responses to His Servants' prayers, and it is not always possible to draw a hard and fast line between Spirit power granted to a person and the divine response to fervent prayer (James 5:17).

It is not always clear from these accounts whether a Spirit gift, once bestowed, was retained and active from its first imparting, or whether it was conferred for but a limited period in order to attain a specific object, and perhaps renewed later. The warlike exploits under item 3 above would appear to have been largely temporary gifts (note, for example, the repeated statements in Judges 14*ff* that the Spirit came mightily on Samson) whereas the needs of wise government and administration would presumably have required a more lasting endowment, such as Moses enjoyed. It is important to notice that the privilege of receiving such supernatural powers did not necessarily guarantee God's approval of the beneficiaries, still less did it promise their salvation. Spirit powers could be abused (such, at least, was Balaam's intention) and even forfeited (as in Saul's case). Further, there were times of great Spirit manifestation, especially in the lives of Moses and, much later, of Elijah and Elisha, but also long periods during which God's "visible hand" remained largely hidden. For example, before Samuel there had been a time of "infrequent vision" (1 Samuel 3:1); much later night fell on the prophetic ministry, throughout the inter-testamental period until just before the birth of Jesus (Ezekiel 7:26; Amos 8:11-12; Micah 3:5-7).

THE URIM AND THUMMIM

A special case of a Spirit gift granted to the nation of Israel but later withdrawn was the oracle called "Urim and Thummim", which was associated with the High Priest's sacred robes, being carried in the "breastpiece of judgment". The exact nature of these "lights and perfections" (as the phrase can be translated) is not known; sufficient to note that by them an immediate answer from God could be obtained through the priest when a ruler needed divine guidance. Thus Moses directed Joshua to seek such guidance through Aaron's son Eleazar.[1] David, although he had the Spirit,[2] frequently had recourse to this oracle.[3] Saul before him had also sought guidance, but fitfully

---

1. Numbers 27:21

2. 1 Samuel 16:13

3. 1 Samuel 23:2,4,9*ff*; 30:7-8; 2 Samuel 2:1; 5:19,23

and inconsistently, so that after his disobedience and rejection this access to divine counsel was denied him.[1] After David's time there is not a single reference to this oracle being consulted, and it is mentioned again only in the days of Ezra and Nehemiah, when it is clear that Israel had lost this privilege altogether.[2] Of course, God still guided the lives of His faithful servants, and answered their prayers in His own good way—but a direct answer to a perplexing situation was no longer guaranteed. We shall demonstrate below that this penalty for disobedience, together with the lapse in the prophetic gift, were precedents for the withdrawal of Spirit gifts in the post-apostolic era.

SPIRIT GIFTS IN THE NEW TESTAMENT

Renewal of the gift of prophecy in New Testament times began with Elizabeth, mother of John the Baptist, and Mary, Jesus' mother, three months before John was born (Luke 1:41-55). John's father, the priest Zechariah, also prophesied just after John's birth, as did the aged Simeon and Anna after Jesus was born (Luke 1:67*ff*; 2:27-38). All four gospels describe the prophetic ministry of John the Baptist, but "John did no sign [i.e. miracle]" (John 10:41). Upon Jesus himself the power of the Spirit was poured out without measure (John 3:34), and it was manifested in a multitude of miracles, signs, healings and inspired discourses. His twelve apostles were granted a limited exercise of these "powers of the age to come" during Christ's three-year ministry, as we have seen (pages 109-112). However we need to go to the "Acts of the Apostles" and certain of Paul's letters to learn in detail about the bestowal of Spirit gifts in the early church. Jesus had promised that he would send these gifts once he had ascended to heaven (John 16:7); the disciples were to stay in Jerusalem until they were "clothed with power from on high" (Luke 24:49).

---

1. 1 Samuel 14:41; 28:6

2. Ezra 2:63; Nehemiah 7:65

In due course the Day of Pentecost dawned and the Holy Spirit was poured out on the Twelve, Matthias having taken the place of Judas.[1] The gift itself was the ability to preach the gospel[2] in all the native languages of the Jews then residing in or visiting Jerusalem, especially those who had been brought up in the Diaspora. Each pilgrim to the feast heard the message clearly in his own mother tongue—and marvelled. Having brought home to the consciences of the assembled multitude the enormity of their behaviour in crucifying their divinely-sent King-Messiah, Peter and his fellow-apostles exhorted every one of them to repent and be baptised, (calling)[3] upon the name of Jesus Christ for the forgiveness of their sins. He added:

> "... and you shall receive the gift of the Holy Spirit. For the promise is to you and to your children and to all that are afar off, every one whom the Lord our God calls to him ... Save yourselves from this crooked generation." (Acts 2:38-40)

An important question of interpretation is posed here. Because the Spirit was poured out upon the Twelve at the outset, the words of Peter in the passage just quoted are almost universally construed as meaning that the Holy Spirit would also be given to all responding to the Apostle's stirring appeal. There are, however, several serious objections to this

---

1. Whether the recipients included the 120 persons of Acts 1:15 is unclear; the original promise was made only to the eleven apostles (Acts 1:4-5; 2:32; 3:15: 4:33; 5:31-32; 10:39-42; 22:14-15; 1 Corinthians 9:1;15:8; 1 John 1:1-3).

2. Defined in Acts 8:12 as the "good news about the kingdom of God and the name of Jesus Christ".

3. Literally: "be baptised *upon* [Greek: epi] the name ..."; Peter was alluding to the Joel prophecy he had just quoted in verses 17-21, which concludes: "... whoever calls on [*epi*-kaleomai] the name of the Lord shall be saved." Later on Paul did just this as he was commanded: "Rise and be baptised, and wash away your sins, *calling on* [again "*epi*-kaleomai"] his name" (Acts 22:16).

interpretation. First, the phrase "the gift of the Holy Spirit" is ambiguous both in Greek and English. Is the Holy Spirit here the giver or the gift itself? If the wording had been "the gift of God" there would be no question that God was the *giver*—and we are convinced it should be similarly interpreted here.[1] The gift itself, promised by the Holy Spirit through Jesus and his apostles, was "the forgiveness of sins". The need for, and the blessing of, sins being "blotted out" or "washed away", will be obvious on a little reflection, for a cleansed sinner, justified by his faith and obedience, becomes a saint in Christ Jesus and an heir of eternal life. On the other hand, reception of one or more of the Spirit's gifts in no way guaranteed eternal life to the one so endowed; it was still possible to depart from the faith, and such conduct would inevitably result in rejection at Christ's judgment seat (see Hebrews 6:4-6). Perhaps Ananias and Sapphira were condemned on such grounds (see below on Acts 5).

Further, the Spirit's promise is to *everyone* whom the Lord calls. Whereas *forgiveness* is clearly granted to *all* who respond to God's gracious invitation[2], it is by no means certain that *Spirit gifts* were granted to every believer, even in the apostolic age, and it is demonstrable that since that era such gifts have ceased.

In confirmation of the above it should be noted that Luke makes no reference to any miraculous powers being exercised by the three thousand converts on the Day of Pentecost (Acts 2:41), only that they all manifested a "spirit" of zeal and thankfulness, sharing with one another both their new-found faith in the Lord Jesus and their temporal possessions (verses 44-45). At this stage it was only the apostles who performed wonders

---

1. A footnote in the NIV Study Bible accepts this interpretation in addition to the usually held views already mentioned.

2. See Acts 10:43, where Peter stresses this all-important fact; and compare Jesus' words in Luke 10:20.

and signs (verse 43); these were obviously "the signs of an apostle" (2 Corinthians 12:12; Romans 15:15-19). Only after the Apostles had their first confrontation with the religious authorities and had returned to their own company, were the latter "all filled with the Holy Spirit and spoke the word of God with boldness" (Acts 4:31), thus extending considerably the number willing and able to bear witness to the gospel without fearing what the authorities might do. Among this company may well have been Ananias and Sapphira, for it is very soon after this that Luke describes in chapter 5 how this couple flagrantly lied to the Holy Spirit, having "agreed together to tempt the Spirit of the Lord" (verse 9). The apostle Peter obviously had the power to discern this spirit of deception and with its exposure both "deceivers" collapsed and died.

Chapter 6 of Acts is specially instructive in its description of the seven deacons selected to oversee "the daily distribution" to widows in the Jerusalem church. Their primary qualification was that they should be "of good repute, full of the Spirit and of wisdom" (6:3). Outstanding among these was Stephen, "a man full of faith and of the Holy Spirit" (6.5), which qualities his adversaries were unable to withstand (6.10). Being "full of grace and power" he "did great wonders and signs among the people" (6.8), although the exact nature of these miracles is unspecified. It was Stephen's inspired witness to Israel's unfaithfulness and obduracy, culminating in the latter's betrayal and murder of God's "Righteous One", which precipitated his own murder by the infuriated mob (chapter 7). The Acts narrative continues with the work of another of the seven deacons, Philip, later styled "the evangelist" (21:8). He too was able to perform healing miracles (8:6-7,13) and he baptised those in Samaria who responded to his preaching of the good news of the kingdom (v.12). What he could *not* do, however, was to impart the Holy Spirit to these new converts, so the apostles Peter and John were sent for to accomplish this by the laying on of their hands and to show they approved receiving Samaritan believers into the Christ body (vv.14-16).

This restriction in Philip's power should be carefully noted. Only very rarely do we read of anyone, other than the Apostles, conferring the Holy Spirit by the laying on of hands. One such instance was when Ananias of Damascus visited Saul of Tarsus (Acts 9:17-18), but this was a unique occasion when Christ's especial 'Apostle to the Gentiles' was commissioned (verse 15). Timothy was warned by Paul not to be "hasty in the laying on of hands" (1 Timothy 5:22), but commentators are in general agreement that this signified no more than the ordaining of elders to oversee the believers at Ephesus. Comparable with this was the occasion when the elders of the church at Antioch laid their hands on Barnabas and Saul before sending them off on their first great missionary journey (Acts 13:1-3)—but as these apostles were already Spirit-filled (Acts 9:17; 11:24), this too was a case of commissioning, and not of imparting Spirit gifts. The plain and inescapable consequence is this: as the apostles passed off the scene, so the power to bestow Spirit powers on others died with them.[1] Chapter 8 ends with the conversion of the Ethiopian eunuch and his baptism—but without any intimation that he also received the Holy Spirit from Philip.[2] Chapter 9 describes the call of Saul of Tarsus to be the apostle to the Gentiles—and as an apostle, to receive the Spirit (verse 17) in abundant measure (Romans 15:18-19; 2 Corinthians 12:11-12).

We move on to Acts 10-11 and the obedience of the first *Gentile* converts to Christianity, viz. Cornelius with his relatives and friends. The occasion was notable in that the Holy Spirit was poured out on these Gentile believers *before* they were baptised into the name of Jesus, and they spoke in tongues

---

1. Thus an editorial footnote on 1 Corinthians 13:4 in Weymouth's New Testament translation states: "The special miraculous gifts which characterised the Apostolic age appear to have ceased at the destruction of Jerusalem in 70 AD."

2. The Western text (but not Codex Bezae, which is defective here) adds "the Spirit fell on the eunuch".

and extolled God (10:44-48). It was a mini-Pentecost (cp 11:15,17), the door of salvation now being opened to *Gentile* believers just as at Pentecost the way of life had been opened to repentant *Jews*. Peter and his fellow Jews needed to have this incontrovertible evidence of God's mercy towards Gentiles to overcome what had been till then their deep-seated opposition to Gentile participation in the gospel on an equal footing with Jewish believers. Peter later refers to this in Acts 15:8.

The only other material reference to Holy Spirit gifts in Acts is the rather puzzling account in chapter 19 of some Christian (?) disciples Paul encountered at Ephesus, who had undergone John's baptism but, according to the RSV text, had "never even heard that there is a Holy Spirit" (verse 2). It is difficult to believe that anyone at all acquainted with the teaching of John the Baptist, or of the Old Testament generally, could be so completely unaware of the Holy Spirit's *existence*. The text of the RV and ASV here have instead: "We did not so much as hear whether the Holy Ghost [Spirit] *was given*"—a very different matter, seeing that the gift of prophecy had been allowed to lapse over the previous four centuries. This rendering is strongly supported by a parallel passage in John 7:39, where the Greek construction is very similar:

"... for as yet the Spirit *had not been given* [literally: "was not"], because Jesus was not yet glorified."

Paul proceeded to fill in this gap in their understanding, doubtless recounting the Pentecostal events and their aftermath, whereupon these disciples were also baptised into (*eis*) the name of the Lord Jesus. Then he confirmed the truth of their newly imparted knowledge in a most practical way, by laying his hands on them, and they too received Spirit powers—speaking with tongues and prophesying.

F.F. Bruce, in his commentary on Acts,[1] refers approvingly to the opinion of Prof. G.W.H. Lampe that the bestowal of these powers was intended to be a second Pentecost. It launched "a new centre of the Gentile mission—the next in importance after Syrian Antioch—and these twelve disciples were to be the nucleus of the Ephesian church".

SPIRIT GIFTS AT CORINTH

Luke's account in Acts traces the geographical spread of the gospel, and records some of the major stepping stones in that process, with special emphasis on the work of Paul as "the apostle to the Gentiles". We have seen how the progress of the gospel message was marked by several outpourings of Spirit power, but Luke does not concentrate on their long-term effects in any one Christian community. This hiatus is amply filled in Paul's first letter to Corinth, where the wise and proper use of Spirit gifts had become a very burning issue in this assembly. In the introduction of his letter the apostle thanks God

> "that in every way you were enriched in him [Christ Jesus] with *all speech* and *all knowledge* ... so that you are not lacking in any spiritual gift ..." (1 Corinthians 1:5-7).

In chapters 12-14 Paul goes into this subject in considerable detail, greatly concerned that these believers should be rightly informed and exercised to use these divine powers with wisdom and discernment. There was, very clearly, dissension in the Corinthian assembly of Christians about which was the most desirable gift. Paul is at pains to point out that all Spirit gifts were helpful if subordinated to the basic needs of "the body of Christ". He likened the gifts to the various faculties and senses of a natural body, all working in harmony for the general good (the same analogy is used in Romans 12:4-8). But some gifts were of greater value than others, and some offices in the

---

1. *The Book of Acts* 1965, p.387 (London: Marshall, Morgan and Scott).

church eldership ranked higher than others. The list in 1 Corinthians 12:28*ff* (see accompanying table) supplies a descending order of spiritual importance, in which "speakers in various kinds of tongues" is the *lowest* of the eight mentioned! In chapter 14 the apostle emphasises that *prophesying*, i.e. speaking God's message in plain language for the upbuilding, strengthening and encouragement of the whole assembly, was a far more desirable gift than speaking in tongues (which edified only the speaker unless an interpreter was also present)—better "five words with my mind, in order to instruct others, than ten thousand words in a tongue" (1 Corinthians 14:19). In the course of his exposition Paul pauses to outline "a still more excellent way" which every Christian believer can and must follow, because these special gifts would later be withdrawn!

SPIRIT GIFTED ELDERS

Ephesians 4:11*ff* 1 Corinthians 12.28

"And his gifts were that some should be	"And God has appointed in the church
apostles,	first *apostles,*
some *prophets,*	second *prophets,*
some *evangelists,*	
some *pastors*	
and *teachers,*	third *teachers,*
	then workers of miracles,
for the equipment of the saints ..."	then healers, helpers, administrators, speakers in various kinds of tongues."

Note the double emphasis on the most important gifts, and that speaking in tongues is the *least* important in the second sequence, and not even mentioned in the Ephesians passage.

WITHDRAWAL OF SPIRIT GIFTS PREDICTED

The wording of chapter 13 should be carefully observed. First the apostle mentions the superlatives of such gifts—tongues as of angels, prophecies to penetrate all mysteries, faith to move mountains, self-sacrifice even to the loss of all possessions and of life itself—but, he stresses, without true Christian *love* accompanying these achievements (a love he goes on to describe graphically in verses 4-7), *nothing* will be gained. Every Bible student learns the all-surpassing value of love— God's great love towards fallen man and the latter's obligation and privilege to reflect that love back to his Maker and also to his fellow man (e.g. Mark 12:30-31; Romans 13:8-10; 1 John 4:7-12). Paul continues:

"Love never faileth: but whether there be prophecies, *they shall be done away*; whether there be tongues, *they shall cease*; whether there be knowledge, it *shall be done away*. [9]For we know in part, and we prophesy in part: [10]But when that which is perfect is come, that which is in part shall be done away. [11]When I was a child, I spake as a child, I felt as a child, I thought as a child: now that I am become a man, I have put away childish things. [12]For now we see in a mirror, darkly; [Greek: "in a riddle"] but then face to face: now I know in part; but then shall I know even as also I have been known. [13]But now *abideth* faith, hope, love, these three; and the greatest of these is love" (1 Corinthians 13:8-13, RV)

The context of these lines (viz. chapters 12 and 14) obliges us to recognise that the apostle is still speaking in chapter 13 about the special gifts of the Spirit, and contrasting their *temporary* status with the *abiding* virtues of faith, hope and love. "Tongues" here must be *the gift* of tongues, and not various languages as such, which are still with us in profusion and now need much time and application to master. Similarly scriptural "knowledge", in apostolic times an instant acquisition (as at Pentecost) is today slowly accumulated over the years. The only true "prophecies" existing today, i.e. inspired expositions of God's mind and purpose, are those that have been preserved in our Bible through the centuries; the prophetic *gift* is no longer manifest. Paul must therefore be referring to powers (such as "tongues" at Pentecost) which were miraculously imparted. They were to be *"done away", abolished* ,[1] whereas faith, hope and love were to *abide*. Ultimately, in God's kingdom, even faith itself will turn to sight, and hope to realisation, but *love* will never end, and is therefore the supreme virtue.

What then does Paul mean by knowing and prophesying "in part" (13:9-10), but only until the coming of "that which is perfect"? "In part" can hardly imply "imperfectly"[2] in view of the superlatives of the first three verses of this chapter! Rather, the apostle was stressing that the distribution of Spirit gifts was uneven, limited in number and nature to some believers but not to others (although all were for the good of the Christ body as a whole); this was, in fact, the reason for the contention which had arisen between the recipients of differing gifts. However, Paul predicted the coming of "that which is perfect" to replace these temporary gifts. Commentators usually conclude that the apostle is looking forward to the "perfection" of God's kingdom, and regard verse 12 as confirmatory. There are at least two objections to this:

1. "Perfect" here means "complete", "mature",[3] and is in contrast to the childish things ("ta tou nepiou") of verse 11;[4] it does not necessarily refer to the kingdom age;
2. Verse 10 foresees "the perfect thing" coming *before* the "knowing" and "prophesying" are "done away".

---

1. The same expression is used in 1 Corinthians 15:24 and 26 of the abolition of all human rule, authority and power and of death itself

2. As rendered by the RSV , as if the opposite of "perfect" in verse 10 - but the Greek words ("ek merous" and "to teleion") are not antithetic concepts.

3. Abbott-Smith Lexicon p.442.

4. So Alford "Greek New Testament", in loc.

It should be borne in mind that, when Paul was writing this letter, the "Holy Scriptures" were still incomplete, and the infant churches *needed* Spirit-endowed elders to guide them in matters of faith and conduct. In due course the gospels were written, as well as Acts, the Epistles and Revelation—quite possibly all of these before AD70.[1] When Paul goes on to refer to his childhood (in direct contrast with the maturity or perfection which was to follow) he is in fact speaking not of himself but representatively of the "infant church" as a whole. The situation is transparently explained in the epistle he later sent to Ephesus:

"And his [Christ's] gifts were that some should be apostles, some prophets, some evangelists, some pastors and teachers, for the *equipment of the saints,* for the work of ministry, for building up the body of Christ, until we all attain to the unity of the faith and of the knowledge of the Son of God, *to mature manhood,* to the measure of the stature of the fulness of Christ; *so that we may no longer be children,* tossed to and fro and carried about with every wind of doctrine ... Rather, speaking the truth *in love, we are to grow up* in every way into him who is the head, into Christ, from whom the whole body, joined and knit together by every joint with which it is supplied, when each part is working properly, *makes bodily growth* and upbuilds itself *in love"* (Ephesians 4:11-16).

It will be obvious that the themes of childhood and growing up into maturity, in connection with the body of Christ, are employed here just as they are in chapters 12 and 13 of 1 Corinthians. Paul envisages here a mature "grown-up" Christian church, motivated by abiding love and no longer a prey to the "deceitful wiles" of unscrupulous men.

---

1. J.A.T. Robinson: "Redating the New Testament" S.C.M. Press 1976.

But what then was to replace the guidance of the Spirit-endowed elders once the apostles had passed off the scene? Paul had in fact told the Ephesian eldership this explicitly when he had earlier bade them a sad farewell:

"And now I commend you to God *and to the word of his grace, which is able to build you up* [cp Ephesians 4:12] and to give you the inheritance among all those who are sanctified" (Acts 20:32).

Timothy, during Paul's final imprisonment, was overseer ("bishop") in Ephesus. To him too Paul commended "the sacred writings":

"... from childhood [babyhood] you have been acquainted with the sacred writings *which are able to instruct you for salvation* through faith in Christ Jesus. All scripture is inspired by God and profitable for teaching, for reproof, for correction, and for training [Greek: "paideia"—"child training"] in righteousness, that the man of God may be *complete*, equipped for every good work" (2 Timothy 3:15-17).

Thus the completed and inspired Scriptures eventually formed the "equipment" of the eldership in the various Christian assemblies, in place of the Spirit gifts once they had ceased. Throughout the centuries the fulness of God's Word—our Bible—has been the guiding star of the believer in Christ because, as Paul said, it is able (empowered) to build him up and qualify him to receive the inheritance of God's kingdom.

THE CLAIM TO SPIRIT GIFTS OR POWERS TODAY

It is impracticable here, and indeed unnecessary, to deal exhaustively with this question. Sufficient to say that such powers are currently claimed by a very wide range of people on the evangelical wing of Protestantism (in both the established church and various non-conformist communions), also by

Roman Catholics and the Greek Orthodox Church—and by many in the minor sects of Christendom too. But, for that matter, we also find claims to Spirit gifts or influence in all kinds of religious groups, both in the major religions of the world such as Islam, Hinduism and Buddhism, and also in "fringe communities" (if that is the appropriate term) like the devotees of voodoo in the Caribbean, the dupes of witchcraft in much of Africa and of Shamanism in Northern Asia, and many others. It would be strange indeed if all these widely varying and, in the main, mutually exclusive religious groups were genuinely guided by the one true Spirit of God! On the face of it the vast majority, being in disagreement with one another, must be in error and therefore their claims to Spirit guidance and control dismissed.

The claims themselves are diverse—from the "inner light" of the Society of Friends ("Quakers") to faith healings at Roman Catholic shrines (e.g. at Lourdes); from the gift of tongues ("glossolalia") of the charismatic movement to exorcism of demons by witchcraft in its many forms.

By no means all evangelicals accept the claims of their brethren, and indeed some have been to the forefront in the investigation and refutation of these notions, carefully documenting their objections. The following books by "mainstream biblical theologians" have drawn together a large number of weighty refutations, although not all of these are acceptable from the authors' understanding of scripture.

(1) B B Warfield: "Counterfeit Miracles" Edinburgh: Banner of Truth Trust 1972.
(2) P Masters: "The Healing Epidemic" London: The Wakeman Trust 1988.
(3) A A Hoekema: "What About Tongue-Speaking?" Exeter: Paternoster Press, 1966,

Warfield's study, first published in 1918, is the oldest and most scholarly of the three. He establishes beyond dispute that the charismatic gifts of the first century ceased rapidly with the passing of the apostles, so that the "church fathers" of the next two centuries, with rare exceptions, always *referred back* to the apostolic era when they discussed miracle working in the Christian assemblies. From the third century onwards there is a progressive *increase* in testimonies of contemporary miracles, reaching a climax in the credulous climate of the middle ages. The wonder-workings of the Roman Catholic "saints" next come in for some very critical scrutiny. After this the Irvingite movement of the 1820's is reviewed, followed by two final chapters on faith-healing (with special reference to Dr. A J Gordon's teaching towards the end of the 19th century) and the "mind-cure" of Christian Science. Warfield's main and sound thesis is that Spirit gifts ("charismata") were intended solely for the authentication of *apostolic* preaching, and once that preaching was established and recorded for all generations in the completed Scriptures there were no grounds or rationality for further endowment.

Masters' book is more concerned with the contemporary scene and the fantastic claims of certain self-proclaimed healers whose "sessions" have all the characteristics of hypnotic trance inductions, and none of the features of New Testament healings. A useful appendix to this book is "A Medical View of Miraculous Healing" by Professor Verna Wright of Leeds University Medical School, who assesses the true (and virtually negligible) improvement in patients "healed" by these evangelical practitioners.

Finally, Professor Hoekema confines his attention to glossolalia, and is equally dismissive of its claims and their supposed Scriptural foundations.

SCRIPTURAL OBJECTIONS TO CURRENT CLAIMS
In our review of Spirit gifts in Old Testament times (p. 119) we have demonstrated how *natural* Israel, although called by God, failed to live up to their high calling, so that the special

privileges of Spirit guidance through inspired men were temporary, with long periods during which they were withdrawn. Israel's failure had been foreseen by Moses and is plainly stated in Deuteronomy 4:26-31; 31:16*ff* and 32:15*ff*; their subsequent recorded history is a sad and full confirmation of Moses' inspired prophecy. The New Testament introduces the concept of a new *spiritual* Israel, constituted of both Jews and Gentiles who recognise in Jesus of Nazareth the long-promised Messiah, one who fulfilled the role of sin-bearer on Calvary and is yet to be the king of the whole world at his second coming (Romans 11:13-32; Ephesians 2:11—3:6; I Peter 2:9-10). But just as Moses warned of the old Israel's apostasy, so Jesus and his apostles foretold a parallel apostasy by the new Israel. Consider the following passages:

"And many false prophets will arise and lead many astray. And because wickedness is multiplied, *most men's love* [sic] will grow cold. But he who endures to the end will be saved" (Matthew 24:11-13).

"For false Christs and false prophets will arise and show great signs and wonders, so as to lead astray, if possible, even the elect" (Matthew 24:24).

"I know that after my departure fierce wolves will come in among you, not sparing the flock; and from among your own selves will arise men speaking perverse things, to draw away the disciples after them. Therefore be alert ..." (Acts 20:29-31).

"Let no one deceive you in any way; for that day [of Christ's return—v.1] will not come, unless the rebellion [Greek: apostasia] comes first, and the man of lawlessness is revealed ..."

"The coming of the lawless one by the activity of Satan will be with all power and with pretended signs and wonders, and with all wicked deception for those who are to perish, because they refused to love the truth and so be saved. Therefore God sends upon them a strong delusion, to make them believe what is false, so that all may be condemned who did not believe the truth but had pleasure in unright-eousness" (2 Thessalonians 2:3, 9-12).

"Now the Spirit expressly says that in later times' some will depart from the faith by giving heed to deceitful spirits and doctrines of demons, through the pretensions of liars whose consciences are seared,.." (1 Timothy 4:1-2).

"For the time is coming when people will not endure sound teaching, but having itching ears they will accumulate for themselves teachers to suit their own likings, and will turn away from listening to the truth and wander into myths" (2 Timothy 4:3-4).

"... no prophecy ever came by the impulse of man, but men moved by the Holy Spirit spoke from God. But false prophets also arose among the people [of Israel], *just as there will be false teachers among you*, who will secretly bring in destructive heresies ..." (2 Peter 1:21—2:1).

In this last quotation the chapter division distracts attention from the interconnection of these two verses. Just as genuine currency is undermined by the circulation of counterfeit coinage, so in all ages wicked men have falsely claimed divine powers, and notably the gift of prophecy (i.e. speaking God's words), by which they have introduced confusion into the minds of multitudes unable or unwilling to distinguish truth from falsehood. From the above warnings it must be obvious that spiritual Israel would follow the bad example of natural Israel before them. It is not surprising therefore that once again God, who does not change, foreseeing this Christian apostasy, reacted in the same way as before, and warned that Spirit gifts would be withdrawn (yet preserving the sure testimony of His Word for the minority that would still earnestly desire to know and do His will).

The claims of false prophets, whether to predict the future or to perform signs and wonders by God's power, is nothing less than rebellion against the Almighty (Jeremiah 28:16; 29:32) and is condemned as either adding to or subtracting from a complete and inspired Biblical record. Moses wrote:

> "You shall not add to the word which I command you, nor take from it; that you may keep the commandments of the LORD your God which I command you" (Deuteronomy 4:2. see also 12:32).

In the same spirit we read in the Old Testament:

> "Every word of God proves true ... Do not add to his words, lest he rebuke you, and you be found a liar" (Proverbs 30:5-6).

Jesus likewise warns, at the end of his last message:

> "I warn every one who hears the words of the prophecy of this book: if any one adds to them, God will add to him the plagues described in this book, and if any one takes away from the words of the book of this prophecy, God will take away his share in the tree of life and in the holy city, which are described in this book" (Revelation 22:18-19).

The words of the true prophets have been preserved in the Scriptures; subsequent claims, which clearly disobey the above warnings, must be viewed with the utmost suspicion and tested by the criteria laid down in the Bible. Let Moses again testify:

> "If a prophet arises among you, or a dreamer of dreams, and gives you a sign or a wonder, *and the sign or wonder which he tells you comes to pass*, and if he says, 'Let us go after other gods,' which you have not known, 'and let us serve them,' you shall not listen to the words of that prophet or to that dreamer of dreams; for the LORD your God is testing you, to know whether you love the LORD your God with all your heart and with all your soul ... But that prophet or that dreamer of dreams shall be put to death, because he has taught rebellion against the LORD your God ... So you shall purge the evil from the midst of

you" (Deuteronomy 13:1-3-5).
"But the prophet who presumes to speak a word in my name which I have not commanded him to speak, or who speaks in the name of other gods, that same prophet shall die.' And if you say in your heart, 'How may we know the word which the LORD has not spoken?'—when a prophet speaks in the name of the LORD, if the word does not come to pass or come true, that is a word which the LORD has not spoken; the prophet has spoken it presumptuously, you need not be afraid of him" (Deuteronomy 18:20-22).

Thus there were, even in Moses' day, two acid tests; the former was essentially doctrinal, and no sign or wonder, however marvellous or inexplicable, was to be taken into consideration if the prophet or dreamer taught disobedience to the very first of the ten commandments (or for that matter, any other). The latter test was a very practical one, and would quickly sort out the wheat from the chaff (Jeremiah 23:28). Jeremiah himself furnishes examples of false prophets whose predictions failed (see chapter 28), and Micaiah before him had clashed with the idolatrous prophets about the outcome of Ahab's war against the Syrians (1 Kings 22). In spite of the vindication of the Lord's true prophets, Israel remained blind and deaf to God's continued appeals to His people to mend their ways.

We have noted the Lord's warnings in Matthew's gospel and elsewhere that false prophets would arise among the Christian community. How then were these to be recognised? Not surprisingly, the New Testament urges all believers to apply the same acid tests, and particularly that of doctrinal purity. At a fairly early stage in the progress of the gospel Paul wrote:

"… I want you to understand that no one speaking by the Spirit of God ever says 'Jesus be cursed!' and no one can say 'Jesus is Lord' except by the Holy Spirit." (1 Corinthians 12:3).

However, by the time John wrote, false teaching had already crept in about Christ's nature, some denying that Jesus had come in the flesh. Hence acknowledgement of the truth about *this* subject became of the utmost importance:

> "Beloved, do not believe every spirit, but test the spirits to see whether they are of God; for many false prophets have gone out into the world. By this you know the Spirit of God: every spirit which confesses that Jesus Christ has come in the flesh is of God, and every spirit which does not confess Jesus is not of God. This is the spirit of antichrist, of which you heard that it was coming, and now it is in the world already" (1 John 4:1-3).

Since John's day the erstwhile Christian church has wandered into many more myths and "destructive heresies". By the same crucial test of doctrinal purity it has suffered shipwreck, for it is no longer built upon the foundation of a Son of God subject to his Father. Virtually every sect of Christendom is wedded to the doctrine of the trinity, which creed the authors believe to be patently false.[1] But "God is not a God of confusion"; He will never authenticate corrupters of His truth and is therefore *not* responsible for the signs and wonders of Christendom (see Revelation 13:13-14).

SPECIAL GIFTS — GREATER RESPONSIBILITIES
The possession of Spirit gifts in Bible times was a great privilege, and carried with it a correspondingly great responsibility. Consequently men and women so endowed were guilty of a more serious betrayal of their trust if they later transgressed God's laws. David's sin with Bathsheba was all the more heinous, and his punishment the heavier, because God

---

1. Unitarians err in the opposite direction, denying as they do the clear scripture that tells of the unique divine sonship of Jesus through the operation of the Holy Spirit upon the virgin Mary. A mere human Jesus would have been unable to save himself, let alone anyone else!

had favoured him with the Spirit and with success in life up to that time (2 Samuel 12:7-8). The summary judgment on Ananias and Sapphira (Acts 5:1-11) could well have been inflicted because they had shared in the outpouring of the Holy Spirit described in Acts 4:31. The sobering words of the apostle in Hebrews put this matter in its true perspective:

"For it is impossible to restore again to repentance those who have once been enlightened, who have tasted the heavenly gift, and have become partakers of the Holy Spirit, and have tasted the goodness of the word of God and the powers of the age to come, if they then commit apostasy, since they crucify the Son of God on their own account and hold him up to contempt" (Hebrews 6:4-6).

Precedents for this condemnation are contained in the Old Testament. Balaam, Saul and Solomon come to mind here—each endowed with Spirit powers yet turning away completely from God's laws to their own condemnation. But the words in Hebrews were exactly fulfilled in several of Paul's earlier fellow-workers who apostatised, either by leaving the faith altogether (2 Timothy 4:10) or—perhaps worse still—by strongly opposing the apostle's doctrine (2 Corinthians 11:12-15; 2 Timothy 2:17-18; 4:14-15). Jesus himself expressly warns that successful prophecy, exorcism and performance of mighty works will definitely *not* suffice to win approval in the Day of Judgment:

"Not every one who says to me, 'Lord, Lord,' shall enter the kingdom of heaven, but he who does the will of my Father who is in heaven. On that day many will say to me, 'Lord, Lord, did we not prophesy in your name, and cast out demons in your name, and do many mighty works in your name?' And then will I declare to them, 'I never knew you; depart from me, you evildoers'" (Matthew 7:21-23).

The present-day desire for Spirit gifts is thus thoroughly misguided, for it concentrates on what is both unnecessary for salvation and indeed unavailable in this present dispensation, and at the same time distracts from what is essential, viz. doing God's will in our daily lives. This "will" has been very fully revealed in the Scriptures, and is in itself a life-time's work in which to attain maturity.

A related claim by some is that faith can only come by the operation of the Holy Spirit upon the heart of a potential believer. As commonly understood, this view does not accurately reflect New Testament teaching. It is of course fundamental that no-one comes to Christ unless the Father draws him (John 6.44). But *how* is a person so drawn? The parables of the treasure hid in a field and of the pearl of great price (Matthew 13.44-46) reflect the two main types of believers. There are, on the one hand, those who unexpectedly stumble across the way of life, having been not consciously looking for it. On the other hand there are those who search keenly for the Truth of God and by their diligent seeking find it. In the twentieth century as much as in the first the only source of enlightenment is God's Word, the Bible, *which is able* to make us wise unto salvation through faith in Christ Jesus (2 Timothy 3:15); as also the Psalmist writes: "Thy word is a lamp to my feet and a light to my path" (Psalm 119:105; cp. Proverbs 6:23). Today God continues doing what He has always done, namely, to direct those who seek Him to the inspired record of His will towards us and of His great purpose centred in His Son. Thus the Holy Spirit's involvement remains wholly in God's control, not in man's—it is God's providential overruling in persons who, in the words of Paul to the Athenians, "seek God, in the hope that they might feel after Him and find Him" (Acts 17:27).

There is another grave danger in claiming personal Spirit guidance today, for such claims undermine the absolute and sole authority of the Bible and pave the way for many aberrations in doctrine and practice, as history has repeatedly shown.

PRACTICAL DIFFICULTIES IN ACCEPTING CURRENT CLAIMS

Having reviewed some Biblical objections, we note now some of the logical objections inherent in current claims of Spirit endowment. First the claims of *glossolalia*, or the ability to speak in foreign tongues right outside the speaker's scope or experience.[1] That speaking in tongues was performed in New Testament times is not in dispute—the fact is borne witness to and the purpose and results (to establish the credentials of God's witnesses to the resurrection of Jesus) clear enough. In present-day "manifestations" there is no comparable purpose or result, and the revelations, such as they are, are puerile, and quite unworthy of serious consideration. In communities claiming these powers there is great mental and moral pressure on "born-again" believers to prove their "renewal" by manifesting this gift, and it is not difficult to understand how many susceptible individuals begin to imagine supernatural stirrings within themselves. Some of these misguided people have later admitted they were misled into making false claims because of this psychological pressure (see Warfield, p 127*ff*). "Speaking in tongues" has often been associated with the gift of prophecy in its more limited sense of predicting future events, especially the date of Jesus' second coming and its related circumstances— and one and all, without exception, have been proved wrong by the non-appearance of Jesus on the date chosen. Thus these claims have been demonstrably proved false, but the lessons have been lost to subsequent generations and the errors repeated, decade after decade.

Gifts of healing refer to claims which over the years have obtained a great deal of notice and often notoriety, when thousands of sufferers have testified that they have been healed of their diseases. The cures may have been effected by healers, men and women who have laid their hands on the sick and

---

1. Another view, which we do not accept, is that New Testament glossolalia refers to "ecstatic utterances", devoid of rational meaning.

prayed over them, perhaps also anointing them with oil (based on the wording of James 5:14-16). Quite remarkable claims have been made; here is just one example, taken from Dennis & Rita Bennett's book "The Holy Spirit and You":[1]

"Blind eyes are opened; cataracts dissolved (yes, and even empty eye sockets filled!); deaf ears are made to hear; tumours disappear; broken bones are instantly mended; damaged hearts restored; multiple sclerosis, tuberculosis, cancer, paralysis, arthritis, and all the ills the flesh is heir to can be and are being healed by the touch of the Master's Hand. Some of these healings have been instantaneous, some progressive, some partial ..."

This summary follows the relation of a few scattered examples of anecdotal cures, in which no proof is offered that the original diagnosis was correct. Alternatively, healing powers have been attributed to some "holy relic", or to a shrine which has been sanctified by a vision of the virgin Mary or some other saint in Roman Catholic hagiology, to which sufferers may repair and seek restoration of health. In both cases (healers or shrines) comparisons are lightly made with the healings by Jesus and his apostles recorded in the New Testament. The comparisons fade when it is discovered that modern claims of healing are deficient in several fundamental respects:

(1) Whereas first century healing worked for everyone coming to Jesus and the apostles, only a fraction of today's sufferers find relief—and very importantly, of those that are relieved most (if not all) have succeeded through faith healing, the triumph of the mind over the body in patients whose maladies are psychogenic and not organic. It must always be borne in mind that faith can be equally effective,

---

1. Pub. Coverdale House, London and Eastbourne, 1971, p.122

whether exercised within a religious group or quite external to one. For example, "Christian Science" and hypnotism, both depending on induced faith, have achieved comparable success, the proportion healed by each being very similar.

(2) Secondly, many so-called healings today are at best only partial and temporary, i.e. some relief only, and but for a limited period. This again is in sharp contrast to the complete recovery of those healed by Jesus and his apostles. In their days there were no residual symptoms to cope with—recovery was full and absolute.

(3) Perhaps most significant of all, there are no substantiated claims today of raising the dead, the kind of miracle which both Jesus and the Twelve performed on a number of occasions. This fact alone is fatal to the pretensions of people claiming the powers of the apostolic age.

Mention above of shrines and relics brings us especially into the world of the Roman Catholic Church and its long association with such things. Many tales are told to the credulous about the efficacy of prayers associated with holy relics, e.g. pieces of the true cross or its nails, the bones of saint X or martyr Y, a phial of the virgin's milk, samples of hair, nail parings and the like from the early martyrs. It has been truly observed that rotten bones have succeeded in effecting cures where their original possessors had failed! True, these claims have long been fading in the churches of the western developed world, but superstitious belief in such things still reigns strongly in the minds of the poorer peoples of the earth—in Asia, Africa and Latin America—a reaction, perhaps, to their hard lot in life.

THE SPIRIT IN TRUE BELIEVERS

There is only one way in which a man or woman can truly be said to possess the Holy Spirit today, and that is by making the teaching of the Bible his or her very own. Jesus said: "The *words* that I have spoken to you *are spirit* and life" (John 6:63). We have his spoken words in the gospels and the book of Revelation and these were recorded by the inspired evangelists. In addition, he fully endorsed the inspiration of the Old Testament as the Spirit word of God, and he also put his seal on the preaching and subsequent letters of his apostles, to whom he said:

"He who hears you hears me, and he who rejects you rejects me, and he who rejects me rejects him who sent me" (Luke 10:16).

Therefore a knowledge of God's purpose in and through Christ places a great responsibility upon those who receive it—but also a great reward for accepting it "not as the word of men but as what it really is, the word of God which, is at work in you believers" (1 Thessalonians 2:13).

A believer's character will be formed, his mind enlightened and his hope sustained, according to the assiduity with which he or she perseveres in systematic daily contact with the Scriptures. Through such daily application the mind and spirit of Christ will be more and more formed within them, and by faithful stewardship according to this word such may confidently look forward to God's mercy, forgiveness and reward in the day when Jesus returns to earth in fulfilment of his explicit and repeated promises.

The Trinity—*True or False?*

APPENDIX TO CHAPTER FIVE: THE HOLY SPIRIT AND THE SPIRIT OF JESUS

The conclusion stated on pages 110*ff*, that the phrases in the above title are synonymous, is further substantiated when we compare a number of New Testament parallels which refer to the function of the two. The following list of equivalences is by no means complete.

OPERATION OF THE HOLY SPIRIT	ROLE OF JESUS
"Having been forbidden by he Holy Spirit to speak the word in Asia (Acts 16.6)	"They attempted to go into Bythinia, but the Spirit of Jesus did not allow them" (Acts 16:7).
"Let him hear what the Spirit says to the churches (Revelation 1:1).	"The Revelation of Jesus Christ ... to show to his servants" (Revelation 2:7).
"It is not you who speaks, but the Holy Spirit" (Mark 13:11).	"I Jesus will give you a mouth and wisdom" (Luke 21:15).
"But the fruit of the Spirit is love, joy and peace (Galatians 5:22).	"He who abides in me ... he it that bears much fruit" (John 15:5).
"Through sanctification by the Spirit" (2 Thess.2:13)	"To those sanctified in Christ Jesus". "Christ Jesus, whom God made our ... sanctification" (1 Cor. 1:2,30).
"The Spirit intercedes for us (Romans 8:26).	"Christ Jesus ... who indeed intercedes for us" (Rom. 8:34).

"But the Counsellor (parakletos), the Holy Spirit, whom the Father will send in my name" (John 14:25).

"We have an advocate (parakletos), with the Father, Jesus Christ the Righteous" (1 John 2:1).

"Through the Spirit in the inner man" (Ephesians 3:16).

"That Christ may dwell in your hearts"(Ephesians 3:17).

"Through him (Jesus) we both have access in one Spirit to the Father" (Ephesians 2:18).

"Christ Jesus our Lord, in whom we have ... confidence of access through our faith in in him" (Ephesians 3:12).
"Through him (Jesus) we have obtained access to this grace in which we stand" (Romans 5:2).

"One and the same spirit, who apportions to each one one individually as he wills" (1 Cor.12:11).

"And his (Christ's) gifts were that some should be apostles, some prophets".(Ephesians 4:11)

We conclude that what Jesus himself did during his earthly ministry, he continued to do, once he was exalted to his Father's side, through the Spirit vested in him without measure. It is the post-Pentecostal antitype to the situation described in the Old Testament, where God is located on His heavenly throne, but aware of and controlling all things by the omnipresence of His Spirit. Further, the breathing of the Holy Spirit into the disciples by Jesus after his resurrection (John 20:22) is a close parallel with the creation of Adam (Genesis 2:7), and shows how Jesus became the beginning of a *new* creation—see chapter 6, page 286*ff*.

Chapter 6

"THE CHRIST, THE SON OF THE LIVING GOD"[1]

Section 1: JESUS THE MESSIAH

Jesus and his disciples were in the far north of the land, commencing the long journey to his crucifixion at Jerusalem. As they walked, Jesus asked the twelve a question: 'Who do men say that I am?' Various replies followed, most of them suggesting that Jesus was a reincarnation of one of the notable Old Testament figures such as Elijah or Jeremiah. But he then turned the question on them: 'But who do *you* say that I am?' Simon Peter's unhesitating answer forms the title of this chapter: 'You are the Christ, the Son of the living God'. Peter's reply distilled into one short sentence all the information he had acquired during the three years in which he had been a constant companion of his Lord. Christ's response shows that Peter had correctly stated the facts. "Blessed are you, Simon Bar-Jona! For flesh and blood has not revealed this to you, but my Father who is in heaven". So we have a firm starting point for a detailed exploration into the person and mission of Jesus. He is 'the Christ', and at the same time the 'Son of God'.

To modern ears the word 'Christ' could easily be regarded as just another name for Jesus, but to a Jew in Peter's day it had a very specific meaning. 'The Christ' (Gk '*Christos*') meant 'The Anointed One', and was the direct equivalent of the Hebrew word 'Messiah'. The coming of this Messiah is one of the themes of the Old Testament and was the earnest expectation of

---

1. Matthew 16:16

148

all pious Jews. So when Peter said Jesus was *the Christ* (Matthew 16:16), or when the high priest asked Jesus if he was *the Christ* (Matthew 26:63), or when Peter later preached that God had made Jesus "both Lord and *Christ*" (Acts 2:36) each time they had in mind the fulfilment of the predictions about the Messiah. So in any enquiry into Jesus, the teaching about the Messiah must be explored.

ASPECTS OF THE MESSIAH'S WORK

If there is one common link between virtually all the books that comprise the Old Testament it is the expectation that there would eventually arise in the nation of Israel a notable man who would be a deliverer and ruler. Many different roles would be combined in this one person, and in each of these aspects the Messiah would be a source of great benefit to the world.

The first book of the Bible reveals that to Abraham, the founder of the entire Jewish race, God promised a descendant who would bring a time of blessing to everyone on earth:

"By myself have I sworn, saith the Lord, ... in thy seed shall all the nations of the world be blessed" (Genesis 22:16-18, RV).

One of these Messianic 'blessings' was to be the forgiveness of sins leading to man's reconciliation to God (Acts 3.25-26). So here we have the promise of a SAVIOUR; although, as will be shown below, this aspect of his mission was not understood by many Jews.

A few hundred years after Abraham's day a different aspect of the work of this future personage was revealed when Moses received an assurance of the coming of a messenger with divine teaching and authority:

"And the Lord said to me, (Moses) ... I will raise up for them a prophet like you from among their brethren; and I

149

will put my words in his mouth, and he shall speak to them all that I command him" (Deuteronomy 18:17-18).

Here the coming of a DIVINE TEACHER is promised.

Some centuries later David, the first king of Israel to have his royal throne in Jerusalem, was told by God that he would have a descendant who would one day occupy that throne for ever:

"I will raise up your son after you, ... and I will establish his kingdom. He shall build a house for my name, and I will establish the throne of his kingdom for ever... And your house and your kingdom shall be made sure for ever" (2 Samuel 7:12-13,16).

So this descendant of Abraham and David would also be an eternal KING.

But as well as being the son of David, this immortal royal ruler would also have another father. God said:

"I will be his father, and he shall be my son" (2 Samuel 7:14)

The promise thus concerned no ordinary man! He would be none other than the SON OF GOD.

By combining these aspects of **Saviour, Teacher, King** and **Son of God**, the work of the promised Messiah emerges as the clear teaching of the Jewish scriptures. The title 'Messiah' means 'the Anointed One'. It is an ancient custom to initiate both civil and religious leaders by anointing them with oil, and the 'anointed of the Lord' was often used to describe Israel's kings. But whilst these were 'messiahs' in this one sense, the future ruler was to be *pre-eminently* the 'Anointed'—'Messiah the Prince' to use Daniel's description (Daniel 9:25, AV).

PREDICTIONS OF THE COMING OF THE MESSIAH

The Old Testament is full of predictions about the coming of this Messiah descended from Abraham through David, and the great work he would do. Many aspects of his life and mission were revealed in advance. The prophet Micah foretold the actual town where he would be born, Bethlehem:

> "But you, O Bethlehem Ephrathah, who are little to be among the clans of Judah, from you shall come forth for me one who is to be ruler in Israel" (Micah 5:2).

Isaiah spoke of his birth and of his success as ruler:

> "For to us a child is born, to us a son is given; and the government will be upon his shoulder, ... Of the increase of his government and of peace there will be no end, upon the throne of David, and over his kingdom, to establish it, and to uphold it with justice and with righteousness from this time forth and for evermore" (Isaiah 9:6-7).

Jeremiah links the Messiah's coming to the final deliverance of Israel:

> "Behold, the days are coming, says the Lord, when I will fulfil the promise I made to the house of Israel and the house of Judah. In those days and at that time I will cause a righteous Branch to spring forth for David; and he shall execute justice and righteousness in the land. In those days Judah will be saved and Jerusalem will dwell securely" (Jeremiah 33:14-16).

These, along with many other similar predictions, formed the basis of the Jewish hope in their coming Messiah. He was anticipated mainly as a deliverer of the nation from a time of extreme trouble, and as a king under whose wise rule Israel and the whole world would live in a state of unparalleled peace, blessing and prosperity. This belief was instilled into Jews from their earliest age, and the coming of the Messiah was the pinnacle of their hopes. It is often overlooked that the first converts to Christianity were Jews who had been brought up in this hope of a coming Messiah. Thus we can understand the obvious excitement of the little group of men that later became the nucleus of Jesus' disciples:

"One of the two who heard John speak, and followed him, was Andrew, Simon Peter's brother. He first found his brother Simon, and said to him, "We have found the Messiah" (which means Christ).

Philip found Nathanael, and said to him, "We have found him of whom Moses in the law and also the prophets wrote, Jesus of Nazareth, the son of Joseph." Jesus saw Nathanael coming to him ... and Nathanael answered him, "Rabbi, you are the Son of God! You are the King of Israel!" (John 1:40- 41,45,47,49).

Notice the terms used to describe the Messiah: the *Son of God*, the *King of Israel*. And all this, those original disciples said, had been gleaned from the writings of Moses (the first five books of the Bible) and the prophets (all the rest of the Old Testament).

JESUS IS THE MESSIAH
The New Testament continues this emphasis on the Messiah, but now as a matter of reality, not prediction. It clearly identifies Jesus of Nazareth, born in Bethlehem, as the Messiah or Christ. The very opening words of the New Testament trace the pedigree of Jesus back to Abraham and David as a basis for the revelation of Jesus as the Messiah:

"The book of the genealogy of Jesus Christ, the son of David, the son of Abraham" (Matthew 1:1).

In confirmation of the identity of Jesus with the long expected Messiah we read that at the annunciation of his birth the angel predicted that he would fulfil all the aspects of the promise to David, viz: be a son of David, be also the son of God, and would reign over Israel for ever on David's restored throne:

"He will be great, and will be called the Son of the Most High; and the Lord God will give to him the throne of his father David, and he will reign over the house of Jacob for ever; and of his kingdom there will be no end" (Luke 1:32-33).

When Jesus grew to manhood his public preaching compelled many to believe that he was indeed the Messiah, or Christ. People on occasions addressed him by Messianic titles: "Jesus, *son of David*" (Luke 18:38), "Hosanna to the *son of David*" (Matthew 21:9), "Tell us if you are the Christ, the *Son of God*" (Matthew 26:63), "Are you the *King of the Jews*?" (Mark 15:2). It is important to note that in each case they were using Old Testament terms attributable only to the Messiah. On at least two occasions Jesus actually affirmed that he *was* the expected Messiah (John 4:25-26; Mark 14:61-62). And because they saw him as the promised Messiah, it is not surprising that they attempted to install him as their king on at least one occasion:

"Perceiving that they were about to come and take him by force to make him king, Jesus withdrew ..." (John 6:15).

Christ's reluctance was because the fulfilment of the Messianic predictions of his kingship was to be at his *second* coming, not the first. Luke records that:

"He proceeded to tell a parable, because he was near to Jerusalem, and because they supposed that the kingdom of God was to appear immediately. He said therefore, A nobleman went into a far country to receive kingly power and then return" (Luke 19:11-12).

153

Clearly the nobleman is Jesus, and the far country heaven. In this way he tried to tell his listeners that although he *was* the Messiah, the promises were not to be fulfilled then, but would await his return from heaven. It was because Jesus did not do immediately the things expected of the Messiah— capitalise on the wave of nationalistic emotion—proclaim himself the King in David's line—rally the Jews to him—expel the Roman overlords from the Holy Land and city—set up the golden age of Messianic rule there and then— it was because of his failure to do all this, that the tide of public opinion turned so rapidly and violently against him. Within a few days of the peoples' rapturous welcome of him into Jerusalem as the son of David, a similar crowd was howling for his crucifixion.

Even the disciples, including Peter who had once so strongly asserted that Jesus *was* the Christ, were disillusioned by the death of their master. "We had hoped that he was the one to redeem Israel" they plaintively said (Luke 24:21). Along with all their fellow Jews they had failed to notice that the predicted Messiah or Christ had the role of redeemer as well as king. After his resurrection Jesus had to educate his disciples to understand that his recent sufferings and death were just as much a part of the Messianic rôle as the kingship:

> "O foolish men, and slow of heart to believe all that the prophets have spoken! Was it not necessary that the Christ should suffer these things and enter into his glory?" And beginning with Moses and all the prophets, he interpreted to them in all the scriptures the things concerning himself.

> Then he said to them, "These are my words which I spoke to you, while I was still with you, that everything written about me in the law of Moses and the prophets and the psalms must be fulfilled." Then he opened their minds to understand the scriptures, and said to them, "Thus it is written, that the Christ should suffer and on the third day rise from the dead, and that repentance and forgiveness of

sins should be preached in his name to all nations" (Luke 24:25-27; 44-47).

So it was with this fuller, indeed complete, picture of the Messiah that the disciples embarked on their mission to convert the world to Christianity. Jesus, whom the Jews had crucified, was the Christ!

"Let all the house of Israel know assuredly that God has made him both Lord and *Christ,* this Jesus whom you crucified" (Acts 2:36).
"But Saul increased all the more in strength, and confounded the Jews who lived in Damascus by proving that Jesus *was the Christ*" (Acts 9:22).
"He (Apollos) powerfully confuted the Jews in public, showing by the scriptures that *the Christ was Jesus"* (Acts 18:28).

These references stress the method of the apostles' preaching. Taking the universally accepted understanding of the expected Messiah as the starting point, they demonstrated from Scripture that Jesus of Nazareth was indeed the promised Christ. When Christianity was first preached it was the Jewish Messiah that was the subject, followed by convincing proof (notably by his resurrection) that Jesus, whom many of them could remember, *was* this promised Messiah. So Peter, in the incident described at the opening of this chapter, was not wrong in styling Jesus "the Christ"— and if we desire to understand the person and mission of Jesus of Nazareth the starting point must be the Old Testament predictions of the coming Messiah. *A system of Christian belief that ignores this basis must inevitably be astray from the original and true teaching about the founder of Christianity.*

CHRISTIANITY VERSUS THE CREEDS
Certainly, the Jews were expecting a human Messiah—divinely sent it is true, but a fleshly descendant of Abraham and David

and in the mould of their great leader Moses. They undoubtedly would not have expected, or been able to comprehend, the individual alluded to in later attempts to define the person and work of the Christ:

> "I believe in one God the Father Almighty, Maker of heaven and earth, and all things visible and invisible: And in one Lord Jesus Christ, the only begotten Son of God, Begotten of his Father before all worlds, God of God, Light of Light, Very God of Very God, Begotten, not made, Being of one substance with the Father" (the Nicene creed).

This chapter will investigate whether the Nicene creed, and the equally famous Athanasian creed, are a true and legitimate interpretation of the Bible references to Jesus the Messiah. It will examine teaching on the person and mission of Jesus under the following Scriptural titles ascribed to him:

The Son of Man
The Son of God
The Word of God
The Lamb of God
The Beginning of the creation of God

Chapter 6

"THE CHRIST, THE SON OF THE LIVING GOD"[1]

Section 2: JESUS THE SON OF MAN

The Messiah as a representative man

This section will examine the Bible teaching about the nature possessed by Jesus at his first coming. Whilst in trinitarian teaching much emphasis is given to Jesus as the Son of God, the many references to him as the Son of Man are largely overlooked. Yet the term was the one almost invariably used by Jesus to denote himself, occurring nearly 100 times in the synoptic gospels. It is only in John's record that the alternative term Son of God is sometimes used by Jesus. The title 'Son of Man' should therefore merit our careful attention as a vital component of our understanding of the Messiah's work.

Jesus was unique in that he had a human mother but no human father. Luke tells us that Jesus was conceived by the direct action of the Holy Spirit on Mary (1:35). Thus God was his father. The implications of the divine sonship of Jesus will be considered in the next section, whilst the significance of his parentage on the human side will be considered now.

"BORN OF A WOMAN"

There is great Biblical emphasis on the fact that the Messiah was to be born to a human parent. Paul introduces Jesus in the opening of his letter to the Romans as having been "descended

---

1. Matthew 16:16

157

from David according to the flesh" (Romans 1:3), and elsewhere states that "when the time had fully come, God sent forth his Son, born of woman ..." (Galatians 4:4). This human parentage is implicit in all the Old Testament descriptions of the Messiah's work. Way back in Eden, after the fall of man and the introduction of sin and death into the world, God made a promise to the effect that Eve should have a descendant who would fatally wound sin's power to destroy mankind. Speaking to the serpent God said "her seed (i.e. the woman's seed, the *Messiah*) ... shall bruise your head" (Genesis 3.15). Similarly, as shown on pp.151-152, the Messiah was promised to be a direct descendant of Abraham and David.

"A PROPHET LIKE TO MOSES"
Further indications of the human parentage of the Messiah are contained in God's promise to His people at Mount Sinai. The context of this passage rules out any trinitarian interpretation. After the young nation of Israel had stood trembling at the foot of Mount Sinai at the awesome voice of God proclaiming the ten commandments, they said to Moses "Let me not hear again the voice of the Lord my God ... lest I die". To which God replied with a promise that ever since has been taken as referring to the coming Messiah:

> "They have rightly said all that they have spoken. I will raise up for them a prophet *like you* from among their brethren: and I will put my words in his mouth, and he shall speak to them all that I command him" (Deuteronomy 18:17-18).

This revealing passage stresses the humanity of the Messiah. He was to be 'like' Moses, and be 'raised up from among their (Jewish) brethren'. Notice he was not to be God Himself, for this is what Israel had said they were unable to face, but a man like Moses who would be the agent through whom God's words would be conveyed, thus obviating the necessity for another open manifestation of divine power and presence as at Sinai.

Jesus fulfilled this role of divine spokesman when he became the "Word made flesh". His comments to the Jews of his day could be a direct allusion to this same Deuteronomy passage when Israel recoiled from hearing God's direct voice:

> "And the Father who sent me has himself borne witness to me. His voice you have never heard, his form you have never seen; and you do not have his word abiding in you, for you do not believe him whom he has sent" (John 5:37-38).

He also said that he was speaking God's words, just as Israel had requested:

> "The word which you hear is not mine, but the Father's who sent me" (John 14:24).

It is important to note in the quotation from Deuteronomy that this future prophet who was to be an agent for God was also to be instructed by God what he should speak to the people—"he shall speak to them all that I command him"— and in the passages above Jesus confirms that this was indeed what he did. This hardly tallies with a Trinity in which "none is afore, or after other: none is greater or less than other".[1] Being told what to say clearly implies a degree of subordination.

THE PHYSICAL NATURE POSSESSED BY JESUS

Turning to the New Testament the same stress is placed on Christ's human parentage, but now with added emphasis upon the physical nature of Jesus. It was identical to his fellow men, enabling him to "taste death for every one" (Hebrews 2:9). Nowhere is this more clearly stated than in the letter to the Hebrews. The inspired writer is at great pains to stress the fact that Jesus possessed a physical nature *identical* with those he

---

1. The Athanasian Creed

159

came to redeem. This was the only basis on which his sacrificial death could be effective:

> "For it was fitting that he ... in bringing many sons to glory, should make the pioneer of their salvation perfect through suffering. For he who sanctifies and those who are sanctified *have all one origin*". That is why he is not ashamed to call them brethren (Hebrews 2:10-11).

This shared origin between the redeemer and the redeemed does not just refer to the fact that Jesus was born of a human mother, but that through her Jesus inherited a physical make-up exactly the same as ours. This is stressed as the Hebrews passage proceeds. After quoting Isaiah to show that the Messiah would be given adopted 'children', i.e. the redeemed, we read:

> "Since therefore the children share in flesh and blood, *he himself likewise partook of the same nature*, that through death he might destroy him who has the power of death, that is, the devil" (Hebrews 2:14).

It is important to note the repeated emphasis in this verse. The writer could have made his point by merely saying "he partook of the same nature", but this would not have been strong enough to stress this vital aspect. The inclusion of both 'himself' and 'likewise' adds weight to the otherwise bald statement. Incidentally, in the original the Greek word for 'also' is included, thus giving triple emphasis: "He *also himself likewise* partook of the same nature". It would be difficult to use plainer words to express the complete identity of the physical natures of Jesus and the common stock of humanity.

A verse or two later the writer reverts to this theme, adding one of the reasons why the Saviour had to partake of human nature:

> "Therefore he had to be made *like his brethren in every*

respect, so that he might become a merciful and faithful high priest in the service of God, to make expiation for the sins of the people" (Hebrews 2:17).

One reason for Jesus sharing our physical nature was for him to be a completely representative man. This will be discussed later in the section headed 'The Lamb of God', but for the present the point of the allusion is that Jesus knows exactly what it is like to be human. In fact his sharing our nature is an essential aspect of his office of Saviour:

> "For because he himself has suffered and been tempted, he is able to help those who are tempted" (Hebrews 2:18).
> "For we have not a high priest who is unable to sympathise with our weaknesses, but one who *in every respect* has been tempted as we are, yet without sinning" (Hebrews 4:15).

Notice again the unambiguous language. Jesus shared 'in every respect' the temptations common to mankind. Specific examples for Jesus were the wilderness temptations (Matthew 4:1-11), and the natural desire to shrink from the ordeal of the cross (Matthew 26:37-44), but in addition to these specific occasions, Jesus received throughout his life the same enticements to sin as ourselves. This was the inevitable effect of sharing man's physical nature. The difference between him and us lies not in the physical make-up but in the response.[1] He never gave way to temptation and remained sinless throughout his life (see also 2 Corinthians 5:21; 1 Peter 2:22; 1 John 3:5).

All this is consistent with Jesus the Messiah being one of our race, but if he was God clothed in human flesh many contradictions occur. For example James emphatically states that "God cannot be tempted with evil" (James 1:14). If Jesus was God, and thus not vulnerable to temptation, one of the

---

1. And especially, of course, in the fact that he was the unique Son of God. This fact must never be lost sight of, even while we consider his humanity.

essential aspects of the Redeemer's work would be absent: he could not be a sympathetic and effective mediator. Scripture also teaches that the life of Jesus was a gradual development in character—understandable if he shared our nature, but something impossible to reconcile with the idea that he was pre-existent God. He "increased *in wisdom* and in stature, and *in favour with God* and man" (Luke 2:52). So at his baptism the voice from heaven could proclaim "Thou art my beloved Son; with thee I am well pleased" (Luke 3:22). The writer to the Hebrews comments that "although he was a Son, he *learned obedience* through what he suffered", as a result of which he was *then* "made perfect" (Hebrews 5:8-9). Clearly a pre-existent all-wise God does not need to increase in wisdom, or to learn to be obedient, nor to obtain the approval of his co-equal God, and certainly does not need to be made perfect at the end of his mortal life.

JESUS IN GETHSEMANE
The context of the Hebrews passage quoted above reveals another facet of the earthly life of the Son of Man:

> "In the days of his flesh, Jesus offered up prayers and supplications, with loud cries and tears, to him who was able to save him from death" (Hebrews 5:7).

The reference is obviously to Christ's distress in the Garden of Gethsemane when "being in an agony he prayed more earnestly: and his sweat became like great drops of blood falling down upon the ground" (Luke 22:44). It is impossible for us to probe the extremity of feeling and tension in the mind of the Saviour as he fought and won the battle against his natural feelings. With the dread of the next few hours haunting him he besought his Father to find some other way of human redemption, if that were possible. Could a pre-existent God, who "knows the end from the beginning" (Isaiah 46:10) have ever had such a battle or ever made such a request? Clearly we have here a man, not a God. We have a man whose emotions were bounded by his present life, without any antecedent knowledge or experiences to come to his aid. Here was one who needed help to weather the crisis that had come upon him. It is inconceivable that if Jesus was God from the beginning, and had therefore devised the scheme of human redemption, he could ask for deliverence from the death he knew was essential.

Help came in the person of an angel. Luke records "there appeared to him an angel from heaven, strengthening him" (22:43). The angels are God's messengers, who "hearken to the voice of his word" (Psalm 103:20), and are clearly of subordinate status to God. Yet here one of their number was able to impart understanding and comfort to one who, if the trinitarian view is correct, was greater and wiser than any angel.

ERRORS PREDICTED BY THE APOSTLES

Failure to recognise the true import of this basic fact that Jesus was the Son of Man and thus *identical* in physical nature to all other men and woman, has led to a lot of what can only be described as playing with words in an attempt to reconcile Scripture with the doctrine of the Trinity. One writer says that while Jesus was "truly Man in every sense, He should *not be subject to the sinful inheritance which had corrupted the whole of mankind"* , and "He differed from us in ... *his freedom from sin, either inherited or acquired.*[1] This difference, he says, was because Jesus' nature was the same as Adam's before the Fall.[2] Yet Scripture says that redemption demands that Jesus was made like us *in every respect*, and this must include our present sin-prone nature.

The teaching that the Messiah was of a different physical nature to the rest of mankind was one of the earliest heresies

---

1. Hammond: "In Understanding be Men", p98,99

2. "All that was characteristic of unfallen man was found in him.", p.98

that the infant church had to combat. Towards the end of the first century the Apostle John had strong words to say about those who denied that Jesus had come in "the flesh", that is, with normal human nature:

"Beloved, do not believe every spirit, but test the spirits to see whether they are of God; for many false prophets have gone out into the world. By this you know the Spirit of God: every spirit which confesses that Jesus Christ has come in the flesh is of God, and every spirit which does not confess Jesus is not of God. This is the spirit of antichrist, of which you heard that it was coming, and now it is in the world already" (1 John 4:1-3).

Reference to any analytical concordance will show that the word translated 'flesh'[1] as well as describing the actual body extends to mean 'human nature'. In this way Paul equates 'flesh' with 'sinful passions', saying that nothing good dwells in the 'flesh', and also that Jesus was in the 'likeness of sinful flesh' (Romans 7:5,18; 8:3). So to believe that Jesus 'came in the flesh' is to say that he shared human nature. In his second epistle John is even more critical of this false doctrine concerning Jesus, and gives stern warnings on how its adherents should be treated:

"For many deceivers have gone out into the world, men who will not acknowledge the coming of Jesus Christ in the flesh; such a one is the deceiver and the antichrist. Look to yourselves, that you may not lose what you have worked for, but may win a full reward. Any one who goes ahead and does not abide in the doctrine of Christ does not have God; he who abides in the doctrine of Christ has both the

---

1. Greek *sarx*. Of this Allman in his *Vocabulary of the Bible* says "In Greek thought the concept of flesh denotes simply a substance, the bodily substance of man; but in the N.T. .. this physical meaning is almost always transcended. N.T. writers use the term 'flesh' to signify the natural man as a whole, with all the characteristics of his weak, impotent, fallen state".

Father and the Son. If any one comes to you and does not
bring this doctrine, do not receive him into the house or
give him any greeting; for he who greets him shares his
wicked work" (2 John 7-11).

This is a solemn warning. Already there were some who
were 'going ahead' by introducing, among other things,
different ideas about the nature of Jesus compared with what
the apostles had taught. The Apostle John described this a
'wicked work', and was emphatic that such ideas rendered
access to Christ and God impossible. In this he is echoing the
words of his Master which state that a knowledge of God and
Christ is essential for salvation: "This is eternal life, that they
know thee the only true God, and Jesus Christ whom that hast
sent" (John 17:3).

"THE MAN CHRIST JESUS"

In keeping with the original views about Jesus, the early
Christians regularly described him as a man, and it is
inconceivable that they would have used this term if all the time
they believed that he was God. In employing this term they
were following the usage of the Master himself. There are
many examples of this. John records that in some sense (to be
considered later p.230*ff*) Jesus refers to himself as coming
down from heaven. But it is the Son of *man* who thus descends.
So in whatever sense Jesus existed before he was born, it was
as a man, not as part of the triune godhead. Here are the actual
references:

> "No one has ascended into heaven but he who descended
> from heaven, the Son of *Man*" (John 3:13).
> "What if you were to see the Son of *Man* ascending where
> he was before?" (John 6:62).

When he wanted to obtain from his disciples the confession of
his Messiahship he used the same term:

"Who do men say that the Son of *Man* is? Simon Peter
replied, You are the Christ, the Son of the living God"
(Matthew 16:13,16)

This same designation describes the attributes and activities
of Jesus in his capacity of God's representative on earth. It is
the Son of *Man* that "has authority on earth to forgive sins"
(Luke 5.24). On the day of Pentecost Peter identified the
Messiah with 'Jesus of Nazareth, a *man* attested to you by God'
(Acts 2:22). It was by this same Man that the resurrection of
the dead has been made possible (1 Corinthians 15:21). But
more than this. Even the glorified Jesus, both in his mediatorial
work now in heaven and in his future glory and exaltation, is
still described as the Son of Man. It is the Son of *Man* that was
to 'sit at the right hand of Power'(Mark 14:62), and that was
seen by Stephen as 'standing at the right hand of God' (Acts
7:56). Meanwhile it is 'the *man* Christ Jesus' who is described
as the mediator between God and men (1 Timothy 2:5), The
Son of *Man* is to return to earth 'with his angels in the glory of
his Father' (Matthew 16:27, 25:31). The same event is to be
heralded by the 'sign of the Son of *Man* in heaven', after which
men will 'see the Son of *Man* coming on the clouds of heaven
with power and great glory' (Matthew 24:30). It is the *Man*
Jesus who is to be the future judge, both of the believers (John
5:27) and of the whole world (Acts 17:31).

The Old Testament uses similar phraseology. In an
undoubted reference to the future role of Christ, Daniel clearly
distinguishes between God the 'Ancient of Days', and the
future Messianic world ruler, the 'Son of *Man':*

"And behold, with the clouds of heaven there came one like
a son of man, and he came to the Ancient of Days and was
presented before him. And to him was given dominion and
glory and kingdom, that all peoples, nations and languages
should serve him; his dominion is an everlasting dominion
which shall not pass away, and his kingdom one that shall

not be destroyed" (Daniel 7:13-14).

Who would gain the idea here of co-equal members of a trinity? The terms used to describe each, and the obvious dependence of the Son of Man on the Ancient of Days for his 'dominion and glory' render such interpretation untenable.

There is no question therefore that the early Christians viewed even the resurrected and glorified Jesus as a Man. If it is as *God* that Jesus mediates for us, or it is as *God* that he returns in glory to rule the world, then the passages cited above would have been a most suitable place to say so. But the term is always *man*, not God, suggesting that they knew nothing of trinitarian dogmas.

The significance of this combined testimony must not be overlooked. Far from regarding Jesus as God, the early Christians saw him firstly as a man. A very special man, truly, but with no claim for him to be a member of an eternal trinity. And it is important to note that this still applied after Christ's glorification and ascension to heaven. Even then he was "the *Man* Christ Jesus".

JESUS NOT MERELY A MAN
But it must be stressed that although Jesus shared the physical nature of mankind with all its proneness to temptation, he was not mere man. By his unique birth he was specially created by God and combined in one person Son of Man and Son of God. As Roberts expressively puts it: "To say that Christ was a man partaking of our sinful nature does not mean that he was the same sort of man as other men. His parentage and education were both divine; and as it was said, "Never man spake like this man", so it has to be said that never man thought as this man, or loved as this man, or felt as this man. He was a special man altogether, though as to nature the same; just as a special vase, got up and gilt for a royal table, is a different article from a common mug, though made, it may be, of the same china

167

clay".[1]

There is a danger that in considering the person of the Messiah under several headings, as in this present study, that we regard each aspect as complete in itself. The true picture of Jesus in all its unique beauty and magnificence is only obtained when all the aspects are combined, and the reader is asked to bear this in mind on proceeding to the consideration of Jesus as the Son of God. At the same time we ask forbearance of the repetition which inevitably must occur when topics and ideas overlap our artificially created Section boundaries.

---

1. Roberts, R. "The Blood of Christ", p28

Chapter 6

"THE CHRIST, THE SON OF THE LIVING GOD"[1]

Section 3: JESUS THE SON OF GOD

The Messiah as a manifestation of God

Many believers in the doctrine of the trinity would accept that Jesus was a man such as we are, but insist that at the same time he was 'fully God'. Unable to explain this apparent contradiction in a way that satisfies reason, we are told that it is a mystery that should be just accepted rather than probed in an attempt to resolve the dilemma. The process by which the Messiah was allegedly both God and man is termed the 'incarnation'. Whilst this is not a scriptural word, it is derived from one that is frequently found there. The Greek for 'in flesh' (*en sarki*) has the Latin equivalent *in carne* and from this comes 'incarnate', with the same meaning. 'Flesh' in biblical usage, whilst primarily meaning the solid matter that makes up our natural bodies, extends to cover more intangible aspects such as mind and thought. Hence the references that use 'flesh' to describe all aspects of humanity, not just physical bodies (e.g. Genesis 6:12). 'Incarnation' as applied to Jesus refers to the process by which it is claimed that one component of the Eternal Trinity came to earth and took on this complete humanity in the form of the Jesus that people knew. Jesus was, according to this view, the Son of God *incarnate*.

In this section we look at Jesus as the Son of God and

---

1. Matthew 16:16

169

examine the Bible teaching about his sonship and its implications for the doctrine of the trinity and the incarnation.

SON OF GOD
This title occurs much less frequently than 'Son of Man', particularly in the Gospels. A comparison of the usage of the two terms shows that whilst 'Son of Man' was the preferred term when Jesus was speaking of himself, 'Son of God' was used predominantly as a form of address *to* Jesus. In other words 'Son of God' reflected who people saw him as, rather than whom he proclaimed himself to be.

ARE 'SON OF GOD' AND 'GOD THE SON' THE SAME?
First, the claim is virtually always made by Trinitarians that the appellation 'Son of God' indicates that Jesus was God in a trinitarian sense. In fact 'Son of God' is regarded as a direct equivalent of 'God the Son'. Quoting Gabriel's announcement of the impending birth of Jesus one writer clearly expresses this view: "The power of the highest shall overshadow thee: therefore that holy one which shall be born of thee shall be called the *Son of God* [i.e., God the Son]". [1] No explanation or justification is given by this author for the juxtapositioning of the words. A similar line is taken by most writers who, having correctly demonstrated that Scripture speaks frequently of the Son of God, assume that they have thereby proved that it is speaking of an eternally pre-existent member of a trinity, God the Son. There is not the slightest justification for the inversion of the words. Son of God is a scriptural title used throughout the Old and New Testaments, whereas 'God the Son' is foreign to the Bible, *not occurring even once*. It was, moreover, never found in the writings of the early Christians for over a century after the founding of the faith.

J.D.G.Dunn, Reader in Theology at the University of

---

1. Baxter, J. S. "Majesty, The God You Should Know", p.63. Pub. Scripture Press Foundation (UK) Ltd., Amersham.

Nottingham, is aware of the misunderstanding that frequently exists when using 'Son of God' in the sense propounded by the creeds:

> "These credal formulations have stamped a clear and lasting impression on Christian thought of subsequent generations up to and including the present day. So much so that it is generally taken for granted ... that to confess Jesus as the 'Son of God' is to confess his deity, and very easily assumed that to say 'Jesus is the Son of God' means and always has meant that Jesus is the pre-existent, second person of the trinity, who 'for us men and our salvation became incarnate'".[1]

After this very timely warning not to read more into the phrase than was originally intended, he goes on to say that the only way to gain the meaning of the term is to find out what it meant to Jesus and the first Christians, and asks the crucial question: "What would those who first used this language about Jesus expect their hearers and readers to understand by the phrase?[2] It is refreshing to find a modern theologian advocating a course of study which seems the obvious way to arrive at an understanding of basic Christianity. It is the invariable rule adopted by the present authors.

'SON OF GOD' MEANS 'MESSIAH'

A careful reading of the New Testament shows that to a first century Christian 'Son of God' *never* conveyed the idea of God appearing in human form in a Trinitarian sense. Dunn comments here: "Certainly 'son of God' as applied to Jesus would not necessarily have carried in and of itself the

---

1. Dunn, J.D.G. "Christology in the Making: An Inquiry into the Origins of the Doctrine of the Incarnation", p12

2. Ibid, p.13

connotation of deity".[1] Rather was 'Son of God' used interchangeably with 'Messiah'. When the Messiah was promised in David's line God said of him "I will be his father, and he shall be *my son*" (2 Samuel 7:14). This Son of God/Messiah was thenceforward expected as the one who would assume the throne of Israel, emancipate God's people and set up the literal kingdom of God on earth. At the birth of Jesus the terms of this promise were alluded to by Gabriel, clearly identifying his Messianic role and equating this with divine sonship:

> "He will be great, and will be called the *Son of the Most High*; and the Lord God will give to him the throne of his father David, and he will reign over the house of Jacob for ever; and of his kingdom there will be no end" (Luke 1:32-33).

Mary undoubtedly saw this as a promise that she would be the mother of the Messiah, who was also going to be 'Son of God'. No attempt was made to explain that the child was to be God incarnate!

Many references confirm the first century understanding that the Son of God was an equivalent term for the Messiah or Christ, with no trinitarian implications. Mark opens his record with "The beginning of the gospel of Jesus *Christ,* the Son of God" (Mark 1:1). John records that early in his ministry first Andrew recognised the role of Jesus—"We have found the Messiah (which means Christ)"—and then Nathaniel acknowledged that Jesus was at the same time the Messiah and Son of God: "Rabbi, you are the Son of God! You are the King of Israel" (John 1:41,49). Later Peter's confession, that elicited such praise from Jesus, expressed this interchangeable use of the terms: "You are the Christ, the Son of the living God"

---

1. Ibid, p.22

172

(Matthew 16:16). In the eyes of the Jewish high priest also the two terms were synonymous, for he asked Jesus at his trial "tell us if you are the Christ, the Son of God" (Matthew 26:63). The same expectation concerning the promised Messiah was expressed by Martha: "Lord, I believe that you are the Christ, the Son of God, he who is coming into the world" (John 11:27). And if any more confirmation were needed there is John's clearly stated objective in recording the miracles of Jesus: "that you may believe that Jesus is the Christ, the Son of God, and that believing you may have life in his name" (John 20:31).

Thus the 'Son of God' in first century teaching was equivalent to 'the Christ', or Messiah, with no built-in trinitarian suggestions. And on the basis that Jesus of Nazareth perfectly matched the Old Testament predictions, the early Christian preaching was also to proclaim that he was the Messiah or Son of God. Paul testified at his trial that in his preaching he had been "saying nothing but what the prophets and Moses said would come to pass: that the Christ (the Messiah) must suffer, and that, by being the first to rise from the dead, he would proclaim light both to the people and to the Gentiles" (Acts 26:22-23). In the first section of the present chapter some of the predictions concerning the Messiah were examined—the 'seed' promised to Abraham, the 'prophet like Moses', the Son of David who would reign eternally on his throne in Jerusalem, the child to be born who would assume government as predicted by Isaiah, and the righteous branch from David's rootstock who would save Judah as promised by Jeremiah. In none of these is there any hint that the Messiah would be God as well as man.

"MIGHTY GOD"

But there are many other prophecies about the Messiah. Do any of these support the contention that the Son of God is in fact God the Son, or Very God, to use the trinitarian term? A frequently used passage is the well known reference in Isaiah:

> "For to us a child is born, to us a son is given; and the
> government will be upon his shoulder, and his name will be
> called 'Wonderful Counsellor, Mighty God, Everlasting
> Father, Prince of Peace'. Of the increase of his government
> and of peace there will be no end, upon the throne of
> David, and over his kingdom ... the zeal of the Lord of
> hosts will do this" (Isaiah 9:6-7).

The full passage clearly is Messianic, looking forward to the
time when the promised ruler will reign for God. What must
not be done here is instantly to read the trinity into this passage,
especially in view of the monotheism of the Jews to whom it
was written. It is worth noting that in the original Hebrew there
is no indication of the capital letters which appear in many
translations. Does 'mighty god' and 'everlasting father' of
necessity say that the Messiah is and always has been God? It is
frequently stated in support of this assertion that the first of
these titles appears to be applied to God Himself in at least one
other passage (Isaiah 10:21). Does this then indicate that Isaiah
regarded the Messiah as a pre-existent God, equal to the
Creator Himself?

First, note the use of the future tense. The child 'will be
called' by these titles; implying that they did not so describe
him in Isaiah's day. This is hardly the language describing an
eternally pre-existing God taking human form. Secondly, we
ask whether the Jews would have understood 'mighty god' to
describe the Messiah as a co-equal and co-existent person of a
trinity. Certainly the original word translated 'god' does not
imply this of itself. It is used of human rulers and judges,
(Exodus 21:6), warriors (Exodus 15:11), angels (Psa 8:5A.V.)
and the idols of the heathen (Exodus 12:12), as well as of the
supreme God.[1] Jesus himself used 'god' in a human sense in
quoting a psalm addressed to evil rulers in the past: "Is it not

---

1. For a more detailed treatment of the use of the word translated 'God' see
chapter 3. p. 58ff, and table on p. 63

written in your law, 'I said, you are gods'? (John 10:34, quoting Psalm 82:6). As shown on p.58*ff* the use of the word 'god' is not necessarily a reference to God Himself. It is also used of 'men of might and rank'.[1] Dunn, in following his path of trying to look at the new Testament through first century eyes, confirms that a wider use of the term was common:

"The language of divine sonship and divinity was in widespread and varied use in the ancient world and would have been familiar to the contemporaries of Jesus, Paul and John, in a wide range of applications. When used in reference to individual human beings it could denote anything from a righteous or pious man ... to a heavenly or semi-heavenly being, including on the way particularly kings and rulers and especially wise or gifted or inspired men".[2]

So the use of the word 'god' to describe the Messiah does not of itself *necessitate,* or even indicate, membership of the Godhead.

The word translated 'mighty' is regularly used in scripture to describe a valiant man, a warrior. So The Oxford Hebrew lexicon defines 'mighty god' as a "mighty hero or divine hero, as reflecting the divine majesty".[3] Indeed, in confirmation of this, one translation of this passage reads "in purpose wonderful, *in battle God-like*"[4] which certainly gives no hint of a trinitarian meaning.

When did the 'child' that was to be born become the 'mighty

---

1. *Oxford Hebrew Lexicon*: Brown, Driver and Briggs, p.42

2. Op. cit. p17

3. Brown, Driver and Briggs, p.42

4. New English Bible

god'? Paul tells us. He says Jesus "was descended from David according to the flesh and designated Son of God *in power* .... by his resurrection from the dead" (Romans 1:3-4). So the Son became mighty or powerful *after his resurrection*, when he was invested with divine nature. He said then to his disciples "all power is given unto me in heaven and in earth" (Matthew 28:18 AV). He thus became a full manifestation of God in might and power in addition to his previous manifestation in disposition and character. There is no indication of pre-existent power. We may safely say therefore that there is nothing in the phrase 'mighty god' that suggests the Messiah was a second person of an eternal trinity taking human form.

"EVERLASTING FATHER"

Similarly this phrase is sometimes glibly quoted and given a completely unwarranted trinitarian meaning. Even a trinitarian would say that it was not the Father but the Son who assumed human flesh! The Hebrew literally means 'Father of eternity',[1] and is so translated in many versions.[2] When the Jews translated this passage they rendered it 'father of the coming age'.[3] This is a very apt description of the role of Jesus, for by his redemptive work he has made possible, or 'fathered' the completed purpose of God.

But many scriptural allusions speak in a more particular sense of Christ's role as a father, without in any way having a trinitarian connotation. Isaiah in ch 53 says "when he makes himself an offering for sin, he shall *see his offspring*, he shall prolong his days" (Isaiah 53:10). The New Testament, quoting Isaiah, puts a similar expression into his mouth: "Here am I,

---

1. Revised Version margin

2. e.g. Darby, Young's Literal

3. LXX

and the *children* God has given me",[1] and speaks of him "bringing many *sons* to glory (Hebrews 2:10,13). These spiritual sons of Jesus are those who believe and obey him. This is the sense in which Jesus is 'the father of the future age'.

This passage has been examined in detail because it is one of the main Old Testament references used to support the doctrine of the trinity. Close examination shows that such claims do not have the backing usually assumed for them. The Messianic prophecies never suggest that the Messiah, the Son of God, was God coming in human form as envisaged by the doctrine of the incarnation.

FATHER AND SON

The very use of the terms Father and Son deny the trinitarian concept of co-eternity and co-equality between the two. A son as old as his father is a manifestly absurd concept. Jesus is described as God's "only begotten Son". Luke says this was achieved by the Father's power, the Holy Spirit, causing Jesus to be formed in the womb of Mary:

"The Holy Spirit will come upon you, and the power of the Most High will overshadow you; therefore the child to be born will be called holy, the Son of God" (Luke 1:35).

Begettal implies a beginning, and there is no hint in the narrative of Christ's birth that the event was anything other than a new life commencing. Truly, the conception of the infant was exceptional, but neither here nor in the continuing use of the terms Father and Son is there a hint that expresses the doctrine of the incarnation, or suggests that the child was already in existence.

---

1. Isaiah 8:18

"My Father"

A notable feature of the gospel records is the term employed by Jesus to address God: "My Father". This is an unexpected expression if the relationship is really one of equality. Especially damaging to the trinitarian view is its continued use by Jesus *after his resurrection and glorification*, where he repeatedly speaks of God as "my Father":

> "Go to my brethren and say to them, I am ascending to *my Father* and your Father, to *my God* and your God" (John 20:17).
> "I will give him power over the nations ... even as I myself have received power from *my Father*" (Revelation 2:27, see also 3:5,21).

Can the conventional view of equality between Father and Son be possibly read into these words? The first quotation seems to be expressing a similar relationship between God and both Jesus and his disciples. And, remember, both occasions were *after* Christ's resurrection and glorification.[1]

How did Jesus express his relationship with his Father? Was it that of an eternally pre-existent and co-equal son who was temporarily experiencing human nature? Far from it. Christ's consistent claim was that he was subordinate to God: he was the one sent, the one speaking God's words, not his own. It is revealing that the gospel of John, used so much in an attempt to justify the trinitarian position, is the gospel above others that emphasises the subordination and dependence of the Son.

"My Father is greater than I"

First, the definite statement by Jesus which of itself effectually demolishes the trinitarian claims:

---

1. The arguments advanced over the next few pages were also used by the majority of Christians in the first three centuries to support the subordination of Christ to his Father. See ch. 8 pp 349,355.

"If you loved me, you would have rejoiced, because I go to the Father; *for the Father is greater than I"* (John 14:28).

This clear affirmation of the Father's superiority has been a thorn in the side of Trinitarians since earliest times. Many ingenious circumlocutions have been used over the centuries to square it with trinitarian dogma.[1] It is interesting to note that the 'official' trinitarian explanation has varied over the years. From the third to the fifth centuries the consensus view was that God was greater than Jesus in the sense that every father is greater than his son, yet they were equal in that they shared the same 'essence'. This then changed to the view similar to that advanced today that only during his incarnation was Jesus temporarily inferior to God. But both of these distort the obvious meaning of the words. The second view is negated by the fact that Jesus' reference goes beyond his earthly life to his ascent to the Father. Even after Jesus had gone to heaven the Father was still greater. In a similar passage Jesus re-affirms the Father's supremacy: "My Father ... is *greater than all"* (John 10:29). Original Christian teaching confirms that the subordinate relationship continued even at the time when Jesus was gloriously enthroned at the Father's right hand in heaven: "The head of Christ is God" says Paul (1 Corinthians 11:4). If the original Christians had set out to demonstrate that the Father was always greater than the Son, they could hardly have chosen more explicit terms.

Throughout his conversations with the Jews, Jesus was at pains to stress that he was not acting on his own authority, implying his subordination to the greater position of his Father. Carefully examine these references:

"Truly, truly, I say to you, the Son can do nothing of his own accord ...".

---

1. The interested reader can find examples in the notes on John 14:28 in the *Speakers Commentary*.

> "I can do nothing on my own authority" (John 5:19,30).
> "But I have not come of my own accord" (John 7:28).
> "I do nothing on my own authority, but speak thus as the Father taught me" (John 8:28).
> "For I have not spoken on my own authority; the Father who sent me has himself given me commandment what to say and what to speak" (John 12:49).

There is clearly no hint of co-equality here.

It is true that Jesus has since been given his own power and authority, but he carefully points out that even then it is a *derived* authority, not an innate possession, and one that will be used after his resurrection and glorification:

> "For as the Father has life in himself, so he has *granted* the Son also to have life in himself, and has *given* him authority to execute judgment, because he is the Son of man" (John 5.26-27).
> "All authority in heaven and on earth *has been given to me*" (Matthew 28:18).
> "Even as I myself have *received power from my Father*" (Revelation 2:27).

Similarly, in conformity with the express predictions of the Old Testament (e.g. the prophecy of the coming of the one like unto Moses, Deuteronomy 18:18, that we considered on pages 150 and 158), the teaching of Jesus was not his own but the Father's. When the Jews were astounded that an apparently untutored man could have such understanding, Jesus expressly stated the source of his knowledge:

> "My teaching is *not mine,* but his who sent me; if any man's will is to do his will, he shall know whether the teaching is from God or whether I am speaking on my own authority" (John 7:15-17).
> "The word which you hear is *not mine but the Father's* who

sent me" (John 14:24).

It is impossible to harmonise these words with the belief that Jesus was a member of an all-knowing and co-equal divine trinity.

As well as the gospel of John, the synoptic gospels also provide evidence from Christ's own lips that he never claimed equality with God. Matthew records the request of the mother of James and John for places of honour for her sons on either side of Jesus in his kingdom. Christ's reply shows that he recognised God's higher authority:

> "To sit at my right hand and at my left is not mine to grant, but it is for those for whom it has been prepared by my Father" (Matthew 20:23).

Referring to the timing of the second coming and that future kingdom, Jesus gives another indication of lack of information that is incompatible with his being the all-knowing God:

> "But of that day or that hour no one knows, not even the angels in heaven, *nor the Son*, but only the Father" (Mark 13:32).

If Jesus was God incarnate it is impossible to conceive of one part of an all-knowing trinity concealing information from the other. On another occasion a ruler addressed Jesus as "Good Teacher". Christ immediately replied:

> "Why do you call me good? No one is good but God alone" (Luke 18:19).

The straightforward meaning of this reply clearly indicates the superiority of the Father with regard to the Son.

"NOT MY WILL BUT THINE BE DONE"

Another strong indication in the gospel narratives of the essential distinction between God and Jesus is the fact that there was the possibility of a conflict of will between them. This is expressed in the poignant words of the Master in the garden of Gethsemane, when he in effect asked if there was any way of achieving human salvation other than the cruel trial ahead:

> "Father, all things are possible to thee; remove this cup from me; yet not what I will, but what thou wilt" (Mark 14:36).

Jesus recognised the fact that there were things possible for God but not to him, and submitted himself to the superior will of his Father. These are not the words of a co-equal deity. The apostolic comment on this shows that in the minds of first century Christians the Son certainly was not God:

> "In the days of his flesh, Jesus offered up prayers and supplications, with loud cries and tears, to him who was able to save him from death, and he was heard for his godly fear (Hebrews 5:7).

Prayer implies subordination and submission. No man prays to an equal. If the trinity is true the concept implicit in this passage is of one member of an eternal trinity praying for salvation to another member of the same tri-unity of gods, and subordinating his will to that member. This is difficult to reconcile with the trinitarian doctrine.

"ANOINTED WITH THE HOLY SPIRIT"

Similar arguments apply to the bestowal by God of the Holy Spirit on Jesus. The Holy Spirit has elsewhere (p.91) been shown to be the power of God rather than a third member of a tri-une godhead. Recipients of this power are able to do supernatural things such as perform miracles, speak God's words and give infallible advice. The process was explained by

David as "The Spirit of the Lord speaks by me, his word is upon my tongue" (2 Samuel 23:2). And just as God could bestow the Holy Spirit, so he could withdraw it. After his grievous sin David prayed that this might not be so in his case: "Cast me not away from thy presence, and take not thy holy Spirit from me" (Psalm 51:11). The bestowal of the Holy Spirit was sometimes marked by special divine action, as in the case of Jeremiah:

> "Then the Lord put forth his hand and touched my mouth; and the Lord said to me, Behold, I have put my words in your mouth" (Jeremiah 1:9).

The prophets foresaw that the Messiah would also be given the power of the Holy Spirit:

> "Behold my servant, whom I uphold, my chosen, in whom my soul delights; I have put my spirit upon him.. (Isaiah 42:1).
> "The Spirit of the Lord God is upon me, because the Lord has anointed me to bring good tidings to the afflicted ... (Isaiah 61:1).

Jesus was anointed with the Holy Spirit on the occasion of his baptism, when

> "the heavens were opened, and he saw the Spirit of God descending like a dove, and alighting on him; and lo, a voice from heaven, saying, This is my beloved Son, with whom I am well pleased" (Matthew 3:16-17).

Thus, as in the cases of the prophets of old, but in much greater measure, the Son was invested with the power of God. Peter comments on this in his preaching:

> "God anointed Jesus of Nazareth with the Holy Spirit and with power" (Acts 10:38).

183

There is nothing in this record to suggest that here was the third person of a co-equal divine trinity being involved, any more than the prophets believed that they were under the influence of a separate divine person when they displayed the power of God. Indeed the reverse is the case. The bestowal of a gift on Jesus, in this case the anointing with the Holy Spirit, implies genuine subordination rather than equality. Jesus recognised that the Spirit was a gift from his Father, donated in fulness:

> "It is not by measure that he *gives* the Spirit; the Father loves the Son, and has *given* all things into his hand" (John 3:34-35).

Surely an all-powerful God cannot receive something that he already possesses in fulness: for according to trinitaran theory "sameness of nature, *equality of power and glory*, oneness in purpose and affection" exists between the members of the Godhead.[1]

FATHER AND SON IN THE EPISTLES
Continuing our review of the relationship between the Son and the Father we come to the New Testament epistles. Here a clear distinction is always made between the two in a way that is irreconcilable with the trinitarian concept. The force of this argument is heightened on realisation that all the epistles were written after Christ's resurrection and ascension, when according to the trinitarian view he had resumed his heavenly position of equality and power as the second person of a co-equal trinity. Why then the continual distinction as expressed, for instance, in the salutations of almost every epistle? The majority of Paul's epistles have this salutation:

> "Grace to you and peace from God our Father and the Lord

---

1. Flint: Encyclopaedia Britannica, Art. "Theism"

Jesus Christ"[1]

The clear distinction between the Father and Son strongly suggests that in the Apostle's mind the two were not co-equal members of a 'trinity in unity'. This is confirmed by the list of the fundamentals of the Christian faith in his letter to the Ephesians:

"There is one body and one Spirit, just as you were called to the one hope that belongs to your call, one Lord, one faith, one baptism, one God and Father of us all, who is above all and through all and in all" (Ephesians 4:4-6).

This is a most important statement. Notice that the Lord (i.e. Jesus) and God are separated in the list— clearly there was no thought of a tri-unity in Paul's mind here. If Jesus was the uncreate God he should not be mentioned separately from Him. Indeed at the end Paul emphasises the supremacy of God as 'above all', including Jesus. And remember, this is after Christ's exaltation to heaven.

"A SON OVER GOD'S HOUSE"
One of the New Testament themes relating to the redemptive purpose of God is the building of a spiritual house in which God will dwell in the future. Jesus alluded to this when he said "in my Father's house are many rooms (John 14:2), and the apostle takes up the theme when he says that the believers were

"members of the household of God, built upon the foundation of the apostles and prophets, Christ Jesus himself being the chief cornerstone, in whom the whole structure is joined together and grows into a holy temple in the Lord; in whom you also are built into it for a dwelling

---

1. For fuller details see Chap. 5, pp. 100-101

place of God in the Spirit" (Ephesians 2:19-22).

In any large establishment in those days there were several tiers of organisation. Lowest were the servants, usually slaves, who did the menial tasks. Then came the children of the house, who occupied a more privileged position; especially the firstborn son who was often given authority over the household. Above the whole house was the owner, whose word was law. In the letter to the Hebrews we are told that God's spiritual house has these same three tiers of responsibility:

> "Now Moses was faithful in all God's house as a servant, to testify to the things that were to be spoken later, but Christ was faithful over God's house *as a son*. And we are his house if we hold fast our confidence and pride in our hope" (Hebrews 3:5-6).

Notice the position of the Son of the house: greater than Moses the servant, yet still not the 'householder', who is God himself. If Jesus was God in the trinitarian sense, then the whole point of this analogy would have been ruined, and we cannot conceive of this perceptive author making such an elementary error. Again, it must be remembered that this epistle was written many years after Jesus had attained his position of exaltation at his Father's side. It is clear that the co-equality of Father and Son found no place in first century theology.

Whilst we are looking at Hebrews it is worth noting that if Jesus were 'Very God' then the Apostle failed to advance what seems to be the most powerful argument in support of his thesis. The purpose of the letter was to demonstrate the superiority of Jesus Christ's ministry over the Law given through Moses. The writer shows that Jesus was greater than the angels who gave Israel the Law, was greater than Moses who received the Law, and was greater than the levitical priests who administered the Law. Detailed arguments and what to us might seem rather obscure Old Testament references were adduced to support this claim of the superiority of Jesus. If the writer all the time believed that Jesus was God incarnate, and that the Old Testament undoubtedly taught this fact, it is legitimate to ask why he did not advance it clearly and boldly as a major argument in support of his case. It would have been a master stroke! This Jesus was God! There all discussion would cease! Instead he is introduced as a Son who whilst now greater than the angels is still dependent on the Father (Hebrews 1:4,9,13).

"HE LEARNED OBEDIENCE"

Continuing in the same letter, there is another clear indication of New Testament teaching about the position of the Son of God. We read:

> "Although he was a Son, he learned obedience through what he suffered; and being made perfect (literally: having been perfected) he became the source of eternal salvation to all who obey him" (Hebrews 5:8-9).

If Jesus was God in a trinitarian sense it is inconceivable that he would have to learn anything, let alone learn how to be obedient through the medium of suffering. And note that it was subsequent to this obedience that Jesus was perfected. Notice the sequence of ideas here. Just as *Jesus* "learned obedience" so those who seek redemption must be obedient to *him*. The parallelism demands that the conditions in which obedience is shown should be the same for the believers as in his case.

"MY GOD"

Another series of references that are fatal to the trinitarian view shows that, *even after his resurrection, glorification and ascent to the Fathers right hand*, Jesus himself and the apostles still regarded the Father as his God. This is incredible if they were co-equal. The evidence for this is incontestable. At the tomb he said to Mary"

"I am ascending to my Father and your Father, to *my God* and your God" (John 20:17).

Similarly in the course of his last message from heaven he refers to the Father as "my God" no less than four times in a single verse (Revelation 3:12). Comparable language is employed by the apostles. Paul speaks of the "*God* and Father of our Lord Jesus Christ" (Ephesians 1:3), and in Hebrews, quoting the Psalms, says "therefore God, *thy God*, has anointed thee with the oil of gladness" (Hebrews 1:9).

THE TRINITY ADMITTED NOT TO BE A SCRIPTURAL DOCTRINE

In view of these repeated and consistent statements and inferences of the subordinate position of Jesus one can understand why most Trinitarians admit that their doctrine of God cannot be found in the Bible. The late Dr. W R Matthews, Dean of St Paul's Cathedral, wrote:

"It must be admitted by everyone who has the rudiments of an historical sense that the doctrine of the Trinity, as a doctrine, formed no part of the original message. St Paul knew it not, and would have been unable to understand the meaning of the terms used in the theological formula on which the Church ultimately agreed".[1]

Or more recently:

"In order to understand the doctrine of the Trinity it is necessary to understand that the doctrine is a *development*, and why it developed. ... It is a waste of time to attempt to read Trinitarian doctrine directly off the pages of the New Testament".[2]

---

1. "God in Christian Thought and Experience", p.180

2. A & R Hanson: "Reasonable Belief, A survey of the Christian Faith, p.171,1980, Italics ours.

FATHER AND SON IN THE FUTURE

It is in reference to Christ's future glory when, according to trinitarian concepts, the Son should have resumed his position of co-equality shared with the Father from eternity, that we have one of the most clear scriptural demonstrations of the true relationship between God and Christ, the Son of God. Paul is writing of the Messianic kingdom that Jesus will set up at his return to the earth, and says that during that reign all opposition will be eliminated, at last even man's grim enemy of death. In support of this he quotes "Thou hast put all things under his feet" (Psalm 8:6). The only power that will *not* have become subject to the Messiah is God himself. Then Jesus will be able to present to his Father a flawless earth that will offer no barrier to his perfect fellowship. But the key point is that even in this state of sublime unity between God and his creation, Jesus *will remain in subjection to God*. This is the way Paul expresses it:

> "Then comes the end, when he delivers the kingdom to God the Father after destroying every rule and every authority and power. For he must reign until he has put all his enemies under his feet. The last enemy to be destroyed is death. 'For God has put all things in subjection under his feet.' But when it says 'All things are put in subjection under him' it is plain that he is excepted who put all things under him. When all things are subjected to him, then *the Son himself will also be subjected to him who put all things under him*, that God may be everything to every one" (1 Corinthians 15:24-28).

Here is a statement of the completed purpose of God with the earth. This is the state of things that is to exist throughout eternity. The Son having presented to God the Father a perfect earth, then will be subjected to the One whose power enabled him to achieve victory over all enemies. Notice that even during the Kingdom Age the Son will still need to draw on the unlimited power of the Father—"the Son himself will also be subjected to him (God) who put all things under him". How then is it possible to suggest that the Father and the Son are equally powerful and that neither is superior to the other? Is it being honest with scripture to maintain that, in the words of the Athanasian Creed, "none is afore, or after other: none is greater or less than other. But the whole three persons are co-eternal together: and co-equal"?

ALLEGED SCRIPTURAL EVIDENCE FOR THE TRINITY[1]

In reply to this cumulative Scriptural evidence that the Son of God is not God the Son, a component of a co-equal trinity of Gods, what evidence do Trinitarians adduce in support of the doctrine? First it must be repeated that many supporters of the Trinity admit that the doctrine as such is not found in the Bible, and that first century Christians did not know of it. For example, one writer says "it is important to be clear that the fully articulated doctrine of the Trinity is not to be found in the New Testament ... this notion of an always existing God the Son is not part of the truth. ... The concept of the preexistence of Christ as an eternal Being distinct from God the Father is an unhelpful myth, akin to a fairy story".[2] Another writes: "Fourth century trinitarianism did not reflect accurately early Christian teaching regarding the nature of God; it was, on the contrary, a deviation from this teaching. ... The dogma of the Trinity owes its existence to abstract speculation on the part of a small minority of scholars. In Tertullian's day, he said that the ordinary rank and file of Christians think of Christ as a man".[3]

---

1. See also Chapter 5, pp.112*ff*

2. Hamilton: *Jesus*, p.8

3. Auer, F: Lowell Institute Lectures, Boston, 1933

But even so it is insisted by some that the doctrine can be *deduced* from scripture even if not explicitly taught there. "The doctrine is an interpretation and development of the witness of the New Testament, not a direct transcription of its words".[1] There are several lines of argument that are used, the majority being discussed below.

1. Jesus is said to have existed before his birth to Mary

The pre-existence of Jesus is considered in detail in a later section of this chapter.[2]

2. Jesus is spoken of as the creator, and the plural word *elohim* is used in Genesis in describing the acts of creation.

The New Testament teaching on the creative work of Jesus forms the subject of another section of this chapter,[3] but the use of *elohim* to describe God in the Genesis account of creation can be considered here. "Then God said, Let *us* make man in *our* image, after *our* likeness" (Genesis 1.26). It is claimed that the use of the plural pronouns together with the plural divine title *elohim* indicates more than one person in the Godhead, and is therefore an indication of the Trinity. The doctrine of God manifestation (see chapter 4) supplies the understanding of this and similar passages. The actual agents of the creation were the angels, the immortal beings through whom God manifested his power. These were the 'Sons of God' that rejoiced at the laying of the foundations of the earth (Job 38:7). In fact in some cases *elohim* is translated 'angels' (Psalm 8:5 A.V., Hebrews 2:7). There is no suggestion of equality among the angels, and the One who energises them, namely God himself, is styled 'the *Most High* El' (singular).

Another example of the use of the plural is found in Isaiah's

---

1. A & R Hanson, Op. cit., p171

2. See p. 219*ff*

3. See page 285*ff*

record of the vision of the enthroned God surrounded by the seraphim:

> "And I heard the voice of the Lord saying, Whom shall I send, and who will go for *us*? Then I said, Here I am! Send me. And he said, Go, and say to this people: Hear and hear, but do not understand; see and see, but do not perceive" (Isa 6:8-9).

It is said that the use of the word "us" indicates plurality in the Godhead. This is assumption only. The "us" could refer to God and the Seraphim.

3. Only God can forgive sins. Jesus forgave sins: therefore he is God.

Sin, by definition, is ultimately an offence against God. Therefore only God can forgive sin, and there are numerous passages that teach that He is willing to extend mercy to sinners on certain conditions. It is true that Jesus also forgave sins, one occasion being when he healed a paralysed man:

> "My son, your sins are forgiven. Now some of the scribes were sitting there, questioning in their hearts, Why does this man speak thus? It is blasphemy! Who can forgive sins but God alone?" (Mark 2:5-7).

But was this forgiveness extended of Jesus' own right, or was his authority to show mercy derived from his Father? The answer is given as the account proceeds:

> "But Jesus, knowing their thoughts, said Why do you think evil in your hearts? For which is easier, to say, Your sins are forgiven, or to say Rise and walk? But that you may know that the Son of man has authority on earth to forgive sins—he then said to the paralytic—Rise, take up your bed and go home. And he rose and went home. When the crowds saw it, they were afraid, and they glorified God,

who had given such authority to men" (Matthew 9:4-8).

Clearly, even the crowd recognised that Christ's ability to forgive had been *given* him by God, and was therefore not an intrinsic possession. The same authority extended to Christ's immediate disciples on receipt of the Holy Spirit from Jesus:

> "He breathed on them, and said to them, Receive the Holy spirit. If you forgive the sins of any, they are forgiven; if you retain the sins of any, they are retained" (John 20:22-23).

On the basis of the trinitarian argument that power to forgive sins makes a person God, the disciples too were members of the eternal Godhead—a proposition that is manifestly absurd.

4. Only God is sinless. Jesus was sinless: therefore he is God.

It is difficult to believe that this is seriously put forward as a proof of the trinity. The case for the defence must be a weak one to be forced to present such evidence! God just *cannot* sin— "Your heavenly Father is perfect" said Jesus (Matthew 5:48). Therefore if Jesus were God, it also would have been impossible for him to sin. Temptations would have been meaningless to him, and succumbing to them out of the question. Yet the wonderful achievement of the Saviour, praised in such appreciative terms by the New Testament writers, was that, whilst possessing sinful human nature, he completely overcame its promptings. All the passages that exult Christ's victory, and all the references to a 'lamb without spot or blemish' in both Old and New Testaments, would be meaningless if Jesus had not the potential to sin. Jesus was faultless in his earthly life not because he possessed divine nature, but because with his Father's help he fought and won the battle against sin. It is gravely lessening his achievement to suggest otherwise.

5. Jesus exercises the divine right of judgment, therefore he is God.

Again the question is whether Christ's rôle in this respect is innate or derived. If the latter the argument loses its point. Whilst God is the ultimate judge, it is obviously within his power to confer his authority on another. This is exactly what he has done. Jesus said:

> "The Father judges no one, but has given all judgment to the Son" (John 5:22).

Once it is accepted that Jesus had to be *given* the authority to judge, the argument that the possession of such power proves his divinity is completely nullified. Scripture also clearly says that when exercising judgment *in the future* Jesus does it on God's behalf, not on his own:

> "On that day when, according to my gospel, *God* judges the secrets of men by Christ Jesus" (Romans 2:16).

6. Jesus accepted worship, therefore is God

It is claimed that because Jesus said "You shall worship the Lord your God, and him only shall you serve" (Luke 4:8), then Jesus must be God in a trinitarian sense as elsewhere he is described as being worshipped.

A clear distinction needs to be made here between events in the mortal life of Jesus and those after his resurrection and glorification. In the first case we frequently read that various people 'worshipped' him, particularly those who had been the recipients of his healing power. The wise men and the shepherds at his birth (Matthew 2:2,11), and the man born blind (John 9:38) are some examples. But did they worship Jesus *as God* or was it simply an act of homage to a superior? A passage in Acts is decisive. When Cornelius received a visit from the Apostle Peter he "fell down at his feet and *worshipped* him" (Acts 10:25). Does this suggest that Peter too was God?

194

Obviously not. On the majority of other occasions where the AV describes people as 'worshipping ' Jesus (or for that matter their fellow men), more recent versions simply say they 'knelt down before him'. The action is obviously one of respect or gratitude to a superior rather than an act of worship to a deity.

But whilst the edict to worship God and no-one else applied up to a certain stage in God's purpose, this does not exclude the later modification of the command. After Christ's resurrection and glorification there is every reason for Jesus to receive "power and wealth and wisdom and might and honour and glory and blessing"[1], although this still need not imply that he is of equal status to God. God himself commands even the angels to worship the Messiah in the future:

> "And again, when he brings the first-born into the world, he says, Let all God's angels worship him" (Hebrews 1:6).

This quotation is from Psalm 97, and clearly relates to the second coming of Christ.[2] The fact that the angels receive from *God* a request to worship the Son demonstrates that the Father and Son are not co-equal. As Paul says to the Philippians, Christ's future worship will be "to the glory of God the Father" (Philippians 2:11).

7. Jesus is addressed as God

On several occasions Jesus is either called or addressed as 'God'. Examples such as the following are invariably quoted in support of the trinity:

> "His name will be called ... Mighty God" (Isaiah 9:6)
> "Thomas answered him, My Lord and my God" (John

---

1. Revelation 5:12

2. 'Speakers Commentary remarks here that this verse "must be referred, both on grammatical and exegetical grounds, not to the incarnation, but to the second advent".

20:28).
"But of the Son he says, Thy throne, O God, is for ever and ever" (Hebrews 1:8).

In addition there are a few occasions where alternative translations or variant manuscript readings use 'God' for 'Lord' when referring to Jesus.

The phrase 'Mighty God' and the use of the word 'God' in a non-divine sense have already been considered (pp. 173-176) to which the reader is referred. To use the other passages as proof of the co-equality and co-eternity of the Son with the Father it needs to be shown that in Scripture the term 'God' is used exclusively of the Father. This cannot be done. As has already been shown (p. 58) in the Old Testament the original word for God, *elohim*, is used of angels, rulers, judges, mighty men, and the idols of the heathen, and its application to the Messiah is therefore no proof of his deity.

Hebrews 1:8 is quoting Psalm 45:6. where the phrase is variously translated "Thy throne, O God" (AV,NIV), "Your divine throne" (RSV), and "Your throne is like God's throne" (NEB), only the first of which would appear to give any trinitarian inference. In the New Testament Christ himself clearly shows that 'God' need not always refer to the Father. Quoting another Psalm (82:6) Jesus said to the Jewish leaders:

"Is it not written in your law, 'I said, you are gods'? If he called them gods to whom the word of God came (and scripture cannot be broken) do you say of him whom the Father consecrated and sent into the world, 'You are blaspheming,' because I said 'I am the Son of God'?" (John 10:34-36).

The exclamation of Thomas "My Lord and my God" does not therefore automatically mean that he was equating Jesus with God. It could have been a confession that by the resurrection he had become convinced that Jesus was indeed the Messiah, and therefore a perfect manifestation of God.[1] Thomas knew that both titles were attributed to the Messiah in the Old Testament (Psalm 45:6, 110:1), and so he could have been expressing his belief in Jesus in these terms. Thus Thomas's avowal can be seen as a further example of John's declared intention to use his gospel record to demonstrate that Jesus was the Messiah, the Son of God (John 20:31).

It is noteworthy that the context of these words of Thomas and those in Hebrews 1:8 excludes the use of God in a trinitarian sense. Prior to the meeting with Thomas Jesus referred to the Father as 'my God', implying his inequality of status (John 20:17). And the Hebrews passage goes on to make a similar point— "therefore God, *thy God*, has anointed thee with the oil of gladness" (Hebrews 1:9). The views of the first-century Christians are therefore clear. They came to realise that Jesus, in a much greater sense than the ministry of the angels as recorded in the Old Testament, was a complete manifestation of the Father, so that divine titles could be appropriately ascribed to him without making him God's equal, any more than the angels who on occasions took God's Name were the Deity Himself. As one writer says:

"When Jesus said "He that hath seen me hath seen the Father also" he did not contradict the statement that "no man hath seen God at any time," but simply expressed the truth contained in the following words of Paul: "Christ is *the image of the invisible God*" (Col. 1.15), "the brightness of His glory, and the express image of His person" (Heb. 1.3). Those who looked upon the anointed Jesus, beheld a representation of the Deity accessible to human vision."[2]

---

1. For an examination of the biblical doctrine of God-manifestation see ch.4

2. Roberts, R: *Christendom Astray* p.139, 1899 ed.

The New Testament English translation is derived from a wide range of ancient manuscripts of Greek and Latin origin, and there are very many copies of the same passage that the translator has to compare, together with scriptural quotations by ancient writers. Over the centuries some slight variations have occurred, usually due to copyist error, but occasionally deliberately done to make a doctrinal point. A notable example of the latter is the fraudulent insertion, probably in the 4th century, of the passage in 1 John 5:7 that asserts the tri-unity of the Father, Son and Holy Spirit (see also p. 32). All commentators without exception now accept that this verse is spurious and recognise that it was a later attempt to demonstrate the trinity. Inferentially the fact that a later hand felt it necessary to insert the passage is of itself an indication that Scriptural support for the trinity was lacking! As Hanson says of this text:

"It was added by some enterprising person in the ancient Church who felt that the New Testament was sadly deficient in direct witness to the kind of doctrine of the Trinity which he favoured and who determined to remedy the defect".[1]

Gibbon in chapter 37 of his *Decline and Fall of the Roman Empire* attributes the forgery to the North African school, followed by a willing connivance by those who saw its propaganda value:

"Even the Scriptures themselves were profaned by their rash and sacrilegious hands. The memorable text, which assert the unity of the THREE who bear witness in heaven, is condemned by the universal silence of the orthodox fathers, and authentic manuscripts. ... After the invention of printing, the editors of the Greek Testament yielded to their own prejudices, or those of the times, and the pious

---

1. Hanson, A & R, op. cit., p.171

fraud ... has been infinitely multiplied in every country and every language of modern Europe."

We can therefore ignore this spurious passage, whilst noting that if the doctrine of the Trinity was clearly taught in the early Church the forgery would not have been needed.

In other instances where Jesus appears to be addressed as God the position is not so clear-cut, and variant readings occur. Hence in the footnotes of more modern translations there are comments such as "other ancient authorities add ...", or "other ancient authorities read ...", or "some witnesses add ...", or "some manuscripts say...". Sometimes the original itself is perfectly capable of being translated in more than one way: here the footnote often gives the alternative. It must be emphasised that these occasions are few, and in the vast majority of general cases make no difference to the sense or the message of the passage for us. But some consider that when fine points of doctrine are being debated such variations can be crucial. It must also be remembered that the translators of the Bible were in the main Trinitarians, and in cases of ambiguity would quite understandably translate in favour of the established beliefs.

As a result of this uncertainty there are half a dozen or so passages that have been translated, or as some allege *could be* translated, to indicate that the first century Christians understood that Christ was God. One example is the AV of Paul's address to the Ephesian elders, which we will examine in detail as an example of the problems, and to show the inadvisability of attempting to establish dogma on the basis of passages where more than one legitimate translation is possible. The passage runs:

"Feed the church of God, which he hath purchased with his own blood" (Acts 20:28).

The trinitarian argument here is that the Saviour who shed his blood is called God. But there is doubt as to whether the original reads 'God' or 'Lord'. The RV margin notes "Many ancient authorities read *the Lord*", as does the NIV footnote . The RSV puts *Lord* into the text and gives *God* as an alternative in the footnote, as does the NEB. In fact the early manuscripts are almost equally divided between the two renderings. The variation is a long-standing one, for it existed in the days of the early fathers. In quoting the passage Ignatius (who died AD109) and Tertullian (AD155-222) use *God* and Irenaeus (born AD130) uses *Lord*. The rest of the verse can also be differently rendered. One translator (Darby) has: "Shepherd the assembly of God, which he has purchased *with the blood of his own*", and adds as a footnote "I am fully satisfied that this is the right translation". This immediately resolves any dilemma, suggesting that God purchased his church with the blood of his own Son, and thus removing any possible trinitarian inference. But whatever the correct version, translators are agreed that this verse should not be used in support of the trinitarian arguments. Darby's footnote continues "to make it (v28) a question of the divinity of Christ is absurd". And *Speaker's Commentary*, warning of the danger of attaching importance to such passages, notes on this verse "the eternal Godhead of Christ cannot be adequately set forth by any number of isolated texts."

Other similar verses can now be examined more briefly. In each case the translation that appears to support the trinity is placed first, the alternative translations appended, and a brief note or comment is appended (usually in the form of translators' or other scholars' explanations).

"The appearing of the glory of our great God and Saviour, Jesus Christ" (Titus 2:13, RSV, RV, NIV, NEB).
Alternatives: "the great God and our Saviour" (AV text; RSV, NEB footnote, RV margin)
Note: "The words will also bear the translation 'of the great

God and of our Saviour Jesus Christ'. It must be admitted that the omission of the article before 'Saviour' does not necessarily require 'God' and 'Saviour' to be understood of the same person" (Speakers Commentary).

> "Theirs are the patriarchs, and from them is traced the human ancestry of Christ, who is God over all, for ever praised" (Romans 9:5, NIV, NEB, RSV footnotes, RV margin).

Alternatives:

> "Whose are the fathers, and of whom as concerning the flesh Christ came, who is over all, God blessed for ever" (AV, NEB footnote).

> "To them belong the patriarchs, and of their race, according to the flesh, is the Christ. God who is over all be blessed for ever" (RSV, NEB similar).

Note: The absence of punctuation in the Greek has possibly led to uncertainty as to how this passage should be rendered.

> "No-one has ever seen God, but God the only [Son], who is at the Father's side, has made him known" (John 1:18, NIV).

Alternatives:

> "No one has ever seen God; the only Son, who is in the bosom of the Father, he has made him known" (RSV. RV, AV, and NEB similar)

Note: Some original manuscripts have 'God' and some 'Son'— "Two readings of equal antiquity" (Speakers Commentary). Darby affirms with considerable emphasis that the translation 'God the only Son' is very doubtful. "In John 1.18 BCL (the texts in question), almost unsupported except by a few versions, and, as to be expected, by many ecclesiastical writers, have the astonishing reading of "God" for "Son" after "only begotten". It is scarcely conceivable that Tregelles and Wescott and Hart should have followed so manifest a corruption and the Revisers have given it a place in their margin".[1] The NIV is clearly wrong here.

> "In the righteousness of our God and Saviour Jesus Christ" (2 Peter 1.1, RV, RSV; NIV, NEB similar).
> *Alternative:* "The righteousness of God and our Saviour Jesus Christ" (AV, RV margin, RSV footnote).

Note: "The translation should be 'of *our* God and *the* Saviour Jesus Christ'. It is indeed possible to explain both *God* and *Saviour* here as titles given to Jesus Christ ... but as the Father and Son are spoken of in contradistinction in the next verse, it is *better to preserve the distinction here also*" (*Speaker's Commentary*).

In view of these ambiguities it is difficult not to agree with one writer who, in a passage outlining the alleged Biblical teaching on the trinity, says: "Admittedly, the name 'God' is not often applied to Jesus. We find it in only seven or eight passages, *some of which can be translated in a different way.*[2]

But in distinction to those 'seven or eight' passages which 'can be translated in a different way' there are literally dozens of occasions in the New Testament where the Father and the Son are mentioned as separate entities and without any hint of ascribing divinity to Jesus. This is particularly true of the salutations to the Epistles, where, if the trinitarian concept were true, it would be the most logical place to indicate that Jesus was in fact God. The almost universal formula, far outnumbering the passages with the ambiguities considered above, is "Grace to you and peace from God the Father and our Lord Jesus Christ". (For further examples the reader is directed to pp.100-101).

---

1. J. N. Darby: *An Introduction to the Bible*. Straw Hill Bible and Tract Depot.

2. "Lion Handbook of the Bible", p.168. Italics ours.

8. Many New Testament passages bring the Father, Son and Holy Spirit in close proximity and sometimes speak of them operating in unison, especially for man's redemption.

The fact that the Father, Son and Holy Spirit are frequently mentioned together is undeniable, but the question has to be asked whether this of itself demonstrates their tri-unity in the sense stated in the creeds. The occasion of Christ's baptism and Paul's benediction to the Corinthians are often mentioned in this connection:

> "And when Jesus was baptised, he went up immediately from the water, and behold, the heavens were opened and he saw the *Spirit of God* descending like a dove, and alighting on him; and lo, a voice from heaven, saying, This is my beloved *Son,* with whom *I* am well pleased" (Matthew 3:16-17).
> "The grace of the *Lord Jesus Christ* and the love of *God* and the fellowship of the *Holy Spirit* be with you all" (2 Corinthians 13:14).

It would be fair to say that only those who had been previously indoctrinated with trinitarian opinions would deduce from such passages the co-equality of the Father, Son and Holy Spirit. The view has to be read into the words rather than derived from them. And even such passages themselves contain indications that the trinitarian view is untenable. How, for example, could the Father be *well pleased* with his Son if they had been all the time co-equal and co-eternal as part of the same indivisible trinity?

9. "In the form of God"

The passage in Philippians that contains this phrase is regarded by Trinitarians as conclusive proof of the pre-existent equality between the Father and the Son. It is the one reference that is immediately quoted whenever scriptural justification for the doctrine is requested. It is now stated, it seems without any real evidence (apart from the possibility of a metrical construction), that the passage was a fragment of an existing and well-known hymn of praise to God the Son which Paul incorporated in his letter. But how substantial is the trinitarian support when it is examined in context and with careful attention to what Paul is actually saying? Here is the full passage:

"Do nothing from selfishness or conceit, but in humility count others better than yourselves. Let each of you look not only to his own interests, but also to the interests of others. Have this mind among yourselves, which you have in Christ Jesus, who, though he was in the form of God, did not count equality with God a thing to be grasped, but emptied himself, taking the form of a servant, being born in the likeness of men. And being found in human form he humbled himself and became obedient unto death, even death on a cross. Therefore God has highly exalted him and bestowed on him the name which is above every name, that at the name of Jesus every knee should bow, in heaven and on earth and under the earth, and every tongue confess that Jesus Christ is Lord, to the glory of God the Father" (Philippians 2:3-11).

This passage is regarded by Trinitarians as incontrovertible proof that the pre-existent Jesus divested himself of his divinity and assumed human form for the salvation of mankind. But is that what Paul intended?

An exhortation to humility

By putting this passage under the theological microscope it is easy to lose sight of the reason why Paul wrote it, so it would be as well to consider his intentions before commencing a detailed examination. What circumstance in Philippi called for this comment? How would its original recipients have read these words? Would they have pored over the meanings and nuances of the individual words in an attempt to deduce the relationship between God and his Son? Surely not. They would have seen Paul's argument to be primarily an exhortation to humility—"count others better than yourselves"—with Paul urging his converts to follow the example of Christ's self abasement. So the first question is: would it be appropriate to reinforce the lesson of humility by using the example of one who was eternally God but chose to become man? It was hardly an example that *they* could follow! This point was made by A.H. McNeile, Professor of Divinity, who had grave reservations about the application of this passage to a pre-existent Christ:

> "Paul is begging the Philippians to cease from dissensions and to act with humility towards each other ... It is asked whether it would be quite natural for him to enforce these simple moral lessons by incidental reference (and the only reference that he ever makes) to the vast problem of the mode of the incarnation. And it is thought by many that his homely appeals would have more effect if he pointed to the inspiring example of Christ's humility and self sacrifice in his human life".[1]

Or as Buzzard comments:

> "Looking afresh at Philippians 2, we must ask the question whether Paul in these verses has really made what would be his only allusion to Jesus' having been alive before his birth. The context of his remarks shows him to be urging the saints to be humble. It is often asked whether it is in any way probable that he would enforce the lesson by asking his readers to adopt the frame of mind of one who, having been eternally God, made the decision to become man"[2]

In all our thinking about this passage it is vital to keep in

---

1. "New Testament Teaching in the Light of St. Paul's, 1923, p.65-66

2. Buzzard, A.: "Who is Jesus", p.20

mind this salient fact that Paul's purpose was to *induce humility after the example of Jesus.*

Both the above writers also make the point that if in fact the Philippians passage taught that Jesus was eternally 'Very God' it would be the only place in Paul's writings to do so. If Paul really did believe and teach even the basic essentials of the trinitarian view, and that this concept of Jesus being God was the one great difference between Judaism and Christianity (as we are now asked to believe), then it is surprising that no clear statement of the doctrine can be found in his writings, and the only place in which it might be even hinted at is hidden in a plea for believers' humility.

It is often argued by Trinitarians that the Apostles played down the deity of Jesus in their preaching so as not to put off the strictly monotheistic Jews. This is a grave reflection on the integrity of the divinely appointed agents of first century preaching, who in other instances disregarded all consequences in the preaching of what they considered to be the truth. It is an even worse reflection on the power of the Holy Spirit which guided these men, for it suggests that the Holy Spirit was unable to meet and successfully deal with any opposition its new teaching might cause. But even this doubtful argument does not apply to Paul, the Apostle to the *Gentiles.* The world at large had none of the prejudices, if they were so, of the Jews concerning monotheism. Indeed, brought up in a culture that paid homage to many gods, the concept of three Gods in one would be neither new nor objectionable. It also could be reasonably expected that if the basis of the new Christian religion—indeed its one distinctive feature—was that Jesus was a member of an eternal trinity of Gods who assumed human form and later died for the salvation of mankind before resuming his place in heaven, then a clear definition of this was needed for these new converts. Paul would have been failing in his duty to them had he not provided this information. Yet, as has been shown above, there is not a hint of the deity of Christ in this sense throughout the Pauline epistles, let alone the clear statement of the doctrine that it would be reasonable to expect. And when it is found that all other essential aspects of Christ's person and mission are elaborated fully in the epistles, this omission becomes the more remarkable.

But, even so, is this Philippians passage the exception? Is it the unambiguous statement of the incarnation that places Paul in the ranks of the Trinitarians? A detailed examination shows the weakness of this view.

"God has highly exalted him"

First some general comments on the passage that throw doubt on the trinitarian interpretation. As a result of Christ's humility and obedience unto death "God has *highly exalted* him". Jesus could not therefore have been God prior to his exaltation. Also, as a result of his humble obedience, Jesus was given *the* name which is above every name". This implies he did not possess it before his exaltation. There is only one Name higher than any other, the Name of God, Yahweh. To have received that Name subsequent to his resurrection suggests that Jesus was not a component of the Yahweh Name before then.[1] But on receiving it Jesus became the first of the 'mighty ones' in whom the Name *Yahweh Elohim*—'He who shall be mighty ones'—would be revealed.[2] And it must also be pointed out that Christ's exaltation was to the *glory of God the Father*, implying the lesser status of the Son.

---

1. "The Name given to the crowned and enthroned Son is not 'Jesus', the Gk. form of the Hebrew name 'Joshua' for that was given to him at his birth as a human baby. It was a relatively common name given to Jewish babies at that time .... The man Christ Jesus ... now shares in the personal name of the Father"—Michael Griffiths, *Down to Earth* p.142. Pub: Hodder and Stoughton, 1986.

2. For the significance of *YAHWEH* see p. 45*ff*, and of God Manifestation, p. 74*ff*.

"He was in the form of God"

Even so the passage is invariably used by Trinitarians who place much emphasis on the phrase "was in the form of God", stating that it refers to the nature of Jesus prior to his birth, at which event he assumed the "form of a servant". The meaning of the original words are crucial to this discussion, particularly the words translated 'form' and 'was'.

Trinitarians insist that *form* conveys the idea of 'essential nature'. The NIV translates the phrase as "being in very nature God", and relegates "in the form of God" to a footnote. The word Paul used was *morphe*, a Greek word that basically means 'form, fashion, appearance, external shape, sort'.[1] The idea is of an external shape that can make identification possible. It has been transferred into English in such words as *morphology*, the study of shape or appearance, and *metamorphosis*, a change of shape. Despite many claims to the contrary, the internal nature or condition of that which is being described does not seem to be implied in the word *morphe*, particularly in everyday speech (the so-called *koine* or 'common' Greek).

But it is the Scriptural use of *morphe* and related words that should be our best guide to their meaning. This usage includes the incident after Christ's resurrection when he "appeared in *another form* (*morphe*)" to the disciples after his resurrection (Mark 16:12). Luke's account of this (24:13-35) shows their failure to recognise him on this occasion was due to the altered *appearance* of Jesus, not an altered 'essential nature'.

In what sense, then, was Jesus in the form (*morphe*) of God? Obviously not in physical appearance. A clue as to Paul's meaning is in the subsequent phrase where Jesus is described as "taking the form (*morphe*) of a servant", i.e. a bondslave (verse 7). 'Form' here cannot mean 'essential nature', for in respect of 'essential nature' there is no difference between the slave and

---

1. Liddell & Scott, "Greek-English Lexicon"

those he serves. What distinguished a slave from his master, and that made him instantly recognisable, was his demeanour and lowly position—his *disposition*. There was no biological difference. So one cannot take Paul's use of the word *morphe* to imply that Jesus had the same physical nature as God. Jesus was 'in the form of God' in the sense that (as has already been exhaustively discussed) he was a reflection of the Father's *character and attributes*. "He who has seen me has seen the Father" (John 14:9) accurately describes the situation, or to use another of Paul's descriptions of Jesus, "Christ, who is the likeness of God" (2 Corinthian 4:4). In other words, in Christ God's character was being revealed to man.

"Was"

The word translated 'was' is another that Trinitarians claim supports the view that this passage speaks of an eternally pre-existent Christ. They contend that "he *was* in the form of God" implies that Jesus possessed God's nature from the beginning of time. Other versions have "being" or "being originally" or "was from the first". The basic meaning of the Greek word (*huparcho*) means 'to exist', but it is the tense of the verb that indicates the *timing* of the existence. In this case it is the imperfect tense, which is defined as expressing "an uncompleted action or state, especially in time past". Thus 'being' or 'was' implies a continuing existence or an existence prior to the present. But the *length* of the previous existence is in no way defined. It is gratuitous to make the existence eternal just on the basis of this word, as other Bible usage shows. When the young man Eutychus fell out of the window "*being* overcome by sleep" (Acts 20:9) none would suggest that he had been asleep eternally. And when Peter said of David "*being* therefore a prophet" (Acts 2:30) it would not be assumed that he had been a prophet from all time. Normal usage demands that the continuing action described had a commencement— Eutychus fell asleep and thus could later be described as 'being' asleep. David was not a prophet from birth, but from the time of his anointing. Similarly Christ's '*being* in the form of God' does not imply eternal pre-existence in possession of the divine nature, but only that *at some time previously* he had assumed the 'form of God' and was still so at the time of writing.

"Did not count equality with God a thing to be grasped"

Continuing with the examination of this passage we come to the phrase "did not count equality with God a thing to be grasped" (verse 6). In the AV this reads "thought it not robbery to be equal with God", and has been understood by Trinitarians to assert that by right Jesus could claim equality in the Godhead. "Inasmuch as he was pre-existent God, He held it as his right to claim equality of Godhead".[1] But again, this is reading the Trinity into the words rather than allowing them to speak for themselves. Whilst 'robbery' is a perfectly valid translation, the underlying idea is of snatching or grabbing at something, and therefore the RSV 'grasping' is to be preferred. The phrase thus translated could mean just the opposite of the trinitarian assertion—that Jesus *refused* to seek equality with God, implying that he did not have it before. This reading is more consistent with Paul's exhortation for the believers to copy the humility of their Lord.

One of the frequent themes of Paul's writing is the comparison between the events in Genesis and the redemptive work of Christ.[2] The old creation contained the symbols of the new creation: the first Adam who brought sin into the world provided a contrast with the last Adam who removes it. Adam was created 'in the image of God', and in Philippians Jesus was described as 'in the form of God'. Paul is here continuing this theme of contrasting Adam with Christ. Thus, in the passage still under consideration, seeking 'equality with God' is clearly a reference to the subtle temptation by which the serpent in Eden induced Eve to eat the forbidden fruit:

---

1. *Speaker's Commentary*

2. See Romans 5:12-18; 1 Corinthians 15:20-28,42-50; etc.

"For God knows that when you eat of it your eyes will be opened, and *you will be like God*, knowing good and evil" (Genesis 3:5).

It was this desire to be equal with God that was the alluring prospect, and so Eve reached out and *grasped* the fruit, with disastrous results. The relevance to Paul's theme of humility is clear. Adam through pride grasped at the opportunity for equality with God, but Jesus, the Second Adam, although a perfect manifestation of the attributes and character of God, did not seek to grasp any short cut to divine equality. Clearly this was the message Paul wanted to get across. Christ, unlike Adam, did not count equality with God a thing to be grasped, or snatched. Paul's allusion was to Christ's *humility*, not to the incarnation.

"Emptied himself"

Paul continues: instead of seeking equality with God, Jesus "emptied himself", or "made himself of no reputation" (AV). According to the trinitarian interpretation this means that God the Son relinquished the outward tokens of his divinity and became man. But it needs to be borne in mind that this is an example the Philippians were being exhorted to copy, which the incarnation certainly was not. The word for 'empty' is also translated 'abase', and one only has to read the gospel records to learn that self-abasement was an important facet of Christ's character. Despite doing many wonderful works, Jesus continually diverted all the praise and honour to his Father in practical demonstration of the humility Paul was enjoining:

> "I do nothing on my own authority, but speak as the Father taught me" (John 8:28).
> "Yet I do not seek my own glory" (John 8:50).
> "He who believes in me, believes not in me but in him who sent me' (John 12:44).

This abasement and subordination to the will of God characterised the life of Jesus, but was particularly demonstrated in the events of the Passion, to which the Philippians passage especially refers. His agony in Gethsemane where he repeatedly said "not my will, but thine, be done" (Luke 22:42) is a further example of his 'emptying himself'. But, Paul continues, his crowning example of humility was his willing submission to his Father's will when he "became obedient unto death, even death on a cross" (verse 8). Isaiah used similar language: the 'suffering servant' "*poured out* his soul unto death", thus completely 'emptying himself'. Seen in this light Christ's example is appropriate to Paul's plea for believers' humility. Here was an example of abasement the Philippians could copy, yes even to the ultimate sacrifice, as John was to say later:

> "By this we know love, that he laid down his life for us; and we ought to lay down our lives for the brethren" (1 John 3:16).

So taken in its scriptural and contextual setting, Paul, by using the phrase "emptied himself", is not describing the process by which God the Son divested himself of his divinity and took human form, but is contrasting Christ with Adam, and illustrating the humility and obedience of the Saviour as an example for those who claim to follow him. As McNeile says again: "In this case the aorist 'ekenosen' (he emptied Himself) does not refer to a single moment of 'Incarnation' but the completeness of a series of repeated acts; His earthly life, looked at as a whole, was an unfailing process of self-emptying".[1]

"In the likeness of men"

Proceeding yet further with the detailed examination of this verse we come to the words "being born in the likeness of

---

1. Op. cit.

men". The idea of birth is not present in the original, which literally translated is "taking in the likeness of men". Much importance is given by Trinitarians to the word *likeness*, alleging that it means that the Son of God assumed a nature *resembling* ours, but not the actual nature itself. The passages in Hebrews alluded to in the section on Christ as the Son of Man are sufficient refutation of this, and the reader is directed to p.160*ff* where this topic is treated in detail.

Is Philippians 2:6-11 a statement about the Incarnation?
In concluding this analysis of Philippians 2:6-11 we therefore deduce that a close examination of the context and the actual phraseology of this celebrated passage gives no support to the doctrine of the trinity. Come to the passage with the trinity already in mind and that doctrine may appear to be given some support; but this is only on a superficial reading. Intrinsically it is teaching something else, and the trinitarian reading is a presupposition rather than a conclusion. This view is supported by further comments of trinitarian theologians on this passage:

> "We cannot with ... confidence say that he (Paul) has left us any statement which is intended to explain the mode of the incarnation".[1]

Dunn warns the superficial reader of the

> "... danger for good exegesis of assuming too quickly that the phrases 'being in the form of God' and 'becoming in the likeness of men' necessarily imply a thought of pre-existence. For the language throughout ... is wholly determined by the creation narratives and by the contrast between what Adam grasped at and what he in consequence became. ... The language was used *not* because it is first and foremost appropriate to *Christ*, but because it was appropriate to *Adam*, drawn from the account of Adam's

---

1. MacNeile, Op. Cit.

creation and fall. *It was used of Christ therefore to bring out that Adamic character of Christ's life, death and resurrection.* ... So when reading Phil. 2.6-11 we should not try to identify a specific time in Christ's existence when he was in the form of God and before he became like men ... (it) *is simply a way of describing the character of Christ's ministry and sacrifice.* In both cases the language used is determined wholly by the Adam stories and is most probably not intended as metaphysical assertions about individuals in the first century AD".[1]

The same writer makes the point that this Philippians passage does not of itself teach the incarnation, and can only be used to support the doctrine if one comes to the passage with the trinity *already in mind*:

"Phil.2.6-11 certainly seems on the face of it to be a straightforward statement contrasting Christ's pre-existent glory and post-crucifixion exaltation with his earthly humiliation. ... However, this straightforward interpretation has to assume that Christ's pre-existence was already taken for granted—an assumption we cannot yet make on the basis of our findings thus far. ... In fact, as J Murphy-O'Connor has recently maintained, not without cause, the common belief that Phil. 2.6-11 starts by speaking of Christ's pre-existent state and status and then of his incarnation is, in almost every case, *a presupposition rather than a conclusion*".[2]

10. "The man that is my fellow"
There is another passage that in the AV is sometimes used to support the idea that the Messiah is equal to God and therefore a component of an eternal trinity. In an undoubted reference to the Messiah, the prophet says:

---

1. Dunn, op. cit. p.120, Italics his

2. Ibid, Italics ours

"Awake, O sword, against my shepherd, and against the man that is my fellow, saith the Lord of hosts: smite the shepherd, and the sheep shall be scattered" (Zechariah 13:7).

Here the word *fellow* is assumed to mean *equal* in the trinitarian sense. A reference to an analytical concordance will readily show the fallacy of this suggestion. The word simply means an *associate* or *neighbour* and is frequently translated as such. The RSV has "the man who stands next to me". In no case is equality expressed or implied, and quoting this in support of the trinity becomes another example of the lengths to which its adherents must go to bolster up a doctrine that is foreign to Scripture. God's *fellowship* is extended to all who associate with His work of redemption and who have a common interest in its completion. So Paul could say "For we are God's fellow workers" (1 Corinthians 3:9, RV), who are "working together with him" (2 Corinthians 6:1). If believers in this sense are the *fellows* of God—and none would suggest that this gives even a hint of equality between them and the Father—then it was even more appropriately used of Jesus, the one in whom God's purpose is centred. Nothing in this passage gives support to the suggestions that Jesus was God incarnate or that he was co-equal with the Father.

11. "I and the Father are one"[1]
One of the 'strong points' of the trinitarian argument is the saying of Jesus "I and the Father are one" (John 10:30). But it would be very poor scholarship to divorce these words from their context and give them a meaning which was never originally intended. There are many ways in which two or more persons can be said to be one without experiencing unity in the trinitarian sense. One scriptural example is marriage: the husband and wife becoming "one flesh" (Genesis 2.24); another is when the early believers were of "one heart" (Acts 4:32). In neither case could the words be given a meaning that

---

1. See also p. 30

215

Trinitarians put on the word "one".

In this passage Jesus is using the familiar analogy of a shepherd and his flock:

> "My sheep hear my voice, and I know them, and they follow me; and I give them eternal life, and they shall never perish, and no one shall snatch them out of my hand. My Father, who has given them to me, is greater than all, and no one is able to snatch them out of the Father's hand. I and the Father are one" (John 10:27-30).

No rational reading of this would suggest that Jesus is here defining the relationship between members of the trinity. On the contrary he stresses that the Father is the greater, even "greater than all". Indeed, this superior greatness of God is the *point of his argument*. Jesus is here comforting his flock by giving them a *double* assurance of their safety. He himself is their powerful defender, evidenced by the "works" he was doing in God's name (v25); but behind him was the *even greater* power of God. And Jesus and his Father are *united* in this intention to preserve the flock from all danger. It is in this desire and ability to defend the flock that they are "one", not in any trinitarian sense.

That the unity between God and Jesus is something different from the orthodox trinitarian meaning is made clear in Christ's prayer to his Father, where he requests that the unity that existed between them should *also* extend to the believers:

> "I do not pray for these only, but also for those who are to believe in me through their word, that they may all be one; *even as thou, Father, art in me, and I in thee*" (John 17:20-21).[1]

No one has ever quoted this verse to suggest that the believers are also components of the Godhead.

---

1. For a development of this see ch. 8

It is the allusions by John to this unity of mind and intention between the Father and the Son that, superficially read, appear to give some support to the trinitarian view. But closer examination shows that the reference is always to the Son being a manifestation of his Father in the way described in chapter 4 of this present work, a reflection of his glory and an extension of his power rather than possessing that glory and power as an inherent property. He is, to use Paul's phrase, "the image of the invisible God" (Colossians 1:15); that is, Jesus is the way in which God's necessarily unseen attributes have been revealed to mankind. John expresses the same idea: "No one has ever seen God; the only Son, who is in the bosom of the Father, he has made him known" (John 1:18). So in Christ all the divine characteristics, essential for man to know and appreciate, have been revealed in a way he can understand. In this sense he is *Immanuel*, God with us (Isaiah 7:14), the Father dwelling in the Son by His Spirit. Note in each of the following examples that the Son, although a manifestation of God, is still dependent on his Father:

"If I am not doing the works of my Father, then do not believe me; but if I do them, even though you do not believe me, believe the works, that you may know and understand that the Father is in me and I am in the Father" (John 10:37-38).

"Philip said to him, Lord, show us the Father, and we shall be satisfied. Jesus said to him, Have I been with you so long, and yet you do not know me, Philip? He who has seen me has seen the Father; how can you say, Show us the Father? Do you not believe that I am in the Father and the Father in me? The words that I say to you I do not speak on my own authority; but the Father who dwells in me does his works. Believe me that I am in the Father and the Father in me; or else believe me for the sake of the works themselves" (John 14:8-11).

This wonderful and absolutely unique relationship between God and Jesus marks out the Son as being different from and higher than every other created being. "In him the whole fulness of deity dwells bodily" (Colossians 2:9). He was a perfect illustration of all the otherwise unknowable attributes of God. He was an extension of the arm of God in the wondrous power that flowed from his word and touch. He was the mouth of God, giving the Father's message to man in a way and with a potency that none of the earlier prophets had achieved. He was beloved of God, experiencing the close and unparalleled intimacy described as being "in the bosom of the Father" (John 1:18) and spending whole nights in prayerful communion with him. And apart from God himself he is the greatest being in the Universe, at whose name "every knee should bow" (Philippians 2:10).

But he was not God in the trinitarian sense. His power was derived, not his own; coming from the Holy Spirit that was given him with a measureless anointing. His words were God's, as he so often declared. His future glory and honour is God's glory, for the Philippians passage goes on to say that every tongue will confess that "Jesus Christ is Lord, *to the glory of God the Father*" (v11).

Chapter 6

"THE CHRIST, THE SON OF THE LIVING GOD"[1]

Section 4: JESUS THE WORD OF GOD

The 'pre-existence' of Jesus'

In this chapter so far we have first considered Jesus as the Messiah, the long promised and long awaited Deliverer of the Jewish race and the Saviour of the whole world. Then in Section 2 the Scriptural teaching about the nature of Jesus was considered. He was unique in that he was both Son of God and Son of man, the latter giving him a physical nature identical to the rest of mankind. He experienced temptation, but never sinned by giving way to it. Section 3 reviewed the early Christian teaching on Jesus as the Son of God, a term which to them was synonymous with 'Messiah'. During his earthly ministry Jesus repeatedly alluded to his dependent role and subordination to his Father. We then examined passages that Trinitarians take to demonstrate the equality of Jesus with his Father and the belief that Jesus, the second person of an eternal trinity, assumed human form. It was shown that none of the passages would have conveyed such a meaning to the earliest Christians to whom the writings were addressed. Most of the alleged 'proofs' of the doctrines of the Trinity and the incarnation are in reality nothing of the sort. It is true that reading them with such doctrines already in mind it is possible to find support for some aspects of the Trinity; but that is very different from saying that such passages deliberately set out to

---

1. Matthew 16:16

219

teach that doctrine, or even reflect the writer's belief of the doctrine. In all cases the incarnation and the Trinity must be read into the words rather than derived from them. What is consistently lacking are scriptural passages that teach the Trinity in words which are incapable of any other meaning.

PRE-EXISTENCE IN WHAT SENSE?

But despite the many references to the subordinate role of Jesus there still remain some passages that appear to refer to his eternal pre-existence with God in heaven, even ascribing the creation of the world to him. This section will examine the question of Christ's pre-existence, and the final section will look at his creative work. Do these passages fulfil the criterion of being *of themselves* unambiguous statements of Christ's personal pre-existence, or do they only appear to teach it if the reader is already preconditioned to read such ideas into them?

One thing is sure: the personal pre-existence of Christ is fundamental to the doctrine of the Trinity. If the concept is doubtful the whole basis of the traditional view of God is put in jeopardy. It is undeniable that a few passages, almost all in the gospel of John, use language that suggests that Christ existed in heaven before his earthly ministry. But what needs to be determined is whether that pre-existence was *as a person* or as an *idea* or *plan* in the mind of God.

OLD TESTAMENT ALLUSIONS

In predicting the coming of the Messiah the Old Testament gives no hint that the promised Saviour was already in existence. In almost every case the future tense is used:

> "I *will* raise up for them a prophet like you from among their brethren; and I will put my words in his mouth, and he shall speak to them all that I command him" (Deuteronomy 18:18).
> "I *will* raise up your son ... I *will be* his father, and he *shall be* my son" (2 Samuel 7:12,14).

"His name *will be* called Wonderful Counsellor, Mighty God ..." (Isaiah 9:6).

In each case the Messiah is seen as a person yet to be born, not a being already existing in heaven who later would assume human form. This is true even when describing the relationship that would exist between God and His promised Son:

"He *shall* cry unto me, Thou art my Father, my God, and the rock of my salvation. And I *will make* him the firstborn, the highest of the kings of the earth" (Psalm 89:26-27).

It is difficult to reconcile these statements with the concept that the Son was already in heaven as the co-equal of God.

"WHOSE GOINGS FORTH HAVE BEEN FROM EVERLASTING"

The well-known passage that identifies Bethlehem as the birthplace of the Messiah is frequently quoted in support of the pre-existence of Jesus:

"But thou, Bethlehem Ephratah, though thou be little among the thousands of Judah, yet out of thee shall he come forth unto me that is to be ruler in Israel; whose *goings forth have been from of old, from everlasting*" (Micah 5:2, AV).

It is alleged that the final phrase indicates the eternal pre-existence of Jesus. But did the prophet really intend that? There are three significant words here: the Hebrew *mikedem* which is expressed as 'old', *olahm* which is rendered 'everlasting', and *motsaah* which in the plural is translated 'goings forth'. The first of these, *mikedem* is from *kedem*, a common word meaning 'old, afore, before in time or in location, past, aforetime' and is often translated as 'ancient times'. *Olahm* is basically an indefinite period of time, and is derived from *alam* 'to conceal'. It is frequently translated 'ever' or 'everlasting' but also as 'old' and 'ancient times'. Neither of the two latter terms necessarily conveys the idea of eternity. Isaiah uses both of these words in a passage that directs Israel to remember their past history—clearly something that did not stretch back into infinite time:

> "Remember this and consider, ... remember the former things of old (*olahm*); for I am God, and there is no other, ... declaring the end from the beginning and from ancient times (*mikedem*) things not yet done" (Isaiah 46:8-10).

Similarly both words are used in describing the events of the Exodus, where to translate them so as to mean 'from eternity' would obviously be inappropriate:

> "Awake, put on strength, O arm of the Lord; awake, as in days of old (*kedem*), the generations of long ago (*olahm*)" (Isaiah 51:9).

Thus *mikedem* and *olahm* in scriptural usage do not necessarily indicate an eternal past.

Those who use this passage to support the trinity assume the third word under discussion, the AV "goings forth", to mean Christ's eternal activity in heaven prior to his incarnation. But the word *motsaah* is a word that simply means 'to proceed from'. Here are some of the ways it is translated:

> '*spring* of water' (2 Kings2:21),
> 'the ground *put forth* grass' (Job 38:27)
> '*that which came out* of my lips' (Jeremiah 17:16).

Of particular interest is the use of the word to describe the son of Abraham who, God said, was to '*come forth* (*motsaah*) out of thine own bowels' (Genesis 15:4, AV), implying birth or physical descent from a forefather. Here we have the clue to the meaning of Micah's words. The Messiah was to come as the 'seed of the woman', as the 'seed of Abraham' and as the 'son of David'—a series of descendants or 'comings forth' that would lead to His appearing. And this purpose had been foretold by God from 'ancient times', even at the very beginning in Eden. These 'comings forth' (i.e. a series of descendants) had certainly been from earliest times, as Christ's genealogies in the gospel records demonstrate. It may be significant that in the Micah passage *motsaah* is in the feminine form of the noun, indicating the female origin of the Messiah, the 'seed of the woman'. Thus it was absolutely true to say of him 'His goings forth have been from old, from everlasting'; or as the RSV more accurately puts it 'whose origin is from old, from ancient days'. It is just another way of saying that his *ancestry* extended back to Adam via David and Abraham. By no rules of biblical interpretation can the personal pre-existence of the Messiah be legitimately read into the passage.

THE CONCEPTION, BIRTH AND EARLY LIFE OF JESUS

Turning to the record of Christ's birth there is a similar silence about his personal pre-existence. Gabriel announced the impending event in the terms of God's Old Testament promises:

> "You will conceive in your womb and bear a son, and you shall call his name Jesus. He will be great, and will be called the Son of the Most High; and the Lord God will give to him the throne of his father David, and he will reign over the house of Jacob for ever; and of his kingdom there will be no end" (Luke 1:31-33).

In view of her unmarried state Mary asked for information as to how this would happen, and was told:

> "The Holy Spirit will come upon you, and the power of the Most High will overshadow you; therefore the child to be

223

born will be called holy, the Son of God" (verse 35).

There was clearly not even a hint in the angel's message that Jesus already existed, and that the babe was to be God coming in human form. Why was this information withheld if it were true? Mary, no doubt because of her godly disposition and outstanding character, had been chosen by God to be the vehicle for the birth of His Son. Would He have concealed any relevant information from her concerning her child? Yet in outlining the Son's work, there is not the slightest intimation that he was already existing as God's co-equal in heaven. Instead the future tense is still used as it was in the Old Testament—he *will be* called the Son of the Most High, etc.

As Jesus grew up he "increased in wisdom and in stature, and in favour with God and man" (Luke 2:52). This statement presents a difficulty for those who believe Jesus had a personal pre-existence. It prompts the question as to what he brought with him when he descended from heaven to earth and assumed human nature. Did he divest himself of all the wisdom and knowledge inherently associated with his divinity and start with a clean slate? Did he so completely relinquish all his perfect attributes that he had to build again from scratch a character that enabled him to re-establish himself in God's favour? The Trinitarians in effect must assume that he did. Yet without irreverence we can surely ask if it were possible for a divine being, one who knows all things and is perfect in every sense, to ever 'forget' everything about his divinity and start again the process of learning and character building?

This dilemma is increased by the generally accepted view that Christ did *not* relinquish any aspect of his deity when he became man:

"When the Word 'became flesh' His deity was not abandoned, or reduced, or contracted, nor did He cease to exercise the divine functions which had been His before. It is He, we are told, who sustains the creation in ordered existence, and who gives and upholds all life, and these functions were certainly not in abeyance during His time on earth. ... The New Testament stresses that the Son's deity was not reduced through the incarnation".[1]

If this is true how did Jesus 'increase in wisdom and in favour with God' if all the time he had never relinquished a divinity that possessed these attributes to perfection?

THE TEMPTATION OF JESUS
The same problem arises with Christ's temptation, both in the specific series of temptations in the wilderness and in his whole life. We read that he 'in every respect has been tempted as we are' (Hebrews 4:15). If Jesus had indeed a personal pre-existence in heaven before his birth to Mary, any recollection of his previous life would have rendered his temptation almost futile. A perfect mind cannot be tempted with evil. A mind that 'knows all things from the beginning' could have foreseen the result of the conflict so as to make it no conflict at all. But could Jesus, as pre-existent and omniscient God the Son have blanked out from his mind all the divine thoughts and feelings that had been his from eternity? We have already seen that Trinitarians believe that Jesus *did* have a recollection of a life in heaven. Indeed according to their view of John 17:5 Jesus could recall the glory he had shared with God before the world was made. So why should he not recall the other aspects of his divinity? Yet if that were so how did he *increase* in wisdom, and why did he need to learn to overcome the 'temptations common to man'(1 Corinthians 10:13) and so be pleasing and obedient to his heavenly Father?

Jesus continued to learn obedience right to the end of his earthly ministry. A most revealing passage in Hebrews reads:

---

1. "New Bible Dictionary". Pub. IVF

"Although he were a Son, he *learned obedience* through what he suffered; and *being made perfect* he became the source of eternal salvation to all who obey him" (Hebrews 5:8).

Again the question must be faced. If Jesus was pre-existent God with an infinite life of perfection behind him how could he 'learn obedience' and as a result of this be 'made perfect'. At what point did the perfect member of the eternal trinity become less than perfect? What form did that deficiency take? These are legitimate questions that Trinitarians seldom, if ever, address.

It is continually alleged that the uniqueness of the Christian message lies in the fact that God became man for the salvation of the human race. It is said that only by this incarnation could man's redemption be achieved. Yet the clear scriptural teaching, as was shown particularly in section 2 of the present chapter and will be emphasised again in a later section, is that Jesus was a man whose physical nature was identical in every respect to ours. And we can now add that this included the need to develop mind and character by a process of normal growth. It is reasonable therefore to query even the relevance of a previous existence. Why is it that the eternal almighty God should deem it necessary to reveal Himself as a man, that is, to become incarnate? How did it help the redemption process? A previous existence in heaven seems in no way an aid to or a preparation for the work he had to do on earth. On the other hand if it is said that it was only through being God that he could triumph in the way that he did, then his personal achievement seems greatly lessened, for God can do anything.

"HE CALLS THINGS THAT ARE NOT AS THOUGH THEY ARE"

The key to understanding the biblical sense in which Jesus pre-existed is the *foreknowledge of God*. His control of future events is so absolute that nothing can prevent His decisions coming into effect. Once He has decided anything it is as good as done:

"I work and who can hinder it?" (Isaiah 43:13).

"I am God, and there is none like me, declaring the end from the beginning and from ancient times things not yet done, saying, My counsel shall stand, and I *will* accomplish all my purpose ... I have spoken, and I *will* bring it to pass; I have purposed, and I *will* do it." (Isaiah 46:9-11).

Because of the impossibility of His plans failing God often speaks of future events as if they had actually happened. This is important to keep in mind. Paul says that God:

"Calls things that are not *as though they were*". (Romans 4:17, NIV).

There are several Scriptural examples of this that are very relevant to this study. For example, when God commissioned Jeremiah to be a prophet He said to him:

"Before I formed you in the womb I knew you" (Jeremiah 1:5).

Here is an example of a man being 'known' by God long before he was born. In this sense it could be said that Jeremiah 'pre-existed'—obviously not as a person but in God's mind and purpose. This is not the only example. All those who are finally redeemed by Jesus have been 'known' to God since before the creation. This point is made many times:

"For those whom he *foreknew* he also predestined (Gk *pro-orizo*, to 'mark out in advance') to be conformed to the image of his Son" (Romans 8:29).

"Even as he chose us in him *before the foundation of the world* (Ephesians 1:4).

"God chose you *from the beginning*" (2 Thessalonians 2:13).

"Who saved us and called us with a holy calling ... which he gave us in Christ *ages ago*" (2 Timothy 1:9).

Note carefully the language used by Paul in these passages. The believers were 'foreknown' and 'chosen in Christ' *before the creation of the world*. None would deduce from this that the believers had a personal existence from eternity. Rather that they existed in the mind and purpose of God and because His purpose is inflexible they could be regarded as real although they had not yet come into existence. Why then should not the reference to Christ's pre-existence be taken in the same way? Dunn, himself a Trinitarian, has a significant comment on how the early Christians would have understood the Ephesians passage quoted above:

"Here too it is the divine choice or election which was made 'before the foundation of the world'—the pre-determination of Christ as redeemer and of those who would be redeemed in and through Christ. We may speak of an ideal pre-existence at this point, but of *real pre-existence of Christ or of believers once again there is no thought*".[1]

Here the distinction is made between the *idea* of Christ's redemptive work ('ideal pre-existence') and the actual *reality* of his existence ('real pre-existence'). The first truly was there from the beginning, and the second patently was not.

In confirmation of this we turn to an important statement about Christ made by Peter:

"He was destined before the foundation of the world but

---

1. Op. cit. p.235, Italics ours

was made manifest at the end of the times for your sake" (1 Peter 1:20).

The word translated 'destined' literally means 'to know beforehand'. It is the word from which we get our word *prognosis* meaning *known in advance*, usually used by doctors in predicting the course of an illness. On the basis of his *foreknowledge* the doctor can offer a good or bad *prognosis* about the outcome of the disease. Thus in this passage Peter is telling us that Jesus was *known in advance* by God in the sense that His plan for him was predetermined; and then at the appropriate time Jesus was born. Clearly there was no thought in Peter's mind that Jesus had personally existed before he was born. Confirmation of this view is found in the opening salutation of this epistle, where Peter describes his readers in identical words:

"Chosen and *destined* by God the Father" (1 Peter 1:2).

None take this to mean *the believers'* personal previous existence.

God's foreknowledge of his purpose in Christ is often likened to an architect's mental picture of a new building. Long before any construction work has started he 'sees' the edifice in his mind's eye. Every detail is planned and recorded so that he knows exactly how the completed building will appear. He could speak of its magnificence and splendour when in fact it did not yet exist. It was in prospect, not in reality. God too has a plan for a house that has not yet been built. Not a literal building but an edifice composed of the redeemed.[1] And the corner stone of this building is Jesus. With an insight greater than any human architect, God can visualise this building in all its glory, and because He is so sure that it will be constructed He can speak of it as already done. It is in this way that it can

---

1. Ephesians 2:19-22; Hebrews 3:2-6 etc.

be said that Jesus had glory with God in the beginning, and that the redeemed were chosen and 'marked out' before the foundation of the world.

THE SON OF MAN'S DESCENT FROM HEAVEN

With these comments about the general Scriptural teaching concerning the sense in which Christ pre-existed we come to the passages, exclusive to the gospel record of John, which seem to suggest Christ's personal pre-existence in heaven. In addition to the classic understanding of the Logos in the prologue (1:1-18), which will be considered later, there are the following passages:

1. "He who descended from heaven, the Son of Man" (John 3:13).
2. "He who comes from above is above all" (John 3:31)
3. "He whom God has sent" (John 3:34).
4. "For the bread of God is that which comes down from heaven, and gives life to the world. ... I am the bread of life" (John 6:33-35).
5. "I have come down from heaven, not to do mine own will, but the will of him who sent me" (John 6:38).
6. "What if you were to see the Son of man ascending where he was before?" (John 6:62).
7. "I am from above" (John 8:23).
8. "I proceeded and came forth from God" (John 8:42).
9. "Before Abraham was, I am" (John 8:58).
10. "I came from the Father and have come into the world; again, I am leaving the world and going to the Father" (John 16:28).
11. "Father, glorify me in thy own presence with the glory which I had with thee before the world was made" (John 17:5).

The fact that all these allusions to Christ coming down from heaven are found only in the gospel record of John should make us pause. Did the other gospel writers know of the pre-existence of Christ but did not mention it? It certainly could be said that their silence suggests they did not believe and teach it. Or could it be that John had a distinctive way of looking at the words of Jesus that bids us look beneath their apparent meaning?

LITERAL OR FIGURATIVE?
There is no doubt that many of Christ's sayings recorded by John were not intended to be taken literally, although sometimes his hearers did just that. When Jesus told Nicodemus that he needed to be "born anew", he first took a literal interpretation—"How can a man be born when he is old? Can he enter a second time into his mother's womb and be born?" (John 3:3-4)—and had to be led gently by Jesus to see rebirth as a *spiritual* process. When Jesus described himself as the "bread from heaven" that a believer had to "eat" (6:50,51), so that "out of his heart shall flow rivers of living water" (7:38) no one would ever think of taking the words at their face value. Jesus himself acknowledged this on one occasion when he said to his disciples "I have said this to you in figures" (John 16:25).

We use figurative speech today almost without thinking about it. We know that a 'heaven-sent gift' has not literally come down from heaven, but expresses the belief that it has been supplied by divine providence. We suggest that many of the references to Christ's descent from heaven were intended to be understood in the same way. For example, the conversation with the Jews (no. 4 in the above list) about the bread of life is a reference to the God-provided manna that fed the Israelites in the wilderness (John 6:31-33). Everybody understood the sense in which manna came down from heaven— not literally dropping from the throne of God, but being God-provided. Why should not the parallel allusion to Jesus descending from heaven be taken in a similar way? Jesus came down from heaven in the sense that he was *provided by God* to be the source of life for the world. The actual body of Jesus was con-ceived by the Holy Spirit in Mary's womb, and thus was 'from

God'. Other references make it clear that the body of Jesus came from God in this sense:

> "Consequently, when Christ came into the world, he said Sacrifices and offerings thou hast not desired, but *a body hast thou prepared for me*.... Then I said, Lo, I have come to do thy will, O God ... And by that will we have been sanctified through the offering of the *body* of Jesus Christ once for all" (Hebrews 10:5,7,10).

References 1,2,5,7,8, can be viewed in a similar way. In addition it should be noted in (1) that it was the Son of *Man* that came down—an unexpected expression if a pre-existent *deity* was intended; for none suggest that Jesus pre-existed as a man.

In references (6) and (10) Jesus couples his coming from God with his ascent to heaven after the resurrection. The way in which he came down has already been established: not a mature figure descending, but a body gradually developed by the Holy Spirit in Mary's womb. But the way in which he ascended is clearly described in the Gospels and Acts. It was with a body and by a *bodily* ascent that he 'left the world and went to the Father' (Mark 16.19, Luke 24:51, Acts 1:9-11). Does not this mixture of meaning suggest that we should not press the words too literally?

"SENT FROM GOD"
Other passages, (3) (5), speak of Jesus being *sent from* God. Do these imply a pre-existence in heaven? By no means. John Baptist is described in similar terms: "There was a man sent from God, whose name was John" (John 1:6). In this passage the original words translated *from God* literally mean *from beside God*; but this emphatic term has never been used to suggest that John had an eternal pre-existence in heaven. It would therefore be inconsistent to use similar passages relating to Jesus to assert *his* pre-existence.

"BEFORE ABRAHAM WAS I AM"

The reference to Abraham (9) is another key passage for Trinitarians, although, as with the majority of such passages, the doctrine has to be read into it rather than deduced from it. It is claimed that when Jesus said to the Jews "Before Abraham was (Gk. *came into being*), I am" he was stating that (a) he existed in Abraham's day, and (b) he could apply to himself the personal name of God revealed in Exodus.

It is not disputed that Jesus had some kind of existence before Abraham was born, but was it a *personal* existence, or one in the mind and purpose of God? The early Christian view was stated by Peter in the passage already considered in detail above (p. 229):

"He was *destined* before the foundation of the world but was made *manifest* at the end of the times for your sake" (1 Peter 1:20).

The word translated 'destined' means *known beforehand*, and from what has already been considered about the promises relating to the coming Messiah it is quite clear that God had marked out beforehand with absolute precision the mission he would accomplish. Thus it is true that before Abraham was born Christ 'was' in the sense that he was envisaged as the one through whom God and estranged man would become reconciled. A glance at the context of the words shows that this was in Christ's mind. The Jews were claiming the privileges of descent from Abraham, whilst Jesus replied that if they were his children they would do what Abraham did (John 8:39). And one of the things Abraham did, in contrast to his unbelieving descendants, was that he 'rejoiced to see my day; he saw it and was glad' (v.56), whereas the Jews who actually were living in the 'day' of Christ did not recognise it. We are specifically told in what sense Abraham *saw* Christ's day. It was in prospect, as an expression of his faith in the coming of Abraham's seed:

"And the scripture, foreseeing that God would justify the Gentiles by faith, preached the gospel beforehand to Abraham, saying, In thee shall all the nations be blessed"
"Now the promises were made to Abraham and to his offspring. It does not say, *And to offsprings*, referring to many; but, referring to one, *And to your offspring*, which is Christ" (Galatians 3:8,16).

We are told that Abraham, on receipt of this promise that he would be the father of the Messiah "*believed the Lord*; and he reckoned it to him as righteousness" (Genesis 15:6). Through this belief Abraham foresaw the coming day of Christ. He foresaw his death and resurrection after the pattern of his own offering of Isaac, and he foresaw the world-wide blessings that would come from that act. But it was all in prospect: Abraham did not believe that his future son was already in existence in heaven. And this too is what Jesus was saying in his reply to the Jews. He re-affirms the fact that he was 'present' in the *plan* of God even before the time of Abraham. He could say this without any suggestion of his personal pre-existence.

The second claim, that Christ apparently applied to himself the divine name I AM, is not as straightforward as appears at first sight. Despite the bias of many translations, there is no textual justification at all for the capital letters. The words *I am* are simply the usual translation of the present tense of the verb 'to be' (Gk. *ego eimi*). In similar grammatical constructions to the phrase under consideration the translators have added 'he' after the 'I am' to give the sense. For example, the identical phrase was used by the healed blind man to identify himself (John 9.9), translated "I am the man". If this translation is consistently applied to Christ's use of the phrase any trinitarian inference disappears. Thus on a rare occasion when Jesus volunteered that he was the Messiah he used an identical construction (*ego eimi*, translated 'I am he') without any hint of pre-existence:

"The woman said to him, I know that Messiah is coming (he who is called Christ); when he comes, he will show us all things. Jesus said to her, I who speak to you am he" (literally *"I am he* speaking to you". John 4:25-26).

Similarly in two other passages in John 8, just prior to where Jesus made the alleged I AM statement, the translators have rendered *ego eimi* as 'I am he", with no suggestion that it represents a personal name:

"You will die in your sins unless you believe that *I am he"* (v24).
"When you have lifted up the Son of man, then you will know that *I am he"* (v28. Other similar examples in John 18:5,8; Luke 22:70).

By stating "I am he" in these three passages Jesus is obviously identifying himself as the Messiah and saying that belief of this fact is essential. If the translators had been consistent they would also have translated John 8:58 as "Before Abraham was, *I am he"*, and no one would have thought it a reference to the divine name. Jesus was not suggesting that he was God, but claiming that he was the Messiah to whose day Abraham looked forward in faith and hope.

But even if this is not admitted, there is no proof that by the use of 'I am' Jesus is claiming to be 'very God'. In fact 'I am' is almost certainly a defective translation of the name of God announced in Exodus:

"Moses said to God ... If ... they ask me, What is his name? what shall I say to them? God said to Moses, I AM WHO I AM. And he said, Say this to the people of Israel, I AM has sent me to you" Exodus 3:13-14).

It has already been shown[1] that this name is really in the future tense—'I WILL BE', and that it can be seen as a statement of God's intention to become manifested in 'mighty ones' of whom Jesus is the first. But if the divine name is 'I WILL BE' it will readily be seen that the whole point of the supposed connection with the 'I AM' of John is lost.

"THE GLORY WHICH I HAD WITH THEE BEFORE THE WORLD WAS MADE"

Here is yet another passage (11) that at first sight appears to suggest that Jesus had a personal existence with God from the beginning. But as with so many sayings of Jesus recorded by John, we need to establish if that is what he really meant. Every time we read 'glory' should we refer it exclusively to literal glory and radiance? This prayer of Christ to his Father as recorded in John 17 contains several references to 'glory', and it is important to have a consistent view of them:

> "Father, the hour has come; glorify thy Son that the Son may glorify thee" (v1)
> "And now, Father, glorify thou me in thy own presence with the glory which I had with thee before the world was made" (v5).
> "All mine are thine, and thine are mine, and I am glorified in them" (V10).
> "The glory which thou hast given me I have given to them, that they may be one even as we are one" (v22).
> "Father, I desire that they also, whom thou hast given me, may be with me where I am, to behold my glory which thou hast given me in thy love for me before the foundation of the world" (v24).

The first thing to notice from these words of Christ is that the glory was something *received* by Jesus and later by the

---

1. p. 46

disciples. It was *not* an inherent possession. God glorifies the Son (v1), and 'gives' glory to him' (vv22,24). Only if Jesus was subordinate to God could he have *received* glory from Him (using 'glory' in the usual sense of the word). "It is beyond dispute that the inferior is blessed by the superior" (Hebrews 7:7).

But does the 'glory' refer only to the physical glory of God who "dwells in unapproachable light" (1 Timothy 6:16), and is it this glory only which is shared from eternity by a second person of the trinity? Clearly not, is the answer to both these questions. For that glory had *already* been manifested to the Jews (John 1:14) and by the time of Jesus' prayer had *already* been given to the disciples (v.22). And no one would suggest that they displayed the Father's physical glory.

In what sense then was Jesus the glory of God even before the creation? We need to understand the way in which John uses the word *glory*. In many New Testament passages the 'glory of God' refers not primarily to physical glory but describes the whole of God's redemptive purpose manifested in Jesus. Although Jesus outwardly was an ordinary man, by his character and mission people saw him as different; they "beheld *his glory*, glory as of the only Son from the Father" (1:14). What glory did they behold? When he did the miracle at Cana it "manifested *his glory*" (2:11) and when Lazarus died and so gave Jesus the opportunity to raise him from the dead, it was "for the *glory of God*, so that the Son of God may be *glorified* by means of it" (11.4). When he was about to perform that miracle Jesus said to the sorrowing sisters "Did I not tell you that if you believe you would see the *glory of God*?" (11.40). In a similar sense the death of Christ himself was an expression of God's glory, for in anticipation of it Jesus said "Father, the hour has come; *glorify thy Son* that the Son may *glorify thee*" (John 17:1). His resurrection was a further exhibition of the glory of God, for as Paul says, he was raised from the dead "by the *glory of the Father*" (Romans 6:4). So the same writer could describe his message as "the gospel of the *glory of Christ*" (2 Corinthians 4:4) and say that the process of believing the gospel is God shining "in our hearts to give the light of the knowledge of the *glory of God* in the face of Jesus Christ" (v6).

Thus the *glory of God* is the gospel—the power and character of God revealed in all that Jesus does for man's salvation. It describes the process by which Jesus will bring "many sons to glory" (Hebrews 2:10), even those whom he has "prepared beforehand for glory" (Romans 9:23). Now this purpose of God, as has been so frequently remarked in this section, has been devised and known by God since the beginning. Jesus was to be the pivot of this gospel plan, and therefore he had glory in the beginning in a *prospective* sense rather than literally. When his disciples believed on Jesus they too partook of this 'glory of God'—"The glory which thou hast given me I *have given* to them" (John 17:22).

So when Jesus prayed that he might now experience the glory which he had with God from the beginning, he was not asserting his pre-existence but asking that God's original purpose with him might now be completed.

But possession of this spiritual and as yet intangible glory leads on to sharing the physical glory of God. Jesus appeared to Paul on the road to Damascus as a "light from heaven brighter than the sun" (Acts 26:13), and to John on Patmos as "the sun shining in full strength" (Revelation 1:16). Likewise Christ's promise to the righteous is that they too will "shine like the sun in the kingdom of their Father" (Matthew 13:43).

THE PROLOGUE TO JOHN'S GOSPEL

We now come to the passage above all which Trinitarians claim teaches the pre-existence of Jesus from eternity and supports unquestionably the concept of the incarnation:

"In the beginning was the Word,
and the Word was with God,
and the Word was God.
He was in the beginning with God;
all things were made through him,
and without him was not anything made that was made.
And the Word became flesh and dwelt among us, full of
grace and truth;
We have beheld his glory, glory as of the only Son from
the Father" (John 1.1-3,14).

From this passage Trinitarians deduce the following about
Jesus:

1. The Word was Jesus in person
2. He personally existed from the beginning.
3. He was God, i.e. the second person of the Trinity.
4. He was the creator of all things, confirming that he was
   God existing from the beginning.
5. He came down to earth to be clothed in human flesh.

It is important to bear at least two points in mind as this
passage is considered. First, it needs to be viewed from the
standpoint of the first century Christian, untrammelled as he
was with all the later arguments and discussions that were based
upon these verses. By the fourth century, after seemingly
interminable conferences and thousands of closely reasoned
manuscripts, a whole edifice of doctrine had been built upon
these few words. But what would *first century* people make of
them?

Secondly, John must not be interpreted in such a way as to
disagree with or contradict the rest of the New Testament
writers. There are some who maintain that whilst (as we have
already seen) the earliest Christian writers had no place for the
pre-existence of Christ or the incarnation, these ideas were
even then being formulated in the early church and toward the
end of the first century were expressed by John. To this view

the present writers cannot subscribe. The Christian message was "once for all (time) delivered to the saints" (Jude 3) and any subsequent variations were examples of the false doctrine that the apostles predicted would develop in their midst.[1] Development in Christian belief certainly did occur towards the end of the first century and during the two centuries that followed, but this was at the expense of the purity of the original message and was roundly condemned and combated by the apostles and their immediate successors. In the writings of the New Testament the apostles speak with an original single voice. If, as we believe, and the church today claims to believe, all the New Testament writers were inspired by the Holy Spirit, to guide them into "all truth" (John 16:13), then the message must be unanimous. One inspired writer cannot be interpreted so as to contradict another.

Thus in view of the absence of proof of the doctrine of the trinity in the rest of the New Testament John's introduction needs to be examined very closely before accepting that it is a departure from the then universally held belief in the unity of God and the subordination of His Son.

THE 'WORD' OR 'LOGOS'

For an understanding of this passage the meaning of the Greek *Logos*, translated 'Word', is crucial. It was the *Logos* that was with God in the beginning, indeed, was God. And it was this *Logos* that became flesh in the person of Jesus Christ.

Logos is a flexible word with a range of meanings. It has given rise to several of our everyday words. It is often combined with another term to mean 'words' or 'a treatise' about a particular subject. For example 'bio*logy*', the study of living things, literally means "words about life" (Greek *bios* = life and *logos* = word). We use the word 'logic' to describe the

---

1. For the historical development of the doctrine of the Trinity see ch.8

reasoning process. And 'word' and 'reason' are the primary meanings of the word as defined by a standard Greek lexicon[1] which contains the following entry for *Logos*:

I. The word by which the inward thought is expressed: also
II. The inward thought or reason itself.

Logos is therefore correctly translated 'word', but has the particular meaning of *expressing an idea that is in the speaker's mind* rather than referring merely to words as such (the Greek has a different term for a 'word' as a part of speech). In the New Testament *logos* occurs frequently, and is the regular term for the *word of God* as spoken or written by Jesus and the apostles. There are some three hundred occasions where *logos* occurs in the original of the New Testament, and it is translated 'word' on about two thirds of these. But *logos* is also variously translated by other terms which express the underlying idea of reason or spoken thoughts, as the following examples show (with the translation of *logos* in italics):

"Therefore let us leave the elementary *doctrines* of Christ" (Hebrews 6:1).
"Jesus said to them, I will ask you a *question*" (Mark 11:29).
"For here the *saying* holds true ..." (John 4:37).
"What is this *conversation* which you are holding with each other ..." (Luke 24:17).
"In the first *book*, O Theophilus ..." (Acts 1:1).
"You have neither part nor lot in this *matter*" (Acts 8:21).
"If it were a matter of wrong ... *reason* would that I should bear with you" (Acts 18:14, AV).

From this usage it can be seen that there are two ideas contained in the word *logos*: the unexpressed thought in the

---

1. Liddell and Scott

mind, and the thought expressed in speech.

'LOGOS' IN FIRST CENTURY CHRISTIAN THOUGHT

It is fortunate for our understanding of this word that we have the writings of Philo, a Jew who was contemporary with the early Christians. We learn from him that the *logos*, and especially the divine *logos*, was the subject of much discussion throughout the non-Christian world of the first century. He refers extensively to it in his writings and so we can gain the sense in which it was used in apostolic times. In one passage Philo writes:

> "... 'logos' has two aspects, one resembling a spring, the other its outflow; 'logos' in the understanding resembles a spring, and is called 'reason', while utterance by mouth and tongue is like its outflow, and is called 'speech' (Migr. 70-85).

But, as this analogy suggests, the two meanings can merge into each other and the distinction between *thought* and *speech* can become blurred. Thus a comprehensive definition of *logos* is *thought coming to expression in speech*.

Philo also shows that the idea of the *logos* was developed further to include not only expression of thoughts by speech but by action as well. He expresses the idea that all created things were originally in the mind of God only, and this *logos* or plan was then put into effect by His creative acts. Because man (unaided by revelation) can see God only in a limited sense by viewing creation, the *logos* makes up the deficiency by describing what man can know of God. He uses another analogy from nature:

> ".. to use Philo's favourite sun and light symbolism, the Logos is to God as the corona is to the sun, the sun's halo which man can look upon when he cannot look directly on the sun itself. That is not to say that the logos is God as

such, any more than the corona is the sun as such, but the Logos is that alone which may be seen of God"[1]

The same writer goes on to summarise Philo's understanding (and therefore probably the first century Jewish understanding) of the Logos:

"God is unknowable by man, except in a small degree by the creation, but the Logos expresses God's ideas to man. There is no idea of personality attached to the Logos."

"The Logos seems to be nothing more for Philo than God himself in his approach to man, God himself insofar as he may be known by man"[2]

'LOGOS' AND THE OLD TESTAMENT

Philo was a Jew with an inevitably strict adherence to the monotheism of God and a devout belief in the Jewish scriptures, our Old Testament. It is far from surprising therefore that his views on the *Logos*, together with those of his Jewish contemporaries, are clearly based on that authority. There the *Word* of God is continually used to describe the inspired prophetic utterances by which God's thoughts were conveyed to His people. "The word of the Lord came unto me" is the almost standard introduction to the prophets' messages. The *Word of God* is also frequently equated not only with God's thoughts and speech, but also with the acts that follow from them. So we find that His creative acts, His control of creation, His purpose in creation, and His declaration of that purpose to man are all attributed to the *Word*. It is significant that in many of these instances when the Hebrew was translated into Greek *Logos* was used as the equivalent to *word*.

Thus it was the Word or Logos, the plan of God in action, that was instrumental in creation:

---

1. Dunn, Op. cit. p.227

2. Ibid, p.228

"By *the word* of the Lord the heavens were made, and all their host by the breath of his mouth". "For he spoke, and it came to be; he commanded, and it stood forth." (Psalm 33:6,9).

The same Word controls the elements:

"He sends forth his command to the earth; his *word* runs swiftly. He casts forth his ice like morsels; who can stand before his cold? He sends forth his *word* and melts them; he makes his wind to blow, and the waters flow" (Psalm 147:15,17-18).

Isaiah expresses the relationship between the Word of God and His plan for the earth:

"For as the rain and the snow come down from heaven, and return not thither but water the earth, making it bring forth and sprout, giving seed to the sower and bread to the eater, so shall *my word* be that goes forth from my mouth; it shall not return to me empty, but it shall accomplish that which I purpose, and prosper in the thing for which I sent it" (Isaiah 55:10-11).

The Word, then, is the *thoughts and purpose of God in action*, either by direct revelation through His prophets or in creating and maintaining the earth to achieve that purpose. Although at first sight it might be thought that the references above give the idea of a separate existence for the Word, closer examination shows that personality is in no way suggested; it is only an idiom of speech that speaks of the *Word* being sent or doing something.

THE SPIRIT OF GOD AND THE WISDOM OF GOD
Alongside the use of *Word* in the Old Testament to describe God's activity in creation or revelation are two other equivalent words: Spirit and Wisdom. These too are described as being the

agents of creation. The Spirit is another term for the *power* of God, the 'power of the Most High' as it is called in Luke 1:35. In the Genesis record of the creation it was "the *Spirit* of God" that moved over the face of the waters, and then God's *Word* brought things into being:

> "Darkness was upon the face of the deep; and the *Spirit* of God was moving over the face of the waters. And God *said*, 'Let there be light'; and there was light" (Genesis 1:2-3).

This equivalence of *Word* and *Spirit* is seen in many instances. Whilst the psalmist could say "by the *word* of the Lord the heavens were made" (33:6), another psalm says "When thou sendest forth thy *Spirit* they are created; and thou renewest the face of the ground" (104:30). So the Spirit of God and the Word of God are often alternative terms.

The same can be said of the *Wisdom* of God. It was also termed the instrument of creation: "The Lord by wisdom founded the earth" (Proverbs 3:19). And this same Wisdom (or Spirit or Word) is personified in Proverbs and shown to be God's agent of creation. In Greek and Hebrew the words for *wisdom* are feminine, and so in personification is represented as a woman (on the other hand *logos* is masculine, hence the NT pronoun 'he'):

> "Does not wisdom call, does not understanding raise her voice? ... I, wisdom, dwell in prudence ...
> The Lord created me at the beginning of his work, the first of his acts of old. ...
> When he established the heavens, I was there .. when he marked out the foundations of the earth,
> then I was beside him, like a master workman,
> and I was daily his delight,
> rejoicing before him always,
> rejoicing in his inhabited world,

and delighting in the sons of men" (Proverbs 8:1,12,22f).

The language here is clearly personification, a figure of speech in which an abstract idea is given the attributes of a person. None would suggest that there was a female deity called Wisdom who was formed by God in the beginning and who then created the world. It is important not to confuse personification with personalisation.

Barclay, one of the most respected Greek scholars of our generation, sums up the first century relationship of *logos, Word* and *Spirit* in Jewish thought that formed the background to John's use of *logos* in his gospel:

"First, God's *Word* is not only speech; it is *power*. Second, it is impossible to separate the ideas of *Word* and *Wisdom*; and it was God's *Wisdom* which created and permeated the world which God made".[1]

To sum up so far. We have seen that the *Word* of God or *Logos* is a term used in scripture and by Jewish writers living in the first century to describe the thoughts and plan of God being put into action. It was applied to the original acts of creation and also to the redemptive purpose God has with the earth. The *Logos* through the ministry of the prophets supplied the essential understanding of God that was not available simply from perusal of his creative acts. The term is used alternatively with Spirit and Wisdom, and in no case is there a suggestion that any of these had a separate personality, i.e. were an actual person.

This is the essential setting of the prologue of John's gospel record. *Any interpretation of the prologue must be incorrect if it fails to acknowledge this background and attempts to impose on*

1. "New Testament Words", p.186. J. Ziesler has a similar association of the three in his *The Jesus Question*. Pub. Lutterworth Press (1980).

John's words a meaning that his original readers probably would not have readily understood. To divorce the prologue from its Old Testament roots, let alone its New Testament contemporaries, is to set off on the wrong path to its understanding.

THE 'WORD' OF JOHN'S PROLOGUE

It is into this background of Old Testament teaching on the Word of God, and the first century Jewish understanding of it based on those sacred writings, that the prologue to John's gospel fits neatly into place:

> "In the beginning was the Word,
> and the Word was with God,
> and the Word was God.
> He was in the beginning with God;
> All things were made through him, and
> without him was not anything made that was made"
> (John 1:1-3)

We can see how John draws on all the Old Testament teaching we have just considered. *Wisdom* is personified in Proverbs 8 (see above) as saying that she was in the beginning, that she was with God, and that she was His instrument in creation. The *Word of God* created the heavens (Psalm 33:6), so did the *Spirit* as described in Job 26:13. The language clearly is of figure and metaphor, of personification, not actual personality. And John is saying exactly the same of the *Logos* or Word. No Jewish reader brought up on the writings of the prophets would have deduced from John's introduction that he was alluding to a person who had existed with God from all time. They would see it instead as a continuation of the imagery by which the *Word* or *Wisdom* or *the Spirit*—those manifestations of God which are inseparable from Him—are described as putting God's intentions into effect.

Bearing in mind the meaning of *Logos* as the thoughts and intentions of God translated into action, we can see that what

John is saying is that from the beginning God had a plan—a plan that was as inseparable from Him as is a thought from the person thinking it—thus, 'the Word *was* God'. That plan necessitated the creation of the world, and so it could be said, in line with the language of the Old Testament, that the *Logos* was the original creative force.

To some readers of the English translations the use of the pronoun 'he' in referring to the Logos indicates that a person is intended. But this is only a quirk of translation. Along with some modern languages ancient Greek and Hebrew had masculine or feminine nouns, with the pronoun being literally 'he' or 'she' respectively. In the majority of cases these pronouns are translated by the neuter 'it'. When Tyndale translated the passage in 1525 he used "it" rather than "he", but the translators of the AV did not follow him in this respect, as was their usual custom (about 90% of the AV is Tyndale's translation).[1] It is understandable that translators with a trinitarian bias should have taken the opportunity to render the pronoun as 'he' in the case of the masculine *Word* of John 1 and of the *Comforter* or *Counsellor* in John 14, but there is clearly no such intention in the original language. On this Dunn says of what he terms the 'poem' of the John 1 prologue:

> ".. we are dealing with personifications rather than persons, personified actions of God rather than an individual divine being as such. The point is obscured by the fact that we have to translate the masculine Logos as 'he' throughout the poem. But if we translated *logos* as 'God's utterance' instead, it would become clearer that the poem did not necessarily intend the Logos in vv1-13 to be thought of as a personal divine being"[2]

---

1. See *The Gothic and Anglosaxon Gospels with the versions of Wycliffe and Tyndale*: J. Bosworth. Pub: John Russell Smith, London 1865.

2. Op. cit. p.243

"THE WORD BECAME FLESH"

Until the time of Jesus the word of God had been revealed through God's prophets. But this was essentially an intermittent activity. The prophets were often raised up to meet an express need at the time and each concentrated on God's message of guidance or reproof, whilst at the same time looking to the future and giving glimpses of the overall plan of God with mankind. In this sense their ministry was fragmentary and partial. In none of the prophets could it be said that the word *became* flesh, but was rather manifested *through* flesh.

But in Jesus the Word *became* flesh—God's plan materialised in all its fulness. Originally His plan to create a race of mighty beings in whom He could be perfectly manifested[1] had only been an idea, a concept in his mind. Then He put the first stages of this plan into action by creating the world and everything in it. But his plan necessitated a redeemer to come in the likeness of humanity. So the Plan, the Word, became flesh in the person of Jesus.

Jesus is the very centre of God's plan for the earth. All God's intentions come to a focus in him. There was no question with him of a *partial* manifestation of God's word as had occurred through the prophets, but Jesus became a complete manifestation of his Father's thoughts and intentions: the "Logos became flesh". Note the use of 'became'—Jesus was not the word from the beginning in the sense that he pre-existed as a person, but he was the 'word made flesh'. He was God's Plan coming into action. He was the complete expression of all the saving attributes of the Father "full of grace and truth".

Looked at in this way—the way of the first century Jew or Gentile to whom John was writing—there was no hint of the personal pre-existence of Jesus, no suggestion that he was Very

---

1. See ch. 4

God clothed in human flesh. The simplest and most straightforward view of Jesus that such a reader would gain from this introduction was that Jesus was the realisation of God's plan for the earth. He would see that Christ's being the *Word made flesh* is no reason for suggesting his personal divinity any more than it would be correct to say that the prophets were God because the Logos was revealed through them. This understanding of the Word made Flesh becomes all the more acceptable because it is completely in harmony with the rest of the early Apostolic writings about Jesus. The greatest apparent anomaly is removed and all the apostles are seen to speak with one voice. It was only later, when influences outside of original Christianity began to obtrude that John 1:1-18 began to be taken as evidence of the personal pre-existence of the Messiah and the incarnation.

Barclay confirms this understanding in passages in which he expounds John's use of *logos* without giving it the trinitarian slant that for centuries has been attached to its meaning:

"Logos has two meanings, which no one English word can express. Logos means word, and Logos means mind. A word is the expression of thought. Therefore Jesus is the expression of the thought of God. Or to take the other meaning, in Jesus we see the mind of God ... In Jesus the mind of God becomes a person".[1]

"In Greek logos means two things—it means word and it means reason ... The Logos of God, the mind of God, is responsible for the majestic order of the world .... He (John) said to the Greeks, "All your lives you have been fascinated by this great, guiding, controlling mind of God. The mind of God has come to earth in the man Jesus. Look at him and you will see what the mind and thought of God

---

1. Barclay *New Testament Translation*, p.191

are like"[1]

"By calling Jesus the *logos*, John said two things about Jesus. (a) Jesus *is* the creating power of God come to men. He does not only *speak* the word of *knowledge*; he is the word of *power*. He did not come so much to *say* things to us, as to *do* things for us. (b) Jesus is the incarnate mind of God. We might well translate John's words, 'The mind of God became a man'. A word is always 'the expression of a thought' and Jesus is the perfect expression of God's thoughts for men.

He then makes a plea that the present writers heartily endorse:

We should do well to rediscover and to preach again Jesus Christ as the *logos*, the *Word* of God"[2]

AN ALTERNATIVE APPROACH

It might be felt that whilst the above explanation might be understood by, say, an educated Jewish Christian of the educational stamp of Philo and well versed in the concept of the divine Logos, Spirit and Wisdom as revealed in the Old Testament, to the average reader the idea might have been well above his head. So it is legitimate to ask if there is an even simpler way of expressing the thoughts contained in the prologue to John's gospel record.

It seems to the present writers that few if any of the expositors of John's prologue have ever sat down and asked the question "Why did John write it?" A prologue by definition is a preface to the main work, an introduction that sets the scene for what follows. It seems never to have been asked how John's prologue serves this purpose. One way to answer this question

---

1. Barclay: *Gospel of John* p.xxii

2. Op. cit. p.188

might be to discover any special feature that is common to both the prologue and the rest of the gospel. And such a feature is easy to find. If there is one characteristic of John's gospel above all others it is that it records the *words* of Jesus. Whilst the other gospel writers record the actions and many of the sayings and addresses of Jesus, John is unique in concentrating on the *words* of Jesus rather than the record of his life.

A glance through the gospel will readily demonstrate this. Chapter three records Christ's conversation with Nicodemus, and chapter four his dialogue with the woman of Samaria. Chapter five is devoted to a discussion about sabbath breaking that led on to Jesus explaining the source of his authority. Chapter six records the miracle of feeding the 5000 as a prelude to a long discourse on the true bread from heaven. Chapters seven and eight record Christ's words to the Jews in the Temple. Chapter nine describes the interchange between him and the Jewish leaders after the miracle of giving sight to the blind man. Chapter ten contains his parable of the shepherd and his sheep. And chapters thirteen to seventeen detail his conversation with his disciples and his prayer to God immediately before his arrest. Clearly John's emphasis throughout his gospel is on the *words* of Jesus.

And in those discourses Jesus emphasises that it is the *words* that he speaks that are important:

> "He who hears my *word* and believes him who sent me, has eternal life" (5:24).
> "If you continue in my *word,* you are truly my disciples" (8:31).
> "He who rejects me and does not receive my sayings has a judge; the *word* that I have spoken will be his judge on the last day" (12:48).
> "I have given them *thy word*" (17:14).

And these words are not Christ's own, they are God's words:

"The word which you hear is not mine but the Father's who sent me" (John 14:24).

Can it be merely a coincidence therefore that the Prologue to this record of Christ's sayings is itself about the *word* of God. It must be reasonable to expect that the use of *word* in the prologue should be similar to its use in the body of the work.

If we then look again at the prologue as if through the eyes of an early reader we can see John's train of thought that made it a suitable introduction to what followed? Moulton in his "Modern Reader's Bible", which lays out the text according to its literary form, divides the prologue into three sections:

I
"In the beginning was the Word:
And the Word was with God:
And the Word was God. (1:1)

II
And the Word became flesh,
And dwelt among us,
(and we beheld his glory, glory as of the only begotten from the Father),
Full of grace and truth. (1:14)

III
No man hath seen God at any time:
The only begotten Son, which is in the bosom of the Father,
He hath declared him" (1:18).

There is a simple connection between these three. In (I) is the statement that God from the beginning has had a plan or purpose or word inseparable from Him. It is a plan to make mortal men and women the eternal sons and daughters of God (verse 12). But because (III) man cannot learn from God *direct* there needed to be a means of 'declaring' the plan to man. This had been accomplished partially by the prophets of old (verse 17) but now especially in the work of His Son, the 'Word made flesh' (II). Having explained by this preamble the reason for Christ's coming, and ended it by the statement that Jesus *declared* God to man, he then proceeds in the rest of the book to record in detail those very *words* of God that are essential for man to know and act upon.

Thus the prologue to John's gospel can be seen to be similar to the introduction to the epistle to the Hebrews:

"In many and various ways God *spoke* of old to our fathers by the prophets; but in these last days he has *spoken* to us by a Son, whom he appointed the heir of all things, through whom also he created the world. He reflects the glory of God and bears the very stamp of his nature" (Hebrews 1:1-3).

Again the topic is the *words* of God, spoken first through prophets and then by his Son. And as in John, Christ is here shown to be a reflection of the glory of God, and His purpose through him the prime reason for the creation.

SUMMARY
In this section we have noted that, apart from a few occasions in the rest of Scripture which are easily explained, the great majority of the passages used to support the idea of Christ's personal pre-existence occur in the gospel record of John. When these are examined in the light of other scriptures, and in comparison with John's use of similar language to describe other situations that clearly have no implication of pre-existence, no support for the personal pre-existence of Jesus can be found. The prologue to John's gospel record was examined in detail, in the light of first century understanding of the *logos*, and the conclusion reached that to the original Christians the *'logos becoming flesh'* was a way of saying that

God's power and wisdom, and His long standing-intentions for man's redemption, were now being manifested in the person of Jesus. No personal pre-existence of the Saviour is demanded by the text or was envisaged by the writer.

Chapter 6

"THE CHRIST, THE SON OF THE LIVING GOD"[1]

Section 5: JESUS THE LAMB OF GOD

The sacrificial work of Jesus

For all Christians the death and resurrection of Jesus on the cross is the cornerstone of their faith; for forgiveness of sins, and the reconciliation between God and man achieved by this event is one of the basic themes of Scripture. But there the unanimity among Christians sometimes ends. The reason why that sacrifice was necessary, and how it actually produced the salvation of mankind, has long been the subject of debate. Those who subscribe to the doctrine of the Trinity see the incarnation, i.e. God becoming man, as the only possible way in which such redemption could be attained. Hammond states 'Scripture, in almost every case of reference to the incarnation, suggests redemption as its purpose'.[2] George Carey, long before his elevation to head of the Anglican Church, wrote 'Christianity stands or falls with the belief that it was God himself in the form of a man who trod this earth, suffered with and for men, and who died for them on the cross'.[3] Prime wrote "It was only by Christ being both God and man that

---

1. Matthew 16:16

2. Hammond, T.C, *In Understanding Be Men*, p97, Pub. IVP

3. *God Incarnate*, p.51, Pub. IVP

salvation could be obtained for sinful men and women".[1]

On the other hand some find the incarnation an obstacle to understanding the redemptive scheme. Granted that the death of Jesus is essential to the redemptive process, they ask how could a divine being really die?—a point that has been debated since the very inception of the doctrine of the Trinity. This section will explore the Scriptural teaching on the atoning work of Christ in the conviction that its testimony will be conclusive.

It is evident that before any decision can be made about the necessity or otherwise of the Saviour being God, an understanding of Bible teaching on how God and man became estranged is vital. Once we grasp the reasons for and the results of the breach we can comprehend the requirements and the process of reconciliation. Only then will we be able to decide if the incarnation fits all the requirements of the case, or whether other explanations must be sought.

In the New Testament the redemptive work of Jesus is inseparably linked to the first member of the human race:

"For as in Adam all die, so also in Christ shall all be made alive" (1 Corinthians 15:22).

In Romans the Apostle Paul goes further and states that Adam typified Jesus: "Adam ... was a type of the one who was to come" (Romans 5:14). The Genesis account of the creation of man is endorsed by Jesus as a factual record (Matthew 19:4-5, etc.), and it is from there that the New Testament writers start their exposition of the office and work of the Redeemer. This must be our starting point too.

Adam was created from the dust of the ground (Genesis 2:7),

---

1. *Questions on Christian Faith answered from the Bible.* p.46

but although in the case of the animals both male and female had been created individually, in man's instance only the male was formed. Eve was not created directly from the dust, but by re-fashioning a part of Adam himself:

> "So the LORD God caused a deep sleep to fall upon the man, and while he slept took one of his ribs and closed up its place with flesh; and the rib which the LORD God had taken from the man he made into a woman and brought her to the man" (Genesis 2:21-22).

The formation of Eve from a part of Adam is the basis of the special sympathy that exists between husband and wife as distinct from the mere pairing of animals. As the record continues:

> "Then the man said, 'This at last is bone of my bones and flesh of my flesh; she shall be called Woman, because she was taken out of Man'. Therefore a man leaves his father and his mother and cleaves to his wife, and they become one flesh" (Genesis 2:23-24).

This identity of nature between man and woman and the sympathy that derives from it is used in the New Testament to describe the relationship between Christ, the Second Adam, and his bride, the Redeemed. In his letters the Apostle Paul quotes the Genesis passage and applies it to Jesus and his church:

> "For no man ever hates his own flesh, but nourishes and cherishes it, as Christ does the church, because we are members of his body. 'For this reason a man shall leave his father and mother and be joined to his wife, and the two shall become one'. This is a great mystery, and I take it to mean Christ and the church" (Ephesians 5:29-32).

So right at the beginning God foresaw the perfect relationship that would one day exist between Christ and his figurative bride, the redeemed. But the important point to note for our present purpose is that in the same way as the original bride and bridegroom shared an identical physical make-up, so the Second Adam and his bride were to come from the same human stock. We will have to refer to this in much more detail later on, but for the moment we note the significant fact that the teaching was there from the commencement of human life on earth.

The Origin of Sin and Death

The newly created human pair were placed by God in an idyllic setting amidst the trees and rivers of Eden. There was nothing to mar their happiness. The beauty of their surroundings, the joy of being alive, and especially the intimacy they experienced with God and the angels must have been a cause of great satisfaction to the newly created pair. No doubt God told them of the sort of life that He expected of them, and they in their turn trusted and desired to please Him.

But such a situation had one drawback. In the very nature of things their service, whilst acceptable, was almost automatic in the sense that there was no incentive to do anything else. A modern robot slavishly following its pre-programmed instructions does not give spiritual satisfaction to its maker. So Adam and Eve needed a further dimension to their relationship with God if the original intention of bringing pleasure to God (Psalm 147:10-11) was to be achieved. This was provided by a simple test of their allegiance. God singled out a tree, beautiful and fruitful, and told them not to eat its fruit or even touch it, on pain of death:

> "And the LORD God commanded the man, saying, 'You may freely eat of every tree of the garden; but of the tree of the knowledge of good and evil you shall not eat, for the day that you eat of it you shall die' (Genesis 2:16-17).

Eve, then Adam, failed this test of character. Prompted by

the enticement of the serpent they both took and ate the fruit. Their disobedience had been induced by the serpent's reasoning, which implanted in their minds a distrust and unbelief in God:

> "But the serpent said to the woman, 'You will not die. For God knows that when you eat of it your eyes will be opened, and you will be like God, knowing good and evil'" (Genesis 3:4-5).

In first accepting this reasoning, and then reaching out to grasp and eat the fruit, Adam and Eve were not succumbing to a momentary lapse. It was a deliberate challenge to God's word and character. There were several aspects to their disobedience:

1. They failed to believe God. They suggested He had lied when He said they would die. In other words they implied God was untrue, unreliable and unjust.
2. They wanted to be like God, and attempted what they thought would be a short cut to achieve this.
3. They challenged God's supremacy, setting up their own will in opposition to His.
4. They had demonstrated pride.

Because of His supreme position and His absolute righteousness, this challenge by man was something God could not merely overlook. He could not simply absolve man's guilt, and fail to carry out the promised death penalty. Yet at the same time one thing is clear: God *wanted* to forgive, but this could not be at the expense of His own preeminence. He could not permit to remain unpunished any who accused Him of being unrighteous, or who in pride set up their will against His. That would be to condone the existence of another will than His own, and would have compromised His claim to sovereignty. The only way to rectify the situation would be for mankind in some way to openly demonstrate that God had been right—that despite what had happened in Eden His supreme position remained unchallenged.

This is the dilemma of redemption. Man, for his part, was powerless to act. Sin (failure to live to the glory of God—Romans 3:23) was now ingrained into his very nature and by his way of life he and his progeny continually challenged God's will. If man could not help himself, could God save him? If without irreverence we can put it in human terms, was it possible for God to devise a scheme by which man could be forgiven, and yet at the same time the Almighty's own righteousness and justice be seen to be preserved? In other words, how could God, to use Isaiah's phrase, be at the same time a 'righteous God *and* a Saviour' (Isaiah 45:21)? That was the issue. It is a measure of the wisdom of God and His love for mankind that He achieved satisfaction of these two apparently irreconcilable objectives. He saved man without any detriment to His supremacy and righteousness.

The New Testament tells us that this demonstration of God's righteousness was accomplished on the cross. Paul wrote concerning the sacrifice of Jesus:

> "This was to show God's righteousness, because in his divine forbearance he had passed over former sins; it was to prove at the present time that he himself is righteous ... " (Romans 3:25-26).

The origin of Jesus and his physical nature have a vital bearing on his ability to demonstrate God's righteousness in the way described here. If Jesus was to vindicate God's position where Adam had failed, it was imperative that he was a man who truly and completely represented the human race in every aspect, and yet at the same time a man who was absolutely sinless and so did not deserve to die.

God, in his love for fallen man, predicted to the original pair the coming of the Saviour. First by a spoken promise and later

261

by a very symbolic act God gave man hope that reconciliation would be made, with the eventual restoration of all that had been lost in Eden. The promise was contained in God's address to the three participants. Whilst He told Adam that after a life of toil and difficulty the death penalty would be certainly carried out, he gave a message of hope in His address to the serpent:

> "I will put enmity between you and the woman, and between your seed and her seed; he shall bruise your head, and you shall bruise his heel" (Genesis 3:15).

The woman's seed is the Saviour

God was obviously using figurative language, so what do the various 'seeds' stand for? First, the serpent's seed. As the instigator of the transgression, the serpent stood for sin. So in figure all the descendants of Adam and Eve whose lives are ruled by sin are the *seed* of the serpent (cp Matthew 23:33, John 8:44). God said that this power of sin was to receive a head (i.e. fatal) wound. By predicting this deadly wound to the serpent's seed God was foretelling the eventual destruction of sin and death that had just entered the world. But who was to actually deliver this lethal blow to sin? Was it to be God? No. It was to be the *woman's* seed who would bring this victory: "He shall bruise your head". However, in fatally wounding the serpent's seed, the woman's seed would himself have to suffer. But it would only be a temporary wound: *in the heel.*

All this clearly pointed forward to the work of Jesus on the cross. By his death he triumphed over sin, killing it and nailing it to his cross. But in achieving this victory he experienced the temporary heel-wound of death, which was healed three days later at his resurrection. As a result of Christ's victory all who believe in him can have their sins forgiven and receive eternal life. In this way the woman's seed was to kill the serpent's seed: or, in plain language, Jesus was to destroy sin and its consequence, death. This victory over sin and man's reconciliation to God is one of the grand themes of the New Testament:

"Christ died for our sins in accordance with the scriptures" (1 Corinthians 15:3).
"And you,who once were estranged and hostile in mind, doing evil deeds, he has now reconciled in his body of flesh by his death ..." (Colossians 1:21-22).

Coats of Skins

The second hint of future redemption is contained in the symbolic act recorded in Genesis 3:21 where God clothes Adam and Eve with coats of skins. In Genesis 2:24 we are told that the newly created Adam and Eve were naked, yet not ashamed. In their innocence they saw nothing unseemly in the absence of clothing. But the record goes on to say that immediately they had sinned, the first pair became conscious of their nakedness, and attempted to conceal it by an improvised apron of fig leaves (Genesis 3:7). Why does God particularly record this? It was a way of giving further details about man's redemption. Clearly they equated their nakedness with their sin and felt an instinctive need to cover that sin from God's sight. They did this with something of their own providing. But by means of this acted parable God showed that they could not cover their own sins. Only He could do that. God substituted another sort of covering in place of the fig leaves:

"The Lord God made for Adam and for his wife garments of skins, and clothed them" (Genesis 3:21).

The skins must have come from a slain creature, possibly a lamb, so here was the first animal sacrifice. God shed the blood of an animal in order to provide a covering for sin. But doing this did not actually achieve forgiveness. It was only a type or figure of the *real* means of forgiveness that would be made possible by the future death of the Lamb of God. So this act also pointed forward to the sacrifice of Jesus.

By these means the record of man's creation and fall defines the principles for redemption. These are:

1. God's righteousness or justice must be demonstrated.
2. Man cannot cover his own sins.
3. Sin can only be covered by God.
4. Blood must be shed.
5. The agent of forgiveness would be a descendant of Eve.
6. That descendant must have the same physical nature as those he will redeem.

The New Testament writers take up these points and apply them to the redemptive work of the Son of God. John Baptist declared that Jesus was the "Lamb of God, who takes away the sin of the world" (John 1:29). Peter, referring to the curse brought by sin upon man from the beginning, says that we were redeemed from the "futile ways inherited from our fathers, not with perishable things such as silver and gold, but with the precious blood of Christ, like that of a lamb without blemish or spot" (1 Peter 1:18-19).

Jesus was like us in every way

But although Jesus was sinless and spotless, he still possessed the nature that in all others produced sin. This was an essential element in being able to inflict the fatal wound on the serpent's seed, or devil as it is sometimes called in the language of personification:

> "Since therefore the children share in flesh and blood, he himself likewise *partook of the same nature*, that through death he might destroy him who has the power of death, that is, the devil" ... "Therefore he had to be made like his brethren *in every respect*" (Hebrews 2:14,17).

And because he shared human nature he was able effectively to sympathise with and save those 'children':

"Because he himself has suffered and been tempted, he is able to help those who are tempted".

"For we have not a high priest who is unable to sympathise with our weaknesses, but one who in every respect has been tempted as we are, yet without sinning" (Hebrews 2:18, 4:15).

Note that the effectiveness of Christ's work depended on his being able to identify himself with us *in every way*.

Christ succeeded where Adam failed

Remembering, as we have already seen, that forgiveness of man must not in any way compromise God's justice and righteousness, we ask how the voluntary self-sacrifice of a sinless member of the human race achieved the remedy for the situation in Eden. It was by Jesus resisting and overcoming the errors introduced by Adam. This is the real teaching of passages such as the celebrated reference in Philippians 2:6, where the believers are exhorted to copy Christ's example of humility:

"Christ Jesus, who, though he was in the form of God, did not count equality with God a thing to be grasped ..."

We have already considered this passage in detail (p. 203*ff*) and seen that it is *not* a definition of the incarnation. Rather is Paul contrasting the attitudes and achievements of Adam and Jesus. Once this is appreciated, his choice of words to make the contrast is striking. The first human pair in their *pride* and their *desire to be equal to God* reached out to *grasp* the forbidden fruit. By contrast Jesus, although a perfect exhibition of God's character, *humbled himself*, and counted *equality with God* not a thing to be *grasped*, and awaited God's reward in His own good time.

Added to these ideas are other New Testament hints of the contrast between Adam and Christ. Adam was *self-willed*, and as a result disobeyed God. Jesus in everything subjected his own will to that of his Father:

> "Lo, I have come to do *thy will*, O God" (Hebrews 10:7).
> "I seek not my own will but the *will of him who sent me*" (John 5:30).
> "For I have come ... not to do my own will, but the *will of him who sent me*" (John 6:38).
> "Not what I will, but what *thou wilt*" (Mark 14:36).

Further contrasts are that Adam was a *sinner*, whilst Jesus was *sinless*, and that whilst death was *demanded* of Adam because of his sin, the sinless Jesus *voluntarily* sacrificed his life.

Putting all these ideas side by side will emphasise the New Testament teaching that wherever Adam failed, Jesus succeeded.

ADAM	CHRIST
Pride	Humility
Desired to be like God: "Grasped" equality	Equality not sought: "Not grasped"
Failed to do God's will	Completely did God's will
A sinner	Sinless
Compulsory death	Voluntary death

Paul summarises the contrasting achievements of the two 'men', Adam and Christ, as follows:

"Then as one man's trespass led to condemnation for all men, so one man's act of righteousness leads to acquittal and life for all men. For as by one man's disobedience many were made sinners, so by one man's obedience many will be made righteous" (Romans 5:18-19).

Why was Christ's sacrifice effective?

It could well be asked how it was that the voluntary sacrifice of this perfect representative of the human race enabled God to deliver man from the thraldom of sin and the bondage of death without compromising His justice and righteousness. The answer seems to be found in those passages that state that the death of Jesus was a declaration of the *righteousness* of God, or, to use the equivalent term, the *justice* of God (the words being the same in the original). Paul told the Romans that the Gospel was:

"The power of God for salvation to every one who has faith ... for in it the *righteousness of God* is revealed" (Romans 1:16-17).

Later in the same letter he elaborates on the way in which Jesus demonstrated the righteousness of God. In chapter 3 the apostle gives three aspects of the sacrifice of the Son of God, each of which was concerned with exhibiting the righteousness of God. The passage is below split into its components, using Young's Literal translation. After saying that sinners will be "declared righteous freely ... through the redemption that is in Christ Jesus", he goes on, by the triple repetition of the word 'for', to emphasise three things that Christ's sacrifice achieved —things past, present and future. By the blood of Christ God showed His righteousness (a) to forgive *bygone* sins, (b) for *present* acceptance of Jesus and (c) to in the *future* declare as righteous those who believe in Jesus. Tabulating the verses may make these three aspects more clear:

267

"whom God did **set forth** a mercy seat, through faith in his blood,

> for the **showing forth** of his righteousness because of the passing over of *bygone* sins in the forbearance of God—

> for the **showing forth** of his righteousness in the *present time,*

> for his being righteous, and declaring him righteous who is of the faith of Jesus" (Romans 3:25-26).

This passage is most important to the understanding of the sacrifice of Christ. Here we have the essence of the matter for our reverential, thankful and joyful contemplation.

The word translated 'set forth' has the meaning of 'to display or put out publicly', and among its common uses was to describe the laying out of a dead body, especially the lying in state of an important person. It was therefore a very appropriate word for Paul to choose to describe the death of Jesus. It indicates that his sacrifice had to be public. A quiet secluded death with no spectators or publicity would not have served God's purpose.

Notice once more that it is all about *righteousness.* Paul says in this passage under consideration that the first two of the three reasons for this public act were to 'show forth' the righteousness of God, both in His past and present actions. Despite the similarity to the phrase 'set forth', 'showing forth' is a different original word, meaning to 'demonstrate' or 'prove'. In what way did the death of Jesus, witnessed by so many, 'demonstrate' the righteousness or justice of God? This, we suggest, is the key to the matter. It can be understood in the following way. The public death of Jesus, a fully representative

man, vindicated[1] the position that God took in Eden. How was
this? In the Garden man was justly condemned to death for his
sin of declaring God to be *unrighteous*. At Calvary Jesus
showed God to be *righteous*. In what way? In the person of
Jesus, the Seed of the Woman, we have one who shared in
every respect the physical nature of all humanity, yet one who
never once sinned. Few would disagree that the death of
sinners is indeed 'just', but was it right that the only morally
perfect man who ever lived should die? "Yes", said Jesus in
effect. In voluntarily offering himself on the cross Jesus
acknowledged that the original death penalty on Adam was also
just. It was as if Jesus had said "God *was* righteous in
punishing Adam. This death of mine shows how condemned
human nature should indeed be treated". Thus as well as
publicly demonstrating the original justice of God, the cross
was also a token of God's supremacy, which Adam had sought
to deny.

Once this righteousness of God had been publicly 'showed
forth' the effect was to reverse the situation in Eden. There
God's righteousness had been impugned, but at Calvary God's
righteousness and sovereignty had been upheld. On this basis
He could now forgive man without any compromise to His
position. To refer again to the words of Isaiah, having been
shown to be a 'righteous God' He could now be a 'Saviour'
(Isaiah 45:21).

The believers in Jesus will also become righteous
With God's position of righteousness and justice now openly
upheld, what was the effect for mankind? This is where Paul's
third point in the Romans 3 passage comes into play. God set
forth Jesus on the cross 'for His being righteous, and *declaring
him righteous who is of the faith of Jesus*'. Here is the grand
result of Christ's sacrifice. Not only did it show God "being

---

1. We use the term only by way of accommodation to our finite
understanding. God needs no vindication for any of His actions.

righteous" but all those who believe in Jesus (and by that is meant more than just a verbal expression of belief[1]) will themselves be accounted righteous by God even though they are sinners. As Paul triumphantly says in another letter:

> "For our sake he made him to be sin who knew no sin, so that in him *we might become the righteousness of God"* (2 Corinthians 5:21).

This is the great achievement of the Cross. Men and women who believe in Jesus will be reckoned righteous by God even though they are sinners. All their personal sins will be willingly forgiven by a loving heavenly Father for Jesus' sake. And being righteous they are thenceforward related to life, as innumerable passages such as the following show:

> "Then the *righteous* will shine like the sun in the kingdom of their Father" (Matthew 13:43).

The Resurrection of Jesus

But the process of making sinners righteous was not completed by the death of Jesus. A Saviour that remained in the grave would be ineffective. Later in his letter to the Romans Paul succinctly describes the whole process: Christ was

> "put to death for our trespasses and raised for our justification (literally 'our being made righteous', Romans 4:25).

Although in one sense God's justice demanded that Jesus should share the fate of all of mankind, whose death-prone nature he had inherited, in another sense it would be unjust for God to condemn a completely sinless man to remain in the grave. As Peter said on the day of Pentecost:

---

1. Belief must be followed by baptism "into his death" (Rom. 6:2) and an acceptable way of life thereafter.

"But God raised him up, having loosed the pangs of death, because it was not possible for him to be held by it" (Acts 2:24).

So Jesus became the 'firstfruits' from the dead—the foretaste of a vastly greater harvest at the general resurrection of all those that had believed on him: "Christ the firstfruits, then at his coming those who belong to Christ" (1 Corinthians 15:23).

DOES THE INCARNATION FIT THE REQUIREMENTS FOR REDEMPTION?

Having established these Scriptural principles concerning the way of atonement we can now turn to consider their implications for the person and nature of Christ, and so examine the feasibility of the incarnation.

The following aspects will be addressed:
1. Was Jesus a completely representative man?
2. Could Jesus have been tempted yet sinless if he was a member of the trinity?
3. The reality of the death of Jesus.
4. His resurrection and glorification.
5. Did Jesus benefit from his own death?

1. *Was Jesus a completely representative man?*

We have seen that for God's righteousness to be declared the sacrifice had to be that of a fully representative member of the human race. Only one who fully shared the nature that had been justly condemned could achieve the victory. Otherwise no forgiveness would have been possible. It is for this reason that the animal sacrifices offered under the Law of Moses were unable to satisfactorily atone for sins. As the writer to Hebrews says:

"For it is impossible that the blood of bulls and goats should take away sins" (Hebrews 10:4).

271

We have already noted that Adam and his bride shared an identical nature, and that this was a figure of the exact match between the nature of Christ and the rest of humanity. As we read again in Hebrews:

> "For it was fitting that he ... in bringing many sons to glory, should make the pioneer of their salvation perfect through suffering. For he who sanctifies and those who are sanctified *have all one origin*. That is why he is not ashamed to call them brethren" (Hebrews 2:10-11).

And because of this shared origin, the physical make-up of Jesus was identical with all mankind:

> "Since the children share in flesh and blood, *he himself likewise partook of the same nature*, that through death he might destroy him who has the power of death" (Hebrews 2:14).

We have previously examined this verse in some detail under the heading 'Son of Man' (p. 158*ff*) but the understanding of the principles of the Atonement now gives the *reason* for Jesus needing to share exactly the nature of those he redeemed. But this sameness, which is vital to the redemptive process, is not admitted by those who believe in the incarnation, as the following show:

> "God sent His own Son in the likeness of sinful flesh—the word "likeness" implies that Jesus was similar to sinful men in His earthly life, yet not absolutely like them, because He Himself was without sin".[1]

> "The Virgin Birth is the guarantee that no entail of birth-sin

---

1. Prime, Op. cit. p45

272

was passed on to Him".[1]

Thus whilst professing to accept the Scriptural teaching on the identity of nature between Christ and mankind, Trinitarians cannot bring themselves to agree it in practice. The present writers believe that the Bible teaches that it was precisely because Jesus *was* 'absolutely like them' in his physical make-up that he was able to be the perfect representative of mankind, through whose death God was able to extend His righteousness to all who believe in Jesus.

2. *Could Jesus have been tempted yet sinless if he was a member of the trinity?*

This aspect has already been covered in detail on p. 160*ff*, to which the reader is referred.

3. *The reality of the death of Jesus.*

This is a problem that advocates of the trinity hardly ever address. There is scarcely a more fundamental doctrine than the necessity of the actual death of the Saviour in order to achieve the redemption of mankind. It would be superfluous to quote even a selection of the many Bible passages that demonstrate this basic Christian belief. And death, by definition, is a cessation of all life, including all mental activity—"the dead know nothing".[2] But an equally fundamental doctrine concerning God is that He is not vulnerable to death.

Here are the horns of a dilemma. If Jesus was a component of the Godhead how then could he die? It must not be argued that the human body died, but the divine mental activity lived on—that is not death of the person. How then did a component of an indivisible trinity—all members of which are alleged to be co-eternal and co-equal, three in one and one in three—how

---

1. *The Catholic Religion*, Op. cit. p167

2. Ecclesiastes 9:5. See also Psa. 6:5; 146:4; etc.

could one member die? On the other hand if it is argued that Christ, as God, could not die, then the basic requirements for atonement could not be met. The Trinitarian has to choose which horn of the dilemma is most comfortable. Either Jesus was a member (albeit a very special member) of the human race who could die in the real sense of the word, or he was part of a single united Godhead for which death is impossible. The voluntary 'death' of someone who couldn't really die is hardly in keeping with Scriptural requirements.

We may further add that even the cursory reader of the records of the passion will gain the impression that Jesus feared his impending death. Why was this if in fact he himself (as distinct from his body) was not actually going to die? Why did Jesus in Gethsemane say "My soul is very sorrowful, even to death", and go on to plead with his Father, "if it be possible, let this cup pass from me" (Matthew 26:38-39)? Even more striking, why did he cry to God to "save him from death" (Hebrews 5:7) if for him death was an impossibility?

When faced with these arguments we are sometimes told that it is wrong to attempt to bring logical thought to bear on this matter. The doctrine of the Trinity is a great mystery which needs to be believed although it cannot be understood.

> "Though a philosopher cannot explain the doctrine of the Trinity in Unity, a child can believe it. This great truth is not one about which we are to trouble our minds. We are simply to believe it, because God has revealed it to the Church, and the Church teaches it. Reason becomes lost in wonder ...".[1]

Notice that no claim is here made for the trinity being a *Bible* doctrine, only one that has been revealed to the Church. But the

---

1. *The Catholic Religion*, Op. cit. p.153

Bible unquestionably claims to do what the Church alleges to be unnecessary—to instruct its readers about God and to give them an *understanding* of the Creator, and the Son's relationship with Him:

> "I strive ... that their hearts may be encouraged ... to have all the riches of assured *understanding* and the *knowledge of God's mystery*, of Christ, in whom are hid all the treasures of wisdom and knowledge" (Colossians 2:1-3).

Similarly Paul wrote to others that the first century spirit gifts were

> "For building up of the body of Christ, until we all attain to ... the *knowledge* of the Son of God ... so that we may no longer be children, tossed to and fro and carried about with every wind of doctrine" (Ephesians 4:12-13).

This insight into God was given by the Holy Spirit power with which Paul and the other apostles were invested. To the Corinthians he wrote:

> "God has revealed to us through the Spirit. For the Spirit searches everything, *even the depths of God*" (1 Corinthians 2:10).

With such a precise indication that the Bible contains all that it is necessary to know about God and Christ, the claim that the Trinity is a mystery only revealed to the Church can be seen to be unfounded. So we can be sure that if the Bible does not address the problem of how God in the person of Christ could die, it is because no such problem existed. Jesus was not God and therefore the dilemma posed by the death of a member of the Trinity did not arise.

4. *The Resurrection and Glorification of Jesus*
To the original Christians the one distinguishing feature of their

275

religion was not (as is alleged today) that Jesus was a member of a divine trinity but that Jesus who was crucified and buried actually rose again from the dead. Thus when the eleven remaining apostles deliberated on appointing a successor to Judas it was the ability to be a witness to the resurrection of Jesus that was the essential qualification:

> "Beginning from the baptism of John until the day when he was taken up from us—one of these men must become with us a *witness to his resurrection*" (Acts 1:22).

So when the first Christians commenced preaching, the resurrection was their theme. On his very first public address Peter made the confident claim that:

> "This Jesus God raised up, and of that we all are witnesses" (Acts 2:32).

And later this was still the burden of their message:

> "And with great power the apostles gave their testimony to the resurrection of the Lord Jesus" (Acts 4:33).
> "Others said 'He seems to be a preacher of foreign divinities'—because he (Paul) preached Jesus and the resurrection" (Acts 17:18).

Undoubtedly, then, the fact of the resurrection formed the basis of the Christian message. And when we come to the *means* by which the resurrection of Jesus was effected, the overwhelming Biblical evidence is that it was an *act of God*. It was a superlative example of the stupendous might of Christ's Father in heaven. To demonstrate the strength and consistency of this claim that Christ was raised by the power of God the following references are compelling in their cumulative testimony:

> "*God* raised him up" (Acts 2:24).

"This Jesus *God* raised up" (Acts 2:32).

"Whom *God* raised from the dead" (Acts 3:15, 4:10).

"The *God* of our fathers raised Jesus" (Acts 5:30).

"*God* exalted him at his right hand" (Acts 5:31).

"*God* raised him on the third day" (Acts 10:40).

"*God* raised him from the dead" (Acts 13:30).

"*He* has given assurance to all men by raising him from the dead" (Acts 17:31).

"(*God*) that raised from the dead Jesus our Lord" (Romans 4:24).

"Christ was raised from the dead by the glory of the *Father*" (Romans 6:4).

"And *God* raised the Lord and will also raise us up (1 Corinthians 6:14).

"*He* who raised the Lord Jesus will raise us also" (2 Corinthians 4:14).

"For he was crucified in weakness, but lives by the *power of God*" (2 Corinthians 13:4).

"*God the Father* who raised him from the dead" (Galatians 1:1).

"Which *he* (God) accomplished in Christ when he raised him from the dead" (Ephesians 1:20).

"To wait for his Son from heaven, whom *he* raised from the dead" (1 Thessalonians 1:10).

"The *God of peace* who brought again from the dead our Lord Jesus" (Hebrews 13.20)

"*God*, who raised him from the dead and gave him glory" (1 Peter 1:21).

It would be difficult to find a more basic aspect of original Christian teaching, or to escape the clear meaning of these words and their implications for the relationship between God and His Son. The Father raised the Son. The first century Christians obviously regarded the two as independent beings, with the Father having the power to raise to life one who otherwise would have remained in Joseph's tomb. Jesus came to life 'by the power of God' (2 Corinthians 13:4), and having been raised up he became glorious—not by his own intrinsic strength, but with a glory received from the Father 'who raised him from the dead *and gave him glory'* (1 Peter 1:21). It is valid to ask the question that if the apostles believed and taught any form of Trinitarian relationship between Jesus and God would they have used this sort of language, and used it so consistently? By no stretch of imagination could one infer from their words that an all-powerful deity needed the aid of a similarly omnipotent co-equal deity to achieve his resurrection.

Subsequent to his resurrection, as some of the above passages have shown, Jesus was *given* glory by God, showing that such glory was not an inherent characteristic. Jesus had been given a brief foretaste of this glory on the Mount of Transfiguration, when "his face shone like the sun" (Matthew 17:2). Now the Father had bestowed it permanently on the Son. Peter emphasised this in his speeches and writings. He told the crowd in the Temple that 'the God of our fathers *glorified* his servant Jesus' (Acts 3:13). This receipt of glory by Christ Peter saw as a reason for our confidence in God:

> "Through him you have confidence in God, who *raised him from the dead and gave him glory*, so that your faith and hope are in God" (1 Peter 1:21).

It is evident that Peter taught that the Father was the superior power, who both raised and glorified Jesus; which fact becomes a source of our own confidence in God. This view of Peter's understanding of the relationship between the Father and the Son is confirmed in his second letter. Referring to the transfiguration, when Jesus appeared in glory, Peter is at pains to point out that Christ's glory was received from God, 'the Majestic Glory' (2 Peter 1:16-17).

This bestowal of glory by God is mentioned frequently in the New Testament. Jesus himself said that at his return to the earth he will come "in the glory of his Father" (Matthew 16:27,

Mark 8:38). The writer of the letter to the Hebrews defines more closely the stages of this glorification process. Applying the words of Psalm 8 to the Messiah he gives three steps by which Jesus has assumed his current position of dominion, second only to that of God Himself:

> "Thou didst make him for a little while lower than the angels,
> thou hast crowned him with glory and honour,
> putting everything in subjection under his feet" (Hebrews 2:7-8).

The fact that Jesus at times *received* glory from God and throughout his subsequent existence displays *God's* glory gives an unmistakable indication of first century understanding of the relationship between the Father and Son. Jesus was not seen as having his glory of his own right, but *received* it from God. There was thus no idea of equality between the two in the minds of the original Christians.

5. *Did Jesus benefit from His own death?*
One of the consequences of Jesus completely sharing the physical nature of mankind with an identical bodily make-up, is that he possessed a body that was sentenced to death.

Jesus, whilst free from committed sins, still shared the dying nature of the rest of mankind. This has been amply demonstrated above (p. 158) and Paul further develops this point in Romans, saying that God sent "his own Son in the likeness of sinful flesh .. and condemned sin in the flesh" (Romans 8:3). To Corinth he wrote in similar vein: "For our sake he made him to be sin who knew no sin" (2 Corinthians 5:21).

The point we are making is that because Jesus was "made like his brethren in every respect" (Hebrews 2:17), he also had this in-built death sentence. His freedom from actual sins did

279

not alter this. This means that Jesus himself needed redemption. He too needed the change from mortality to immortality. To most of those who subscribe to the conventional view of the deity of Jesus this would appear an extreme, even heretical, statement. But there are references in the New Testament that strongly suggest that the first century Christians endorsed this view.

One example is found in the letter to the Romans, in which Paul implies that death once had *dominion* over Jesus:

> "For we know that Christ being raised from the dead will never die again; death *no longer* has dominion over him" (Romans 6:9).

Why would Paul have written "no longer has dominion" if death did not have dominion over Jesus at some previous time? Does not this suggest that Jesus himself needed saving from the power that death had over him?

The theme of the Epistle to the Hebrews is the contrast between the Law of Moses which *symbolised* the process of redemption, and the actual *achieving* of redemption by the work of Jesus. One of the examples cited is how the ritual of the Day of Atonement foreshadowed the complete forgiveness of sins made possible by Christ's death and resurrection. The Day of Atonement was the most sacred day of the Jewish calendar, on which atonement was made for the sins of the whole nation. In the innermost section of the holy tent called the Tabernacle was the Most Holy Place. Here stood the Ark of the Covenant which symbolised the place where God and man might meet. By a complex ceremony which culminated in the High Priest sprinkling the blood of an animal sacrifice on the golden lid of the Ark the nation's sins were forgiven. Full details of the events of this day are given in Leviticus chapter 16.

The key figure in all the ceremonial was the High Priest, who was the only one allowed into the figurative presence of God in the Most Holy. A notable detail of the ritual was that the High Priest actually went *twice* into the Most Holy, each time with the blood of a sacrifice. The first occasion was with the blood of a "sin offering *for himself*" (Leviticus 16:11), and the second with the blood representing *the people* (v15). Why did the High Priest need to make a separate atonement for his own sinful condition? There must have been some underlying meaning to the ceremony, a meaning that was part of the way in which Israel could be instructed about their coming Redeemer.

This figurative meaning is expounded in the epistle to the Hebrews, where the High Priest is clearly identified with Jesus, whose dual atoning function is retained. In contrasting his work with that of the Mosaic priests we read:

> "He has no need, like those high priests, to offer sacrifices daily, *first* for his own sins and *then* for those of the people; he did this once for all when he offered up himself" (Hebrews 7:27).

Speaking particularly of the Most Holy Place on the Day of Atonement the writer says:

> "But into the second only the high priest goes, and he but once a year, and not without taking blood which he offers for *himself* and for the *errors of the people*" (Hebrews 9:7)

What was the reason for this repeated reference to the fact that the High Priest had to make atonement first for himself and then for the people? Why is this aspect of the Day of Atonement ritual stressed when many others are ignored? Is there a reference here to the fact that, although free from committed sins, Jesus himself needed redemption?

This suggestion is confirmed when the climax of the contrast between the typical and the real High Priest is reached:

"But when Christ appeared as a high priest of the good things that have come, then through the greater and more perfect tent (not made with hands, that is, not of this creation) he entered once for all into the Holy Place, taking not the blood of goats and calves but his own blood, thus securing an eternal redemption" (Hebrews 9:11-12).

In the Authorised Version the words *for us* are inserted after the word "redemption", but this is without any textual authority. The insertion maybe identifies a dilemma of the translators, for the original suggests that Jesus achieved redemption *for Himself*—something that is suggested by the Day of Atonement symbology but something their theology could not accept. Roberts comments on this verse as follows:

"You will observe that the two italicised words, *for us*, are not in the original. In the Authorised Version of 1611 they are added to the translation, and they are added in defiance of grammatical propriety. In the Revised Version of 1881 they are omitted. The verb is in the middle voice, and the meaning of that is remarkable in this connection. We have no middle voice in English: we have passive or active voice: you either *do* or are *done to* in English; but in Greek, there is another voice—a middle voice—a state of the verb in which you do a thing *to yourself.* "Having obtained *in himself* eternal redemption".[1]

Knowing the meticulous use of the Greek language by the writer of this epistle to the Hebrews it is inconceivable that he would have deliberately chosen to use the verb in this form if he was not conveying the idea that Jesus himself benefited from his own death. His "own blood" achieved his own salvation as well as the salvation of those who believe on him.

---

1. *The Blood of Christ* p.8

Apart from the typology of the Law of Moses, there is at least one other reference in the Old Testament that suggests Jesus achieved his own salvation by his sacrifice. In AV of Zechariah 9:9, a prophecy of Christ's triumphal entry into Jerusalem, the marginal alternative rendering reads:

> "Rejoice greatly, O daughter of Zion; shout, O daughter of Jerusalem: behold, thy King cometh unto thee: he is just, and *saving himself*: lowly, and riding upon an ass, and upon a colt the foal of an ass".

This will be recognised as very similar language to that of Hebrews 9:12, and supports the reasoning that Christ's sacrifice accomplished his own salvation.

This view that Christ needed to obtain salvation is confirmed by another passage in Hebrews. In two places we read of Jesus being *made perfect* after his death and resurrection—with the obvious inference that he was not perfect before.

> "For it was fitting that he ... in bringing many sons to glory, should *make the pioneer of their salvation perfect* through suffering" (Hebrews 2:10).
> "The word of the oath ... appoints a Son who has been *made perfect* for ever" (Hebrews 7:28).

This is hardly the language of one who believed that Jesus was an immaculate pre-existent member of a trinity of Gods appearing in human form.

A further pointer to early Christian belief on this is found in the closing benediction of the letter to the Hebrews:

> "Now may the God of peace who brought again from the dead our Lord Jesus Christ, the great shepherd of the sheep, *by the blood of the eternal covenant*, equip you with everything good that you may do his will" (Hebrews 13:20-21).

The *eternal covenant* is an Old Testament phrase used of the divine scheme of redemption embodied in the Promise to Abraham.[1] The mission of Christ was to "confirm the promises given to the patriarchs" (Romans 15:8), which Jesus did by his death and resurrection. Thus the *blood of the eternal covenant* was Christ's own blood shed at Calvary, and the passage tells us this blood was the means of his resurrection.

We submit that there is unequivocal evidence that the early Christians saw Jesus as a man of their own race, specially raised up by God it is true, and far superior to every other man, but at the same time a man who because of his Adamic stock (though not for his personal sins) needed redemption as much as any other, and who achieved it for himself as well as for others by his death on the cross. If this is accepted then the case for Jesus being God incarnate simply cannot be sustained.

THE GRACE OF GOD AND THE LOVE OF JESUS
Because the nature of this study has necessitated a detailed examination of the principles of the Atonement through the work of Jesus, it is possible to have given the impression that this is a theoretical, almost technical subject. But Scripture does not treat redemption in this way. Nothing that has been said by the present writers is intended to obscure the most amazing fact, joyfully proclaimed from the lips of the Redeemer and the pens of the Apostles, that forgiveness of sins and consequent salvation is first and foremost a demonstration of love and grace towards man. The gift of the Saviour was because God loved the world. It was Christ's love that made him lay down his life for his sheep. It is by the grace of God, not because of any achievement on their part, that all the sins of those who believe in Jesus will be forgiven. It is by the goodness and loving mercy of God that those thus made righteous will be

---

1. Genesis 17:7, Genesis 22:16-18, Acts 3:25-26, Galatians 3:8,16,27-29) and in the Promise to David (2 Samuel 23:5, 2 Samuel 7:12-16, Isaiah 55:3, Luke 1:32-33, Romans 1:3 etc.

given immortality. And it is for the believer to receive this wondrous offer with joy and thankfulness, and to try to respond with a love that will give us "confidence for the day of judgment" (1 John 4.17).

when immortality. And it is for the believer...
wondrous story with Joy, and the sublimes, and to try to respond
with a love that will give its confidence for the day of
redemption is at hand.

Chapter 6

"THE CHRIST, THE SON OF THE LIVING GOD"[1]

Section 6: JESUS "THE BEGINNING OF GOD'S CREATION"[2]

Jesus as Creator

In Section 4 of this chapter we have demonstrated that the passages usually advanced to support the doctrine of the personal pre-existence of Jesus can readily be interpreted as a pre-existence in the mind and purpose of God only, and that the early Christians certainly understood them in this way. But there are still a series of allusions scattered throughout the New Testament that refer to Jesus as a Creator, and these are usually taken by Trinitarians to support their contention that Jesus, as the second component of an eternal trinity, was present at the beginning and involved in the work of the physical creation.

PASSAGES THAT ALLUDE TO A CREATIVE ROLE FOR JESUS

> "All things were made through him (the Word), and without him was not anything made that was made" (John 1:3).

> "The world was made through him" (John 1:10).

---

1. Matthew 16:16

2. Revelation 3.14

"One Lord, Jesus Christ, through whom are all things and through whom we exist" (1 Corinthians 8:6).

"God, who created all things by Jesus Christ" (Ephesians 3:9, AV).

"He is the image of the invisible God, the first-born of all creation; for in him all things were created, in heaven and on earth, visible and invisible, whether thrones or dominions or principalities or authorities—all things were created through him and for him. He is before all things, and in him all things hold together" (Colossians 1:15-17).

"(God) has spoken to us by a Son, whom he appointed the heir of all things, through whom also he created the world" (Hebrews 1:2).

"Thou, Lord, didst found the earth in the beginning, and the heavens are the work of thy hands; they will perish, but thou remainest; they will all grow old like a garment, like a mantle thou wilt roll them up, and they will be changed" (Hebrews 1:10-12).

These are the majority, if not all, of the references which refer to Jesus as a Creator. The Ephesians passage can be excluded immediately, for the final phrase "by Jesus Christ" is omitted from later translations, as it does not appear in the best and oldest manuscripts. Is this another example of the work of an over-zealous Trinitarian scribe attempting to lend support to the doctrine?

'OLD' AND 'NEW' CREATIONS

Care must be taken not to immediately assume that in all these passages the reference is to the literal creation of the earth as described in Genesis 1-2. The Bible speaks of more than one creation. There is the physical creation of the heavens and earth and their contents, but also many references to a new, spiritual creation. This new creation will not be a replacement of the literal earth, but the creation upon the existing earth of a new perfect order. And because the terms used to describe the spiritual creation and its various processes and effects are often based upon those used of the literal creation, it is only by examining the context of the reference that it becomes clear which of the two creations is intended.

In the beginning, as described in Genesis 1, the heavens and the earth were formed, followed by the creation of Adam from the dust of the ground. Man was made in the image or likeness of God (Genesis 1:26) and in this sense was the son of God (Luke 3:38). The woman was formed from the side of Adam whilst he was asleep and presented to him as his bride. The pair were placed in a paradise, or garden, but were banished from it when they sinned, thus denying access to the Tree of Life which could have made them to live for ever.

All these aspects are picked up by the rest of Scripture and are referred to the *new creation*. They are regarded as pre-figuring the redemptive process by which God and man will be reconciled and united, mankind becoming a glorious and eternal component of the Yahweh Name.

Thus God says through Isaiah "Behold, I create a new heavens and a new earth; and the former things shall not be remembered" (65:17). This is no reference to a new literal earth to replace the existing one, for that "abides for ever" (Ecclesiastes 1:4), but to a new order being developed in the physical world. This new creation was the hope of the early Christians, for Peter says: "According to his promise we wait for new heavens and a new earth in which righteousness dwells" (2 Peter 3:13).

THE OLD CREATION THE BASIS FOR THE NEW

This perfect state represented by the new creation will be reached by processes corresponding to events of the literal creation. In the literal creation a new man was created, in the figurative new creation a new man was also created, Jesus, the Second or Last Adam, the Son of God in a greater sense. His work contrasts with the achievements of the original man:

"Thus it is written, The first man Adam became a living being; the last Adam became a life-giving spirit. The first man was from the earth, a man of dust; the second man is from heaven" (1 Corinthians 15:45,47).

Like the first Adam who was created in the image of God, Jesus was "the express image of his (God's) person" (Hebrews 1:3 AV). It has already been shown the way Jesus did this—by being a perfect manifestation of the attributes of God. Unlike the first man, who brought death, the last man will bring life:

"For as in Adam all die, so also in Christ shall all be made alive" (1 Corinthians 15:22).

The analogy is continued in the creation of Eve:

"The Lord God caused a deep sleep to fall upon the man, and while he slept he took one of his ribs and closed up its place with flesh; and the rib which the Lord God had taken from the man he made into a woman and brought her to the man. Then the man said, This at last is bone of my bones and flesh of my flesh; she shall be called Woman, because she was taken out of man" (Genesis 2:21-23).

The New Testament parallels this with the future relationship between Christ, the Bridegroom, and the redeemed, the Bride. She will owe her existence to his side wounded at Calvary. The correlation here with the literal creation is explicit in Paul's writings. Continuing the Genesis account quoted above he says:

"For this reason a man shall leave his father and mother and be joined to his wife, and the two shall become one.

This is a great mystery, and I take it to mean Christ and the church" (Ephesians 5:31-32).

Revelation describes the union of Christ and the redeemed under the figure of the marriage of the Lamb:

"The marriage of the Lamb has come, and his Bride has made herself ready; it was granted her to be clothed with fine linen, bright and pure—for the fine linen is the righteous deeds of the saints" (Revelation 19:7-8).

Thus the union of Father, Son and the redeemed, as prayed for by Jesus—"That they may be one even as we are one, I in them and thou in me, that they may become perfectly one" (John 17:22-23)— will be achieved by this new creation.[1]

The above references clearly show that Jesus is the starting point of this new creation, just as Adam was of the old. Hence he is "the beginning of God's creation" (Revelation 3:14), and the "first-born of all creation" (Colossians 1:15), in the sense that through him God originated His plan for the new order. And just as Adam was the first of a race of mortal men and women, so through Jesus a *spiritual* race is being developed. God through him is fathering a new race of sons and daughters whose identity is determined by a new heart and mind. "You have put off the old nature with its practices and have put on the new nature, which is being renewed in knowledge after the image of its creator" (Colossians 3:9-10). Thus those who are 'in Christ' as opposed to those who are 'in Adam' are components of this new creation:

"Therefore if any one is in Christ, he is a *new creation*; the old has passed away, behold, the new has come" (2 Corinthians 5:17).

---

1. For elaboration of this theme see Ch. 7

This newness is shown by the way of life of the believer:

> "For we are his workmanship, *created* in Christ Jesus for good works" (Ephesians 2:10).

The literal creation was the result of God's *word*—every creative act was preceded by "And God said". In the same way the spiritual creation comes about as a result of the word of God:

> "You have been *born anew*, not of perishable seed but of imperishable, through the living and abiding *word of God*" (1 Peter 1:23).

PARADISE RESTORED

Finally, as a result of the work of Jesus in bringing about this new creation of a race of immortal perfect beings, the paradise of Eden will be restored in a symbolic sense. By the literal creation described at the beginning of the Bible God brought order out of chaos, illumined the world by the light of the sun, created a beautiful environment of plants, trees and rivers and placed in it the newly created human pair. But a curse followed because of man's sin. The Tree of Life, that special tree that could bring eternal life, was put beyond their grasp as they were banished from the face of God into a life of estrangement, trouble and death.

In contrast to the creation account at the beginning of the Bible, the inspired record closes with a picture of the completed *new creation* when the great barrier of sin will no longer prevent perfect fellowship between God and man. This symbolic Garden of Eden will restore all the representative components of the original literal creation. The river is one that brings endless life, the Tree of Life heals eternally, the earth's curse is removed, God's face will again be revealed to the adoring worship of the new race of the redeemed, and the light of the sun will be replaced by the radiance of His presence:

291

"Then he showed me the river of the water of life, bright as crystal, flowing from the throne of God and of the Lamb through the middle of the street of the city; also, on either side of the river, the tree of life ... and the leaves of the tree were for the healing of the nations. There shall no more be anything accursed, but the throne of God and of the Lamb shall be in it, and his servants shall worship him; they shall see his face, and his name shall be on their foreheads. And night shall be no more; they need no light of lamp or sun, for the Lord God will be their light, and they shall reign for ever and ever" (Revelation 22:1-5).

In the previous chapter of Revelation is a similar symbolic representation of the completed new creation that will replace the old Adamic order:

"Then I saw a new heaven and a new earth; for the first heaven and the first earth had passed away. And I saw the holy city, new Jerusalem, coming down out of heaven from God, prepared as a bride adorned for her husband; and I heard a great voice from the throne saying, Behold, the dwelling place of God is with men. He will dwell with them, and they shall be his people, and God himself will be with them; he will wipe away every tear from their eyes, and death shall be no more, neither shall there be mourning nor crying nor pain any more, for the former things have passed away. And he who sat upon the throne said, Behold, I make all things new" (Revelation 21:1-5).

So it can be seen that God's purpose from the beginning was to bring about through His Son a new creation of a race of immortal beings in whom He could dwell. The prayer of Jesus recorded in John 17 will then be answered:

"That they may all be one; even as thou, Father, art in me, and I in thee, that they also my be in us." (John 17:20).

JESUS THE BEGINNING OF THE NEW CREATION

With this insight into the new creation, and with the understanding that it has no reference to the original literal creation (although its imagery is firmly based on the Genesis record), the passages quoted at the commencement of this section which speak of Christ's creative role can be re-examined. When Paul spoke of "One Lord, Jesus Christ, through whom are all things and through whom we exist" (1 Corinthians 8:6) he was plainly referring to the *new creation* that will arise from his redemptive work rather than to the original creation. It is in this sense that Christ is "the beginning of the creation of God" (Revelation 3:14).

Similarly the two passages in Hebrews do not imply that Jesus was present at the literal creation or that he took part in it. In 1:2 where we read "through whom also he created the world" the word translated 'world' is not *kosmos*, the word for the literal earth, but *aiōnias*. This is the plural of *aion* which simply means an 'age', and teaches that God had Jesus in mind from the beginning, and all the subsequent 'ages' through which the world has passed have been organised with God's messianic purpose in mind. No trinitarian inference can therefore be drawn from the allusion, especially in view of the context of this phrase, where it is stated that Jesus was *"appointed* heir of all things", which of necessity indicates authority of the Father over the Son, thus ruling out any suggestion of eternal co-equality between them.

The passage in Hebrews 1:10 that alludes to Jesus as a creator needs to be read with the purpose of this epistle clearly in mind. The prime purpose of the epistle was to demonstrate the superiority of the ministry of Christ over the Law of Moses. The first of many examples of this superiority is that Christ is greater than the angels through whom the Law was originally given (2:2). To sustain this argument the writer quotes several Messianic psalms, one of which is Psalm 102 which undoubtedly refers to the future rule of the Messiah when the "new" heavens and earth of his rule are established. The psalmist speaks of God's appointed time to favour Zion (v13), of the time when God will appear in glory and all the rulers and nations of the world will do homage to him (vv15,16,21-22), and also of the time when a "people that *shall be created*" shall fear the Lord (v18,AV,NIV). The psalm is looking forward to the *new creation* established by Jesus and which will be revealed at his second coming. It is in this context that it goes on to describe a *change* of heavens and earth in the words later quoted in Hebrews:

> "Of old thou didst lay the foundation of the earth, and the heavens are the works of thy hands. They will perish, but thou dost endure; they will all wear out like a garment. Thou changest them like raiment, and they pass away; but thou art the same, and thy years have no end" (Psalm 102:25-27).

In the context of the establishment of the new creation it would be inappropriate to refer this passage to the literal creation, which elsewhere is described as lasting for ever (Ecclesiastes 1:4). It must refer to an existing *order of things* on earth that is to be replaced. Heavens and earth are often used in this figurative sense in Scripture. God described the success of the Babylonian army against the nations using the same imagery as Psalm 102:

> "All the host of heaven shall rot away, and the skies roll up like a scroll" (Isaiah 34:4).

The same figure was used of the fall of Babylon itself:

> "Therefore will I make the heavens tremble, and the earth will be shaken out of its place" (Isaiah 13:13).

It is this identical figure that is being used in Psalm 102 to describe the major change in the world's organisation effected by

Jesus at his return. The existing 'heavens and earth' of human rule will be removed, and the new creation instituted. The point of the Hebrews allusion can now be seen. One of the reasons why Jesus is greater that the angels is that whilst they created the *literal* world, Jesus is the founder of this *new order*. The reference therefore is not primarily to the literal creation as a superficial reading might indicate.

Moving on to the Colossians reference, where it states that "in him all things were created", we have a similar situation. Paul actually defines what created things he is talking about. They are not the literal earth and sky of the physical world, but "thrones or dominions or principalities or authorities" all of which have been "created through him and for him ... and in him all things hold together" (Colossians 1:15-16). The key words here are "in him". As Jesus ascended to heaven he said "All authority in heaven and on earth (i.e. the 'thrones and dominions') has been given to me" (Matthew 28:18), teaching us that from the moment of his exaltation all the human organisations on earth exist by the will of and in the purpose of Christ. He is using them to forward his development of that plan to create "a *new heavens and earth* in which righteousness dwells" (2 Peter 3:13). Again, to use this passage to say that Christ as "very God' was responsible for the literal creation of the earth is to grossly misread the Apostles intentions and arguments.

GOD'S CREATIVE POWER FOCUSED IN CHRIST
An alternative view of these 'creation' passages is that Christ is revealed not as the actual pre-existent creator but the embodiment of the power and wisdom of God which was the creative force. Any Trinitarians who feel that such passages (particularly Colossians 1:16-17 and Hebrews 1:10-12) support the pre-existence of Jesus as part of an eternal trinity would do well to ponder the following quotations from Dunn, himself a Trinitarian theologian, who attempts to listen to them with the ears of their original recipients, rather than with the ears of

later readers who have been conditioned to assume from such
passages the fully fledged doctrine of the incarnation:

"What does this mean, to say that Christ is the creative
power (= wisdom) of God by means of which God made
the world? Is the intention of the writer to ascribe pre-
existence to Christ as such? Despite its obvious attract-
iveness that interpretation does not necessarily follow. This
may simply be *the writer's way of saying that Christ now
reveals the character of the power behind the world.* ... In
other words that language may be used here to indicate the
continuity between God's creative power and Christ
without the implication being intended that Christ himself
was active in creation".[1]

"... Probably (in Colossians 1:17) we do not have a
statement of Christ as pre-existent so much as a statement
about the wisdom of God now defined by Christ, now
wholly equated with Christ".[2]

"*Is then the Colossian hymn writer trying to say any more
than that the creation and Christ must be understood in
relation to each other: now that Christ has been raised from
the dead the power and purpose in creation cannot be fully
understood except in terms of Christ, and so too Christ
cannot be fully understood except in terms of the wise
activity of God* which has made the world what it is, which
gives the world its meaning, and which will bring the world
to its appointed end.
"Once again then we have found that what reads at first
sight as a straightforward assertion of Christ's pre-existent
activity becomes on closer analysis an assertion which is

---

1. Dunn, J.D.G, "*Christology in the Making*", second edition, p.190. In this
and in all subsequent quotations on this head the italics are original.

2. Ibid. p.191

rather more profound—not of Christ as such present with
God in the beginning, nor of Christ as identified with a pre-
existent hypostasis or divine being (Wisdom) beside God,
but *of Christ as embodying and expressing (and defining)*
that power of God which is the manifestation of God in and
to his creation".[1]

"Since the point is so important, let me attempt to put it in
a slightly different way. We must grasp the fact that Paul
was not seeking to win men to a belief in a pre-existent
being. ... What he was saying is that Wisdom, whatever
precisely that term meant for his readers, is now most fully
expressed in Jesus—*Jesus is the exhaustive embodiment of*
divine wisdom: all the divine fullness dwelt in him".[2]

"*Christ fully embodies the creative and saving activity of*
God, that God in all his fullness was in him, that he
represents and manifests all that God is in his outreach to
men. We can express this as the *divinity* or even *deity* of
Christ, so long as we understand what that means: the deity
is the Wisdom of God, for the Wisdom of God is God
reaching out to and active in his world. So the deity of
Christ is the deity of Wisdom incarnate; that is, to
recognise the deity of Christ is to recognise that in Christ
God manifested himself, his power as Creator, his love as
Saviour, in a full and final way. But, to make the point one
last time, we should use the language of *incarnation* at this
point only if we use it properly. For whilst we can say that
divine wisdom became incarnate in Christ, that does not
mean that Wisdom was a divine being, or that Christ
himself was pre-existent with God, but simply that Christ
was (and is) the embodiment of divine wisdom".[3]

---

1. Ibid p.193-4

2. Ibid. p.195

3. Ibid p.212

Whichever of the two interpretations outlined in this section is accepted—Christ as the originator of the new creation, or Dunn's view that Christ was a later bodily manifestation of the one wisdom and power of God that originally created the world—does not alter the fact that there is no room at all for the conventional view that these passages attribute the literal creation to Jesus, and that therefore he is a pre-existent member of an eternal trinity. Our studies do however confirm the greatness of Jesus Christ as a manifestation of the one true God and the originator of that new creation, developed over the ages, that will at last be revealed in the earth.

SUMMARY
In the six sections of this chapter we have closely examined the biblical teaching about Jesus and have found that, when viewed from the perspective of first century Christianity, the passages usually taken to teach the deity of Jesus in fact do nothing of the sort. Jesus existed from the beginning only in the mind and purpose of God, as the one who would reconcile Himself with fallen man, thus making a 'new creation'. Jesus Christ was, and still is, subordinate to the Father, and will continue to be so even when God's purpose with the earth and man is completed. Both before and after his glorification he was termed 'man', and his physical nature was identical to ours; his temptations as authentic, and his death as real as any man's. Yet at the same time he was the Son of God by begettal by the Holy Spirit, though never termed 'God the Son'. By his victory over sin he has been exalted to the place of highest honour at the Father's right hand, everything in heaven and earth being now subject to him—except the Almighty Himself. As our redeemer he deserves our highest thanks and praise: we should 'honour the Son even as we honour the Father'. But Scripture does not permit us to go further and describe him as God the creator, or to envisage him as a member of an eternally pre-existent and co-equal trinity.

Chapter 7

"THAT THEY MAY ALL BE ONE"[1]

The true Divine family

In the previous chapter it has been fully demonstrated that the Lord Jesus occupies a unique position in the purpose of God. On the one hand the Scriptures are unanimous in showing him to be always in subjection to the Father, both in his life on earth and after the resurrection (and even post-millennially); on the other hand he is presented as uniquely Son of God by his divine begettal. He also developed in full measure the moral traits, i.e. the perfect character, of his Father. Because of his obedience even to death on a cross he has been granted the divine titles and honours appropriate to such a victor over sin. These scripturally balanced assessments of the nature and mission of Christ completely rule out the unitarian dismissal of his divinity, and also refute the trinitarian concept of equality with the Father.

We have already seen[2] that Jesus' own words which he had spoken earlier, "I and the Father are one" (John 10.30), are to be understood as meaning that he was always of *one mind and purpose* with God his Father. In 1 Corinthians 3:8 there is a parallel statement: "Now he that planteth and he that watereth are one" (AV & RV) but which the NIV translates: "The man

---

1. John 17:21

2. pp.30,215

299

who plants and the man who waters *have one purpose"*. Jesus' words describing his unity with God are *not* therefore an assertion of equal *status with the Father,* as this would contradict so many testimonies to the contrary in John's gospel and also in the letters of Paul.

But there is another threefold relationship which also is a theme of biblical revelation. This is clearly expressed in the words of Jesus when he describes the unity that will exist between himself, his Father and the redeemed:

"That they (i.e. those who are to believe in Jesus) may all be one; even as thou, Father, art in me, and I in thee, that they also may be in us ... The glory which thou hast given me I have given to them, *that they may be one even as we are one, I in them and thou in me, that they may become perfectly one"* (John 17:21-23).

So we find that this basic teaching of unity is not restricted to the *two* persons of the Father and Son. Rather is the concept of unity extended to include *all* true believers, as the 'one body' of Christ. This is particularly evident in John's gospel record. Compare the following passages:-

"... that you may know and understand that the Father is in me and I am in the Father." (John 10.38)

"Believe me that I am in the Father and the Father in me...." (John 14.11)

"In that day you will know that I am in my Father, and you in me, and I in you" (John 14.20)

"If what you heard from the beginning abides in you, then you will abide in the Son and in the Father" (1 John 2.24)

These references speak of a perfect fellowship between the

Father and the Son, but they also contain a promise of its *extension.* "In that day"—the day of judgment and reward—all who "walk in the light" of the revealed "Word of life" share that unity. This is evident by putting more words of Christ alongside the full passage quoted on the previous page:-

"I and the Father *are one*". (John 10.30);

"I do not pray for these only, but also for those who are to
believe in me through their word, *that they may all be one;*
even as thou, Father, art in me, and I in thee, that they also
may be[1] in us, so that the world may believe that thou hast
sent me. The glory which thou hast given me I have given
to them, that they may be one even as we are one, I in them
and thou in me, that they may become perfectly one .... "
(John 17.20-23)

Thus the concept of unity between God and his Son is extended to include *all who believe in the apostolic teaching concerning the Son.* The attainment of such a unity is, of course, no sudden achievement but a *process,* as the words of verse 23 above imply: "*may become* perfectly one" or, more literally: "may be perfected into one." This will be realised only in "the last day" (John 6:44). When this aspect of the process is appreciated, other verses in John's record become more significant in revealing and explaining the growing relationship between the Father, the Son and the believers. For example:

".... I know my own and my own know me, as the Father
knows me and I know the Father, ... " (John 10.14-15)

"... If a man loves me, he will keep my word, and my
Father will love him, and *we* will come to him and make

---

1. AV 'one' omitted by the RSV and most modern versions, but the manuscript evidence is pretty evenly divided. Either way the fact of unity is plainly asserted.

our home (literally: 'abode') with him" (John 14.23)

".... all that I have heard from my Father I have made known to you" (John 15.15)

The same basic truth is also conveyed in other words, especially in the use of the term 'fulness'. Applied to God this expression denotes the sum of the glorious and majestic attributes of God. But this *fulness* is not only extended to Christ, but to the believers as well. Note in the following passages how the divine fulness extends to all God's family:-

"And the Word became flesh and dwelt (literally: 'tabernacled') among us, *full of grace and truth*...(inherited from his Father—see Exodus 34.6) *And from his fulness have we all received*, grace upon grace" (John 1.14, 16)

"(God) ... has made him the head over all things *for the church*, which in his body, the *fulness* of him who fills all in all" (Ephesians 1.22-23)

"... to know the love of Christ which surpasses knowledge, that you may be *filled with all the fulness of God*" (Ephesians 3.19)

"... until we all attain to the *unity* of the faith and of the knowledge of the Son of God, to mature manhood (literally: 'to a perfect man'), to the *measure of the stature of the fulness of Christ*" (Ephesians 4.13)

"For in him (Jesus) all the fulness of God was pleased to dwell" (Colossians 1.19)

"For in him the whole fulness of Deity dwells bodily, and you have come to *fulness of life in him* (NIV: "you have been given fulness in Christ"), who is the head of all rule and authority" (Colossians 2.9-10)

302

The prophet Isaiah had a vision of the future glory of Christ.[1] Speaking of this future time the seraphim saw this *fulness* of God extending to embrace the whole earth:-

> "Holy, holy, holy is the LORD of hosts; the whole earth is *full of his glory"* (literally, as in the RV margin "the fulness of the whole earth is his glory") (Isaiah 6.3)

Further back, in the days of the Exodus wanderings, God strongly affirmed to Moses His ultimate purpose, using a similar expression:-

> "... but truly, as I live, and as *all the earth shall be filled with the glory of the LORD* ..." (Numbers 14.21)

In short, God's "eternal purpose" (Ephesians 3.11) will reach its consummation when every 'saint' (i.e. every sanctified believer) is perfected in mind and body by being transformed into the divine nature, i.e. each one becomes fully united with God and with the Lord Jesus in the resurrection on the last day (2 Peter 1.3-4). As glorious Spirit beings equal to angels (Luke 20.36), they will then shine with God's glory, as Jesus and the angels do now, and will inherit a cleansed and glorified earth for all eternity. Then will be fulfilled the promise spoken to Daniel:-

> "... those who are wise *shall shine like the brightness of the firmament*; and those who turn many to righteousness, *like the stars for ever and ever"* (Daniel 12.3)

words fully confirmed by Jesus:-

> "Then the righteous will *shine like the sun* in the kingdom of their Father" (Matthew 13.43)

---

1. "Isaiah said this because he saw his glory and spoke of him". John 12:41

This is the true three-fold relationship—not the Father, Son and Holy Spirit, but the Father, Son, and the perfected company of the Redeemed who will enjoy throughout eternity a perfect unity, when God will be "all in all" (1 Corinthians 15:28 AV,NIV).

One could cite other Bible statements embodying the same promise of incorporation into this ultimate unity, e.g. "I, the LORD, the first, and *with the last*; I am He" (Isaiah 41.4), which is relevant because "the last" here is plural, and refers to the same divine purpose. Again, God's declared intention to dwell in a sanctuary in the midst of Israel (Exodus 25.8. Note the description in Exodus 40.34 [and also in Solomon's temple—1 Kings 8.10-11] that God's glory *filled* the tabernacle), finds its ultimate fulfilment in the heavenly temple *on earth,* the holy city Jerusalem, identified as the Lamb's wife, i.e. the redeemed (Revelation 19.7; 21.2, 9). This temple is also defined as "the Lord God the Almighty and the Lamb" (Revelation 21.22). It has been:-

"built upon the foundation of the apostles and prophets, Christ Jesus himself being the chief corner-stone, in whom the *whole structure* is joined together ... into a holy temple in the Lord ... in *whom you also are built into it* for a dwelling place of God in the Spirit" (Ephesians 2.20-22).

See also 1 Peter 2.4-6 in this connection, where both Jesus and his followers are described as "living stones" in God's "spiritual house".

SPIRIT, WORD AND TRUTH

The concept of three entities in one—Father, Son and believers— which we have just defined and expounded, may be further illustrated by a different approach, viz. from the interchangeability of the three terms that form the heading of this section. It is striking to note how the following three-way equivalents are established by more than one supporting text.

Consider this diagram:-

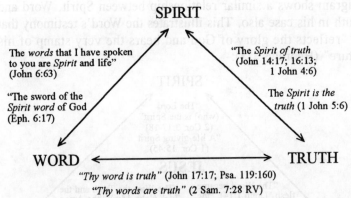

SPIRIT

The *words* that I have spoken
to you are *Spirit* and life"
(John 6:63)

"The sword of the
Spirit word of God
(Eph. 6:17)

"The *Spirit of truth*
(John 14:17; 16:13;
1 John 4:6)

The *Spirit is the
truth* (1 John 5:6)

WORD ←————————→ TRUTH

"Thy word is truth" (John 17:17; Psa. 119:160)
"Thy words are truth" (2 Sam. 7:28 RV)

In their Biblical context these terms are sometimes used virtually interchangeably, perhaps because it is by God's *Spirit* that the *Truth* becomes known through the spoken and written *Word*. The fact that at least two distinct passages affirm each equivalent adds some additional support to their interrelationship. Further evidence that these are valid equivalents springs from the close connection between the three terms and the Deity Himself. This is depicted in the next diagram, in which we retain the same outline triangle, but insert into it additional scriptural statements about the Father:-

SPIRIT

"God is a Spirit"
(John 4:24; cp.
Isa. 31:3)

GOD

"The Word was
God" (John 1:1)

"The God of truth" (Isa 65:16;
Psa 31.5 RV)

WORD ←————————→ TRUTH

Thus the Father is characterised here as Spirit and the Word. He is also "the God of Truth", who never lies (Titus 1.2)

305

As Christ was a perfect manifestation of God, the following diagram shows a similar relationship between Spirit, Word and Truth in his case also. This illustrates the Word's testimony that he "reflects the glory of God and bears the very stamp of his nature" (Hebrews 1.3):-

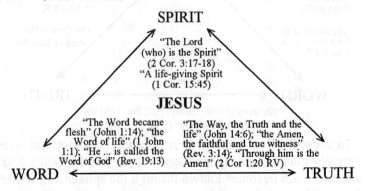

It is clear from these parallel testimonies that Jesus too, although subordinate to his Father, has been granted the rank and status appropriate to his divine Sonship: like his Father he is the embodiment of Truth, being the Word once made flesh, but now become spirit.

Finally, a similar relationship applies to the believers.

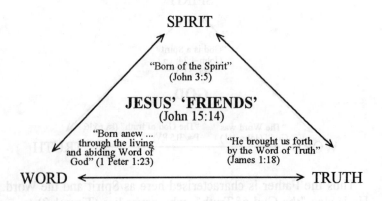

If *we* claim to be true Christians and therefore "in Christ" (Galatians 3.27—29), then the Spirit/Word/Truth increasingly absorbed from the "Word of Truth" must be active in our own hearts and minds, ruling our whole lives to render them consistent with the 'godliness' (i.e. *God-likeness*) we profess. Thus the final diagram illustrates how believers, if truly "born again", will reflect even in this life the same godly principles which characterise their Master, in anticipation of that day of redemption when mind and body will be fully perfected in and through the Father and the Son.

Then the true 'three in one' will be revealed—the Father, the Son and the Redeemed. This is the promise of the Gospel held out to believers who 'endure to the end'. May it be the true hope of all who read these pages.

Chapter 8

"THEY SHALL WANDER INTO MYTHS"[1]

The historical development of the Doctrine of the Trinity

400 B.C. TO 300 A.D.—THE PHILOSOPHICAL BACKGROUND

To the ordinary reader it may seem a little strange to commence a review of the history of a Christian doctrine with a survey of the teachings and views of Greek philosophers. But in fact it is impossible to understand the development of the Trinity without this background. It was not mere rhetoric when St. Augustine confessed that he was in the dark about the Trinity until he read the writings of Plato; or when he told some to go and learn the Trinity from the Platonists.[2] And Gibbon, in speaking of the Trinity, remarks that Platonic philosophy 'marvelously anticipated one of the most surprising discoveries of the Christian revelation'.[3]

Philosophy, literally 'love of wisdom', concerns man's search for an understanding of the world and himself. By means of human thought it attempts to explain what knowledge is and how it is gained. It advances propositions and tries to deduce conclusions from them by reasoned arguments. It is

---

1. 2 Timothy 4:4

2. Quoted by Stannus, p24. (For detailed bibliography see Appendix 3 at end of chapter).

3. *Decline and Fall*, ch.21

essentially a deductive process, no external revelation being admitted. The early Greeks specialised in this type of abstract reasoning, which was first established by Socrates and elaborated by his disciple, Plato.

PLATO

Plato commenced his voluminous writings in the early 4th century B.C., covering a wide range of topics. As far as theology was concerned, his deductions led him to the belief in a Supreme Being who, because of his absolute transcendence was detached from and outside the universe, but who manifested himself in two ways: as Ideas and as the Soul of the Universe. All created things he brought into being by means of his 'Ideas', also called the Demiurge. There was also the Soul or Spirit of the Universe, of which the soul of man was a part. These three, Supreme Being, Demiurge and World Soul, comprised the relationship between God and created things, although Plato himself did not define their relationship with any clarity.

Neo-Pythagorism, a revision of the famous 6th century B.C. philosopher's ideas, adopted a similar division into 'Principle of Being', the Demiurge who acted as creator, and the 'World'.

One effect of Plato's ideas is worth noting. Because all humans participated in the 'World Soul' he believed that the individual souls of men were not only immortal but had also pre-existed.

STOICISM

This was an extremely moralistic philosophy founded by Zeno of Citium in Cyprus around 300 BC. In contrast to the Platonists they believed that the Supreme God was within creation ('immanent') and that all creation was permeated with Divine Reason which they called *Nous* ('Mind') or *Logos* ('Word'). A part of this *Logos* was thought to reside in each human individual, from which he derived his reasoning ability, the *spermatikos logos*.

MIDDLE PLATONISM

In the first century B.C. followers of Plato defined more closely the relationship between Plato's components of the 'threefold One'. The Supreme Godhead was the originator of the other two, who preceded or 'emanated' from him. Later these came to be known as the *Protos Theos* ('First God'), *Nous* and *Psyche*. By using the term *Nous* for the 'second god' Middle Platonists effectively combined the teaching of Plato and the Stoics.

NEOPLATONISM

This was the final form of Platonism, reached at the beginning of the third century A.D., and developed especially by Plotinus (a fellow student of the famous Origen) at Alexandria. It combined most of the elements of the preceding philosophies, propounding the tripartite god of the *One,* the *nous* and the *psyche.* However, the relationship between the first two seems to be more closely defined:

'The original Being first of all throws out the *nous*, which is a perfect image of the One and the archetype of all existing things. It is at once being and thought, ideal world and idea. As image, the *nous* corresponds perfectly to the One, but as derived it is perfectly different.'[1]

This *nous* ('a sort of second god'[2]), which 'corresponds perfectly to the One' is the creator of all things, and within it is included the gods of the pantheon, and the stars, who were also considered to be gods.

Dominant in their teaching was the idea of a World Soul, which bore a similar relationship to the *nous* as the *nous* did to the One. This World Soul embraced innumerable individual human souls, which could either submit to be ruled by the *nous* and survive, or turn aside to sensuality and lose themselves in

---

1.*Encyclopaedia Britannica*: Art. 'Neoplatonism'

2.ibid.

the infinite. In either event, as part of the World Soul, the individual ones pre-existed and were immortal. It is relevant to our present study that the Christian Neoplatonists believed in a tripartite division of man into *soul*, *mind* and *body*: a relationship that was thought to be derived from a similar tripartite division in the Godhead, seeing that man was made 'in the image of God' (Genesis 1.27. see also p. 349).

Gibbon's rather acerbic comments on the Neoplatonists, whilst possibly an example of his trenchant prose, no doubt contain more than a grain of truth:

'.. by mistaking the true object of philosophy, their labours contributed much less to improve than to corrupt the human understanding. ... they exhausted their strength in the verbal disputes of metaphysics, attempted to explore the secrets of the invisible world, and studied to reconcile Aristotle with Plato, on subjects of which both those philosophers were as ignorant as the rest of mankind'.[1]

Thus it can be seen that, whatever the differences in detail among the various theories of the philosophers, one almost common concept was that the Deity was composed of, or manifested himself through, *three* agencies. This idea was to prove of great significance to the development of the doctrine of the Trinity. Little sums up the effect of first and second century philosophy on the evolution of this doctrine:

'There was then evolved the conception of an Intermediary Divine Being, identical with the Supreme in essence, yet in dynamic relation with the generated world, who expressed the Divine will in the Creation, and continued to act as the Divine Agent in the administration of the universe. This Being was variously designated the Idea of Ideas, the First Principle, the Divine Potency, the Second God, or the Logos, according to the philosophical prepossessions of the

---

1.Gibbon, *Decline and Fall* Chap.13.

writers. *It was this Logos of the philosophers which was taken up into Christian theology and made to represent the historical Jesus Christ, son of God ...*'[1]

IMPACT ON JUDAISM

After the almost universal spread of Greek culture and learning following the conquests of Alexander the Great, the teaching of the philosophers began to be incorporated into Jewish thought. In the apocryphal work described as the *Wisdom of Solomon*, dating from the 3rd century B.C., concepts such as the immortality and pre-existence of the soul, hitherto foreign to the Jewish religion, are introduced (3:1, 8:19-20). As Millman later said 'Platonism had already modified Judaism'.[2] Thus by the first century A.D. the Jewish historian Josephus could describe their belief in Hades and Abraham's bosom as the respective abiding places of evil and good of departed souls.[3] It is this importation from Greek philosophy that Jesus uses in the parable of the Rich Man and Lazarus (Luke 16:19-31). Other examples could be given to show that Judaism had already become tainted with Greek thought; and it was inevitable that the newly founded Christian Church should be subject to a similar process. Some see the denial of the bodily resurrection by a few in the church at Corinth as a direct result of early Christians embracing or, more likely, not discarding Platonic views.[4] As Stead has recently noted:

'Moreover the clash between Platonic and biblical views of the soul confused the Christian teaching on the afterlife. The Hebrews looked forward to a resurrection of the body; only so could consciousness be restored; and it would take place on a day of judgement after a period of absolute non-

---

1. V.A.S. Little: *The Christology of the Apologists* pp.20-21. Pub. Duckworth (1934). Italics ours.

2. *History of Christianity* Vol. II p.355

3. *Against Apion*

4. e.g. Chadwick: *The Early Church*, p34.

existence. But Christians tended (as many still do) to accept also the survival of the soul as Plato conceived it, so that consciousness continues without interruption beyond the moment of death. But granted the promise of a fully surviving consciousness, it is hard to see the point of a subsequent resurrection of the body, which Christians were bound to accept in accordance with their Creeds.'[1]

If Plato's idea of the immortality of the soul could thus be imported into Christian thought, it is far from surprising that his views on the Deity should also find a foothold in the early church.

In concluding this section it might be well to stress (without any slur upon the exceedingly able and perceptive minds of those great thinkers) the fact that philosophy is only the product of human intellect. Despite the claims that were later made for philosophy, it is not divine revelation such as is contained in Scripture. As Gibbon again says:

'They meditated on the Divine Nature, as a very curious and important speculation; and in the profound enquiry, they displayed the strength and weakness of the human understanding'.[2]

35-90 A.D. THE APOSTOLIC CHURCH

The whole thrust of this book is an attempt to demonstrate that the original Christians' beliefs and teaching about God and Christ were not Trinitarian. It is therefore unnecessary to restate here the arguments of other chapters. However, at this juncture it is useful to note that historians and commentators all down the centuries have acknowledged that the Trinity formed

---

1.Stead, C: Art. 'Greek Influence on Christian Thought', in *Early Christianity*, Ed. Hazlett.

2. Gibbon, *Decline and Fall* chap.2

no part of the original Christian message, and that all New Testament evidence is that the first Christians regarded God as a unity and Jesus as subordinate to Him. The following are a sample of comments of such writers (almost all of whom were or are Trinitarians), and any who claim to find the Trinity implicitly, even if not explicitly, taught in Scripture are invited to ponder the evidence.

Hooker (1593): 'Our belief in the Trinity, the co-eternity of the Son of God with his Father, the proceeding of the Spirit from the Father and the Son, these with such other principal points are in Scripture nowhere to be found by express literal mention; only deduced they are out of Scripture by collection.'[1]

John Milton (1608-1674): 'For my part I adhere to the Holy Scriptures alone, I follow no other heresy or sect. If, therefore, the Father be the God of Christ, and the same be our God, and if there be none other God but one, there can be no God beside the Father.'[2]

'Milton's arguments against the Trinity are ultimately logical and commonsensical: Why create mystifications which are not to be found in the Bible? John Locke and Isaac Newton, with Milton the three greatest names of the period (c.1650), could not find Trinitarianism in the Bible'.[3]

Dr. Neander (1850): 'The Doctrine of the Trinity does not, it appears to me, belong strictly to the fundamentals of the Christian faith; as it appears from the fact that it is explicitly set forth in no one particular passage of the New Testament; for the only one in which this is done, the

---

1. Hooker, Richard, *Ecclesiastical Polity,* Bk. i, para 14.

2. Quoted by Stannus, p29.

3. Christopher Mill, *Milton and the English Revolution* pp.286,295

passage relating to the three that bear record (1 John 5) is undoubtedly spurious, and in its ungenuine shape testifies to the fact, how foreign such a collection is from the style of the New Testament writings. We find in the New Testament no other fundamental article besides that of which the apostle Paul says that other foundation can no man lay than that is laid, the preaching of Jesus Christ as the Messiah; and the foundation of His religion is designated by Christ himself as the faith in the only true God and in Jesus Christ whom He hath sent'.[1]

Dr. Joseph Priestly (1871): 'Why was not the doctrine of the *Trinity* taught as explicitly, and in as definite a manner, in the New Testament at least, as the doctrine of the divine *Unity* is taught in both the Old and New Testaments, if it be a truth? And why is the doctrine of the *Unity* always delivered in so unguarded a manner and without any exception made in favour of the Trinity, to prevent any mistake with respect to it?.'[2]

'It is well known, and mentioned by Eusebius,[3] that the Unitarians in the primitive church always pretended to be the oldest Christians, that the Apostles themselves had taught their doctrine, and that it generally prevailed till the time of Zephyrinius, bishop of Rome'.[4]

'Christians retained the same faith, believing in the strict unity of God, and the proper humanity of Christ, all the time of the Apostles and of those who conversed with them, but began to depart from that doctrine presently afterwards; and the defection advanced so fast, that in about one century more, the original doctrine was generally

---

1.Neander, *History of Christian Religion*, vol. ii, p286

2. Priestly p.321

3.Bk. 5 para 28

4.Priestly, p7

reprobated and deemed heretical.'[1]

Bishop Smallridge: 'It must be owned, that the doctrine of the Trinity as it is proposed in our Articles, our Liturgy, our Creeds, is not in so many words taught us in the Holy Scriptures. What we profess in our prayers we nowhere read in Scripture, that the one God, the one Lord, is not only one person, but three persons in one substance. There is no such text as this, 'That the Unity in Trinity, and the Trinity in Unity is to be worshipped'. No one of the inspired writers hath expressly affirmed, that in the Trinity none is afore or after other, none is greater or less than another.'[2]

Mozeley (the brother-in-law of the famous nineteenth century Cardinal Newman) 'I ask with all humbleness where the idea of Threeness is expressed in the New Testament with a doctrinal sense and force? Where is the Triune God held up to be worshipped, loved and obeyed? Where is He preached and proclaimed in that threefold Character? We read 'God is one' as too, 'I and the Father are one'; but nowhere do we read that Three are one, unless it be in a text long since known to be interpolated ... To me the whole matter is most painful and perplexing, and I should not even speak as I now do did I not feel on the threshold of the grave, soon to appear before the Throne of all truth .... Certainly not in Scripture do we find the expression 'God the Son', or 'God the Holy Ghost'. Whenever I pronounce the name of God, simply and first, I mean God the Father, and I cannot help meaning that, if I mean anything.'[3]

Paine (1900): 'The Old Testament is strictly monotheistic.

---

1. Priestly p.7

2. *Sixty Sermons*, No. xxxiii, p348.

3. Reminiscences of Oriel College and the Oxford Movement.

God is a single personal being. The idea that a trinity is to be found there, or even in any way shadowed forth, *is an assumption that has long held sway in theology, but is utterly without foundation.*[1]

'In the Synoptic gospels ... there is no hint anywhere of a pre-incarnate life, ... or of a divine incarnation. He calls God his Father, but he also teaches that God is Father of All, and gives his disciples the *Pater Noster*. ... There is no evidence that the idea of a peculiar metaphysical union with God ever entered his mind. At least it did not appear in his synoptic teaching.[2]

'With this critical explanation, we take the New Testament writings as we find them, and ask what evidence they give us on the question of the evolution of the doctrine of the Trinity. The earliest stratum of the evolution is contained in the Book of Acts, and in the Synoptic gospels. The doctrine of Christ in the first stratum is distinctly that of *Messiahship*. Jesus is a man of God, sent of God to declare his gospel .... There is no assertion of Christ's divinity, or of his pre-existence or incarnation.'[3]

'That Paul ever confounded Christ with God himself, or regarded him in any way as the supreme Divinity, is a position invalidated not only by direct statements, but also by *the whole drift of his epistles*.'[4]

Dr. W. Matthews (1940): 'It must be admitted by everyone who has the rudiments of an historical sense that the doctrine of the Trinity, as a doctrine, formed no part of the original message. St. Paul knew it not, and would have

---

1. *A critical History of the Evolution of Trinitarianism*, p4 (italics ours).

2. ibid, p5

3. ibid, p6-7.

4. ibid, p22. (italics ours)

been unable to understand the meaning of the terms used in the theological formula on which the Church ultimately agreed'.[1]

Encyclopedia of Religion (1987): 'Exegetes and theologians today are in agreement that the Hebrew Bible does not contain a doctrine of the Trinity, even though it was customary in past dogmatic tracts on the Trinity to cite texts like Gen. 1.26 "Let us make humanity in our image, after our likeness". Although the Hebrew Bible depicts God as the father of Israel and employs personifications of God such as Word, Spirit, Wisdom, and Presence, it would go beyond the intention and spirit of the Old Testament to correlate these notions with later Trinitarian doctrine. ... Further exegetes and theologians agree that the New Testament also does not contain an explicit doctrine of the trinity ... In the New Testament there is no reflective consciousness of the metaphysical nature of God ("immanent trinity") nor does the New Testament contain the technical language of later doctrine.'[2]

Dunn (1989): 'All this raises the question whether the pre-existence-incarnation interpretation of these key passages in Paul and Hebrews is properly grounded in the exegesis of these passages. Has that interpretation properly understood the character and thrust of earliest Christianity's Adam christology? It is quite true that once the context of the original Adam theology faded from the immediate perspective the language which derived from that theology lent itself to a pre-existence-incarnation interpretation, particularly in the case of Phil. 2.6-11. ... but from what we have seen of the Adam christology in Paul and elsewhere in the early decades of Christianity, that interpretation *goes beyond the meaning and intention of the original*

---

1. Matthews, W.R. (Dean of St Paul's), *God in Christian Thought and Experience*.

2. Art. 'Trinity'

Philippian hymn and its use by Paul' .[1]

Speaking of Paul's reference in Col. 1.15-20, 'It is at least questionable whether ... he intended to assert the pre-existence of Christ, or to affirm that Jesus was a divine being personally active in creation.'[2]

'Paul was not seeking to win men to belief in a pre-existent being'.[3]

We *repeat* that with the exception of Dr. Priestly all the above writers are Trinitarians or members of the established church, and it is salutary to learn that even they acknowledge that the Scriptural basis for the doctrine of the Trinity is virtually non-existent.

DEVIATION FROM APOSTOLIC TEACHING PREDICTED[4]

One of the features of the early Christian movement was the fact that almost from its inception some of its basic tenets were challenged, and the Apostles had continually to be on their guard lest the variant ideas should take root. In Corinth the bodily resurrection was denied; in Colosse the unique position of Jesus in God's purpose was challenged, and throughout the Christian world the Judaisers were attempting to retain the new faith within the confines of the Law of Moses. The Apostles foresaw that such processes would intensify after their death and so gave many warnings to the flock to beware of departing from the truths they had been taught.

Paul gave this warning to the Ephesians on his final visit to them:

1. Dunn, J.D.G. *Christology in the Making*, p 128 (our italics).

2. ibid, p194

3. ibid, p195

4. See also pp. 135*ff*

'Take heed to yourselves and to all the flock ... I know that after my departure fierce wolves will come in among you, not sparing the flock; and from among your own selves will arise men speaking perverse things, to draw away the disciples after them.' (Acts 20:28-30).

A few years later, in his letter to Timothy, his warnings became more emphatic:

'Now the Spirit expressly says that in later times some will depart from the faith by giving heed to deceitful spirits and doctrines of demons, through the pretensions of liars whose consciences are seared, who forbid marriage and enjoin abstinence from foods which God created to be received with thanksgiving by those who believe and know the truth' (1 Timothy 4:1-3).

About the same time Peter gave similar warnings:

'But false prophets also arose among the people, just as there will be false teachers among you, who will secretly bring in destructive heresies, even denying the Master who bought them, bringing upon themselves swift destruction. And many will follow their licentiousness, and because of them the way of truth will be reviled. And in their greed they will exploit you with false words' (2 Peter 2:1-3).

As the guiding hand of the Apostles was gradually withdrawn, these predictions came to pass. In the closing years of the first century the very aged John had to write against those who were promulgating false views about the person of Christ (1 John 4:1-3; 2 John 7-8). In the final book of Scripture, in a message from Jesus himself, we learn of the false doctrines and evil practices that were already in his church (Revelation 2:14-16,20; 3:1-3).

Of course, the question has to be decided as to whether the doctrines that survived into the succeeding ages were the true original ones or the 'destructive heresies' that had been 'secretly brought in'. Daille's comment is very relevant here:

> 'Now I cannot believe that any faithful Christian will deny but that Christianity was at its zenith and perfection at the time of the blessed Apostles. ... It will follow then, that those times which were nearest to the Apostles were necessarily the purest, and less subject to suspicion of corruption, either in doctrine or in manners of Christian discipline: it being reasonable to believe that if any corruptions have crept into the Church, they came in little by little, and by degrees, as it happens in all other things ... but .. after the death of the Apostles the conspiracy of error began to discover itself with open face'.[1]

In later years Tertullian had a rule by which he detected heresy— 'What was true was first, what was spurious afterwards'[2]—and we will use a similar approach.

The problem is that variations to the original teaching poured in thick and fast in the second and third centuries so that what later times repudiated as heresies were in fact the original views. As one writer says: 'Many scholars believe that in some regions views later condemned as heresy predominated at first'.[3] As most of the early 'heresies' concerned the position of Christ, it is reasonable to conclude that they were in fact the original Christian teaching. When the Church later discarded these early beliefs did it discard an important element of the Apostolic faith? We will submit evidence that it did.

THE EARLY 'RULES OF FAITH'
What, then, were the earliest beliefs about the relationship of God to Jesus? From almost the beginning it was felt necessary

---

1. Daille, *The Right Use of the Fathers*, p.2

2. Quoted in Blunt's *Early Fathers*, p155

3. *History of Christianity*, Lion, p.107

to define the basic items of faith, particularly in a form that could be used as a confession by baptismal candidates. From these developed more extensive rules of faith which in turn were enlarged into the creeds.

The earliest declaration of belief was probably a simple 'Jesus is Lord' (1 Corinthians 12.3) or 'Jesus is the Christ' (1 John 5:1). A slightly later confession runs: 'Jesus Christ, the Son of God, is the Saviour'. The initial letters of this phrase in Greek produce the Greek word *ichthys*, i.e. "fish", and therefore probably from a very early date a fish was chosen as the symbol of Christian faith. Soon the need was felt for a more comprehensive statement, or creed (from *credo*, I believe), such as an early one found in Egypt:

I believe in God, the Father, the Almighty;
And in Jesus Christ, his only begotten Son, our Lord,
And in the Holy Ghost, the holy church, the resurrection
of the flesh.'[1]

By combining several references the creed of Justin (c.A.D. 150) has been deduced:

I believe in the Father of all things and the Lord God.
And in our Lord Jesus Christ, the first-born son of God, according to the Father's will born through a virgin and become man and crucified under Pontius Pilate and dead and risen from the dead and ascended into heaven, and will come again in glory as judge of all men.
And in the Holy Spirit of prophecy.[2]

Several similar creeds have been preserved from a similar date.

In the church at Rome in the fourth century was an already ancient Latin creed known as the Old Roman Creed, and which

---

1. *Encyclopaedia Britannica*, Art. 'Creeds'.

2. *Encyclopaedia Britannica*, Art. 'Creeds'.

subsequently became known as the Apostles Creed. Its Latin form has been shown to be a translation from the Greek, and as this language ceased to be the language of the Roman Church in the middle of the third century, it must be dated before about A.D.250, and is almost certainly much older than that date. Although it is now believed that the title 'Apostles Creed' is a misnomer in the sense that there is little evidence that it was first written by the immediate disciples of Jesus, it is admitted by all that the creed is of great antiquity, and probably accurately reflected their teaching. It was added to over the centuries, but its earliest form is as follows:

> I believe in God the Father Almighty;
> And in Jesus Christ his only begotten Son, our Lord,
> Who was born of the Holy Ghost, and the virgin Mary,
> Who was crucified under Pontius Pilate and buried:
> on the third day he rose from the dead,
>
> ascended into heaven,
> sat down at the right hand of the Father;
> from whence he will come to judge the living and the dead;
> And in the Holy Ghost, the holy church, the forgiveness of
> sins, the resurrection of the flesh.

Up to the beginning of the fourth century these creeds and rules of faith were essentially local statements by individual communities, and thus varied in detail from place to place. There was considerable flexibility of belief and opinion. It was not until later that creeds, such as the Nicene Creed, were drawn up by the whole church and used as a test of orthodoxy, with excommunication as a penalty for non-compliance.

It will be readily seen that none of these early statements of faith describe the relationship between God and Jesus in anything approaching Trinitarian terms, and are therefore strongly suggestive—on Tertullian's rule that 'what was true was first'—that subsequent developments were a modification of the immediate post-Apostolic faith.

A.D. 90-120. THE POST-APOSTOLIC PERIOD

In the immediate post-apostolic years—conventionally called the times of the Apostolic Fathers—little written evidence has come down to us that enables us to establish the then current beliefs. Just a few passing references and allusions are often all that we have to guide us. However, all that is extant is in line with the view that Trinitarian ideas were not yet being expressed; but at the same time the nature of Christ and his relationship to his Father was already engaging the minds of some, with widely differing views emerging.

DOCETISTS, EBIONITES AND NAZARENES

From the later standpoint of the official church historians of the *fourth* century (by which time the Church was virtually trinitarian) these three sects represented heretical movements as early as the latter years of the first century, each not believing that Jesus Christ was God. The Docetists believed that Jesus during his life on earth had not a real human body, but only an apparent one.[1] This can be regarded as a genuine heresy, and appears to have been combated by the aged apostle John when he warned his readers that 'many deceivers have gone out into the world, men who will not acknowledge the coming of Jesus Christ in the flesh; such a one is the deceiver and the antichrist' (2 John 7).

But can one place the Ebionites and the Nazarenes in the same category? The two names possibly describe but one group of early Christians in southern Syria. Mosheim[2], however, regards them as two separate groups, the Hebrew 'Nazarenes' being interchangeable with the Greek term 'Christians'. When Jerusalem was attacked by Titus in A.D. 66-70 the Christians in Judea, heedful of the warning of Jesus in his Mount Olivet Prophecy (Luke 21:21) fled the region before the Roman

---

1. *Encyclopaedia Britannica*, Art. 'Docetae'

2. Vol. 1, ch.5

armies closed in. They moved north to Pella where they established a church that lasted for the next few hundred years. This group of Christians called themselves Nazarenes, but those outside, noting with disparagement their poverty, called them Ebionites ('poor men'). Does this very early group of Christians, cut off from the mainstream of developing Christianity, furnish us with clues to original beliefs?

One thing noted about the Nazarenes and Ebionites[1] by the early writers was that they 'saw Jesus as an ordinary man indwelt by God's power at his baptism'[2] The word 'ordinary' here needs some qualification. Certainly some of the Ebionites went so far as to say that Jesus was the actual son of Joseph, but another section within them held Jesus to be the Son of God by his conception through the Holy Spirit, but not pre-existent. 'They obstinately rejected the preceding existence and divine perfections of the *Logos* or the son of God'.[3] Eusebius, the church historian of the 4th century, although his knowledge of and interest in Syrian Christianity was minimal and biased,[4] describes them in these terms:

'Ebionites they were appropriately named by the first Christians, in view of the poor and mean opinions they held about Christ. They regarded him as plain and ordinary, a man esteemed as righteous through growth of character and nothing more, the child of a normal union between a man and Mary. A second group went by the same name, but escaped the outrageous absurdity of the first. *They did not deny that the Lord was born of a virgin and the Holy spirit, but nevertheless shared their refusal to acknowledge His*

---

1. They also retained the original Christian belief in the future reign of Christ on earth, which was enough to ensure the censure of 3rd and 4th century Christianity, which by then had largely abandoned this element of Apostolic teaching.

2. *History of Christianity*, Lion, p110

3. Gibbon, *Decline and Fall*, ch. xx

4. Louth, A, *Eusebius*, p.xxiv-xxv.

pre-existence as God the Word and Wisdom[1] (our italics).

Moeller suggests that this second group within the Ebionites were in fact the Nazarenes and says they closely represented apostolic Christianity:

> 'The survival down to a later age, of a Judaeo Christianity more closely approximating to that of the apostles, but through its isolation and seclusion taking on the character of a backward sect, distinguished from the more abruptly heretical character of the Ebionites, is attested by the fact that Epiphanius in his age[2] distinguishes, under two names which were originally general names for Christians, between Nazarenes and Ebionites'.[3]

But how did the mainstream Christians of the time regard the Ebionites and Nazarenes? Did they condemn them for their failure to preach that Christ was pre-existent? There is no record of this, rather the contrary. Hegesippus, one of the earliest Christian writers 'who belonged after the first generation after the apostles'[4], and who 'in five short books gave an authentic account of the apostolic preaching',[5] makes no mention of this supposed heresy of the Nazarenes and Ebionites. This suggests that rejection of the pre-existence of Christ was then standard teaching[6] throughout the Christian world. About the same time other prominent Christian writers also noted the existence of the Ebionites and Nazarenes without denouncing their opinions as heretical:

---

1. Book III.27

2. 4th century

3. *History of the Christian Church*, p.100

4. Eusebius Bk.II.23

5. ibid, Bk.IV,7

6. Priestly, p.3

'It is remarkable, however, that those who held the simple doctrine of the humanity of Christ, without asserting that Joseph was his natural father, were not reckoned heretics by Irenaeus ... and even those who held *that* opinion are mentioned with respect by Justin Martyr, who wrote some years before'.[1]

Of the few pastoral letters written which can be accepted as genuine in this immediate post-apostolic period is the First Epistle of Clement. Writing from Rome to a troubled Corinth community, he concludes with this benediction:

'Finally, may the all-seeing God and Master of spirits and Lord of all flesh, who chose the Lord Jesus Christ, and us through him for his own people, give to every soul that is called by his excellent and holy name, faith, fear, peace, patience, and long suffering, self-control, purity, and sober-mindedness, so that they may be well-pleasing to his name through our high priest and defender Jesus Christ, through whom unto him be glory and majesty, might and honour, both now and forever and ever. Amen.'[2]

Clearly to Clement God was supreme, above all. His is the 'excellent' name. It was He who 'chose' Jesus, and it is only He who receives praise 'through' Jesus. As Lamson says of this letter of Clement: 'What traces, then, does it contain of the modern doctrine of the Trinity? It contains not the faintest trace of the supreme divinity of the Son or of the Spirit'.[3]

So as the first century closes there is no evidence in Christian writing of belief in the personal pre-existence of Jesus, or that he was held to be equal to God or worshipped as God.

---

1. Priestly, p.6.

2. ch. 64.

3. Lamson op. cit. p.4.

SECOND CENTURY DEVELOPMENTS

IGNATIUS

Ignatius was bishop of Antioch and was put to death in the Coliseum at Rome sometime between the years 110 and 117. On his fateful journey to Rome he wrote epistles to various churches that had sent emissaries to cheer him on his way, and to one individual, Polycarp of Smyrna. Of the epistles once attributed to him, seven are now regarded as genuine, although they may contain some interpolations.[1] In all these letters the essential distinction between God and Jesus and the subordination of the Son to the Father is evident. He speaks of God as the 'Father of Jesus Christ',[2] of 'one God, who has manifested himself through Jesus Christ his Son'[3], exhorts his hearers to 'subordinate yourselves to the bishop and to one another, as Jesus Christ in the flesh did to the Father',[4] and refers to the 'God of Jesus Christ'.[5] In the following passage, by the repetition of the word 'truly', Ignatius was clearly attacking the Docetians in stressing the reality of the person of Jesus, but at the same time gives a summary of then Christian belief, which contains no hint of any co-equality or pre-existence but rather stresses the dependence of Christ on God ('his Father raised him', etc.):

> 'Stop your ears therefore when anyone speaks to you apart from Jesus Christ, who was descended from David, who was the son of Mary, who was truly born, who both ate and drank, was truly persecuted under Pontius Pilate, was truly crucified and died, in the sight of those in heaven and on earth and under the earth; who was also truly raised from

1. For discussion on this see Moeller, pp.112-114; Mosheim, Vol. I. Cent I, ch.II, para 20 and footnotes.

2. Magnesians 3:2

3. Ibid, 8:2

4. Ibid, 13:2

5. Trallians 7:1

the dead, when his Father raised him, and his Father in like manner will raise us up also who believe in him through Jesus Christ, without whom we can have no true life'.[1]

There is clearly no hint here of any relationship between God and Christ as is demanded by Trinitarian dogma. If Ignatius believed the modern idea of the Trinity he could and almost certainly would have used other arguments to combat the errors of the Docetians.

But on the other hand elsewhere in his letters Ignatius does seem to go further than the Apostles in that he describes Jesus as 'God', using phrases such as 'Jesus our God', and 'our God Jesus Christ'. We say 'seem' advisedly, because there is some possibility that here we have examples of the later interpolations alluded to above; although probably few would go along with Lamson's view that the text is 'hopelessly corrupt'.[2] The uncertainty arises because in a Syriac version Ignatius' Epistle to the Romans closes with 'Jesus Christ our God', whilst the other versions simply says 'Jesus Christ'. Similarly in his Epistle to the Ephesians 'blood of Christ' was changed into 'blood of God'. This raises suspicions that other occasions where Jesus is called God may have been similarly edited to suit later beliefs. (As we have already seen from a consideration of 1 John 5, this is by no means uncommon, see pp.32,198). Alternatively Ignatius could have been using the term in the sense that Justin and Tertullian did some years later. Speaking of Jesus they said: 'Who, since he is the first-begotten ... of God, is God',[3] and 'whatever is born of God is God'[4]; Here they are saying that Jesus is God, not in the trinitarian sense, but in same way that one born of human parents is human.

---

1. Ibid 9:1-2

2. Lamson, op. cit. p.16.

3. Justin, *Apol. I* p.81

4. Tertullian, *Apol.,* adv. Gentes,c.21

Even so, could it be said that we have here the very beginnings of the process that led to the full doctrine of the Trinity? Whilst Ignatius in no way regarded Jesus as God in the Trinitarian sense, we might detect a slight shift of emphasis away from the Apostles' teaching. As Leitzmann says:

'John preached that the logos had become flesh, but Ignatius goes further and says without hesitation that God had come in the flesh or had appeared as man, and this characterisation of Christ as divine, leads him, in the end, actually to speak of the sufferings of God and the blood of God'.[1]

But even this was but a first step on the long road to the Trinity. As the same author continues concerning Ignatius' views:

'Nevertheless the person of the Son is clearly distinguished from that of the Father ... The difference between the Father and the Son becomes still more evident when the subordination and the exemplary obedience of the Son are emphasised. ... Both in the abstractions of theology, and in the concrete religion of Ignatius, the Risen Lord is a person clearly separated from the Father, the one God of his monotheism'.[2]

So whilst Ignatius might have used the word 'God' in referring to Jesus, he was not using the term in its highest sense and saying that Father and Son were equal.

THE LETTER OF POLYCARP
When Ignatius left Philippi on the last stage of his fateful journey to Rome he left the Philippians instruction to write to Polycarp at Smyrna asking for copies of Ignatius' other letters. In complying with this request Polycarp sent his own epistle to

---

1. Leitzmann: *History of the Early Church,* Vol. 1, p242

2. Ibid, p243

them as well. Unlike the epistles of Ignatius, in Polycarp's letter there is nothing with the slightest Trinitarian implication. He never speaks of Christ as God, and always maintains a clear distinction between the Father and the Son. The Father is Christ's God, the 'Almighty', and Jesus the 'Saviour';[1] God is the 'Father of our Lord Jesus Christ'[2]; Christ received glory from God at his resurrection;[3] and belief must be 'in our Lord Jesus Christ and in his Father who raised him from the dead'.[4]

It would thus seem from Polycarp that Ignatius was expressing a far from universal viewpoint when he termed Christ 'God'; or maybe there is some truth in the suggestion that his original text was modified later.

THE SHEPHERD OF HERMAS

The next example of early Christian literature dates from about 140. It is a rather whimsical book of visions described by Hermas, written in an attempt to stir up the Christians in Rome to greater spirituality. Although not part of the canon of Scripture, it was highly regarded by later writers such as Irenaeus. Here, possibly for the first time, we have the pre-existence of Christ firmly stated:

'The Son of God is far older than all his creation, so that he was the Father's counsellor in his creation'.[5]

But the subordination of the Son to the Father, and his dependence on Him is not questioned. Jesus received the law 'from the Father', and 'received all power from his Father'.[6]

---

1. Chapter 1

2. Chapter 12:2

3. Chapter 2:1

4. Chapter 12:2

5. Parable 9, chapter 12.

6. Parable 5, ch.6

THE EPISTLE OF BARNABAS

Probably the next document, chronologically speaking, is the Letter of Barnabas, circa 150. Like the above work it was highly regarded in the early church. When Tischendorf found the Codex Sinaiticus in the convent of St Catherine at the traditional site of Mt. Sinai, this epistle was bound in with the rest of the New Testament, coming after the book of Revelation. By now the doctrine of the Son's pre-existence is firmly established, and he is designated creator:

> '.. he (Jesus) was Lord of all the world, to whom God said, at the foundation of the world, "Let us make man in our image and in our likeness"'. ....' .. when as they look at the sun ... which is the work of his (Christ's) hands'.[1]

NO *LOGOS* DOCTRINE

At this point in our study of the history of the Trinity it is worth noting that nowhere in the 'Apostolic Fathers' (as the writers we have so far studied are called) has the *logos* doctrine been referred to. It is highly significant that the opinions which were later to become the essence of Justin Martyr's teaching have received not the slightest attention. Lamson comments on this:

> 'The absence of all traces of the (Logos) doctrine in these writings can be explained only on the supposition that the authors "did not", in the words of Souverain, "find it in the Christian religion, nor in the Jewish; and, not having studied in the school of Plato, they could not import it from that school into the Church of Christ". Hagenbach concedes that the authors of these writings "do not make any particular use of the peculiar doctrine of the Logos". Semisch, after observing that the most ancient Fathers of the Church, in their speculative inquiries into the person of Christ, took their direction from Philo, whose doctrine of the Logos was their starting point, adds, "*We except, however, the so-*

---

1. Chapter 5:5,10

*called Apostolic Fathers. Every such application of the idea
of the Logos was foreign to their minds"*.[1]

JUSTIN MARTYR

Up to this point of our historical review the detail of the lives
and the beliefs of the early Christians have been fragmentary
and obscure. But with the advent of Justin Martyr we enter a
period well chronicled with writings that are universally
accepted as genuine. Justin was born probably about the turn of
the century, and continued until about 165, when he suffered a
martyr's death. Before his conversion to Christianity he was
devoted to studies of philosophy, and even afterwards he
continued to preach Christianity dressed in the conventional
robe of a philosopher.[2] His main works consist of two
Apologies (i.e. defences of Christianity) addressed to the
Emperor and a *Dialogue with Trypho*, a Jew antagonistic to
Christian beliefs. As a person of high ideals, intrepidly
witnessing to his beliefs, and showing fearless courage even to
the sacrifice of his own life, he must command our respect and
appreciation.

Yet to a modern reader Justin's somewhat abrasive style of
writing, his rather unexpected beliefs, his poor mustering of the
arguments, his inaccurate quoting or even modification of
scripture, his belief that even philosophers like Socrates and
Plato were inspired by God through the *logos*,[3] give rise to
disappointment if a systematic and vigorous defence of
Christianity is expected. According to Justin all the evils in the
world are traceable to the demons who sprang from the illicit
union of the angels with the daughters of men.[4] These
antagonists of God and of all that is good were responsible

---

1. Lamson, p.25

2. Eusebius IV,11

3. First Apology, 46

4. The reference is to Genesis 6:1-3—but few today would accepts Justin's
interpretation of this passage.

throughout history for all the lies, fraud and false religions such as paganism; but their deceptive practices had now been discovered and exposed by the coming of Christ. In this we can see that Justin was influenced by the thinking of his age rather than Apostolic and scriptural Christianity, for demonology was of the essence of pagan religions.[1]

This is even more true of his statements about Christ, where it is universally acknowledged that he derived his views from the philosophers rather than scripture. It was Justin who invested the word *logos* with the meaning that Trinitarians give it today, i.e. a pre-existent person rather than a thought or purpose that became reality at the birth of Jesus. Justin reinterpreted the O.T. passages which previously had been regarded as Hebrew idioms or figures of speech[2] to mean that the Logos was bodily present from old time. Thus passages such as 'By the word (LXX *logos*) of the Lord were the heavens made'(Psalm 33:6) and the creative acts of wisdom in Proverbs 8:22-31 he regarded as descriptions of Christ's actual operations in creation.

To ensure that we are not misrepresenting the 'philosopher turned Christian', in alleging Plato as the real source of his views on the relationship of God and Christ, we give just a small selection of comments by historians on the source of Justin's ideas:

'These apologists, the most notable of whom was Justin Martyr, defended Christianity ... Their defence was that if there was any truth in traditional religion, it lay ... in a lofty philosophical piety, and that the truth glimpsed by the philosophers (especially the Platonists) was grasped more surely by Christianity. ... The appeal to philosophy,

---

1. For a detailed critique of Justin's writings see Lamson, pp26-60, and Leitzmann, Vol. II, p183-185; and a briefer comment in Mosheim, Vol. I Cent. II, Ch. II, para 5.

2. Lamson, pp.70-74 deals extensively with this.

especially to Platonism, and the claims that Christianity was vindicated by what was best in the philosophers .... most appealed to Eusebius'[1]

'The earliest Christian philosophers, particularly Justin and Athenagoras, likewise prepared the way for the speculations of the Neoplatonists ... by their attempts to connect Christianity with Stoicism and Platonism'[2]

'Justin was converted, but did not understand this to mean the abandonment of his philosophical enquiries, nor even the renunciation of all that he had learnt from Platonism. ... The transcendent God of Plato, beyond mortal comprehension, is the God of the Bible. ... Justin's debt to Platonic philosophy is important for his theology in one respect of far-reaching importance. He uses the concept of the divine Logos or Reason both to explain how the transcendent father of all deals with the inferior, created order of things, and to justify his faith in the revelation made by God through the prophets and in Christ.'[3]

'It is obvious that Justin's Christianity is divided into two halves; one is a philosophic religion which clothes Greek ideas and conceptions in a loose Biblical garment, ... and the second aspect is that of the unreasoned faith of the Church in which words of Jesus, sacramental mysticism, and church-life combine to form an active unity'.[4]

Thus it is indisputable that if we seek the source of Justin's theology we need to look no further than the philosophical concepts outlined at the beginning of this chapter. It came from Plato rather than the Jewish and Christian scriptures. The

---

1. Louth, A, Eusebius, p. xiv-xv

2. *Encyclopaedia Britannica,* Art. 'Neoplatonism'

3. Chadwick, pp 75-77.

4. Lietzmann, Vol. II p.185.

Platonic concept, now revised by the emerging Neoplatonists of Justin's age, of a transcendent, unknowable God who revealed himself to the material world by means of a 'second god', the Logos, was transported into Christianity to produce the Father and the pre-existent Son, the creator and redeemer of the world.

But, let it be noted, this is still far from the full Trinitarian concept as it was later developed. Justin's views differed from the final church position in several respects. First, Justin clearly states that Jesus was a being *created* by God. Using the words of later controversy, "there was a time when he was not". He taught that the Logos or Reason, originally an attribute of God, was converted into a real being by a voluntary act of the Father; and this took place some time before the creation of the world. His words are:

> 'In the beginning, before all creatures, God begat of himself a certain rational power, which, by the Holy Spirit, is also called the Glory of the Lord, ... Son, Lord, and Logos'[1]

Thus, because the Son was created, Justin regards him as a distinct person, inferior and subordinate to the Father. He speaks of the Father as 'Lord of that Lord who appeared on earth' and the source of all his power.[2] He frequently applies to the Son such phrases as 'next in rank' or 'next after God'; the Son is 'the first power after God the Father and sovereign Lord of all'.[3] Thus Justin recognised a great difference between the Father and Son. There was no belief in Jesus forming one of three co-eternal and consubstantial 'persons'; rather he was distinct in essence and nature, having a real individuality, separate from God, from whom he derived all his power and

---

1. *Dial.* c.61, Otto's translation.

2. *Dial* p.222

3. *Apol.* I p.63.

authority, and was subject to his Father's will in all things.

Although the germ of the Trinity had now been firmly introduced, it does not mean to say that the teaching about the preexistent Logos was universally accepted by the Church. Justin was probably an *avant garde* thinker, similar to some of the Church leaders of our day who propound controversial ideas. In support of this suggestion we have the comment of Leitzmann who mentions that Tatian, a disciple of Justin, and Athenagoras, a later second century writer, both felt unable to wholeheartedly accept Justin's views:

> '... the doctrine of the logos is only dealt with in a passage (of Tatian's) that requires it, and with much restraint as compared with Justin. ... Apparently neither of these two men (Tatian and Athenagoras) was willing to recognise, in the extra-biblical world, "the seed-corn of the logos", which Justin had brought into discussion'.[1]

In fact Justin himself implies that his views about Christ did not reflect the universal belief of his time. He recognises that there were some who rejected them, being believers in the simple humanity of Jesus. To these Justin accords respect even if he cannot agree with them—something his present day successors could copy with profit. In his dialogue with Trypho he admits the possibility of his being wrong; but that even if he could not prove the Son's pre-existence, the latter's position as Christ is not affected. Trypho had protested:

> 'For as to your assertion that this Christ pre-existed, being God, before the ages, and then submitted to be born and made man ... appears not only paradoxical, but foolish'.

To which Justin replies:

> 'I know that this assertion appears paradoxical, especially

---

1. Leitzmann, Vol. II, p186

to you Jews. Nevertheless, Trypho, the proof that he is the
Christ of God stands, if I cannot show that he pre-existed,
the son of the Creator of the universe, so being God, and
that he was born of the Virgin as man. But, since it is fully
demonstrated that he is the Christ of God, whatever be his
nature, even if I do not succeed in proving that he pre-
existed .... in the latter respect only would it be just to say
that I have erred. You would still not be authorised to deny
that he was a man, born of human parents, and should it be
shown that he became Christ by election: for there are
some of our race who acknowledge that he is the Christ,
but affirm that he was a man ... from whom I dissent'. [1]

This is a most important passage. Justin admits the possibility
of his ideas being unproveable; and accepts that there were
some who disagreed with him, but he does not term them
heretics. Clearly Justin did not believe, as was later held and is
maintained until this day, that the divinity and pre-existence of
Christ were essential for the accomplishment of his mission,
and belief in it essential for salvation. There were sufficient
proofs to demonstrate that Jesus of Nazareth was the Christ.
This for Justin was the all-important fact: whether or not Christ
pre-existed could be left as a matter of opinion.

There is possibly another reason for the shift in emphasis in
the public presentation of Christ's origin. Put ourselves in
Justin's position. His objective was to present Christianity in
the best possible light, first in an attempt to reduce persecution,
but ultimately to convert the world. Yet the pagans were asked
to believe in someone who appeared to them to be a common
criminal, and who after being condemned at a civil trial was
slain in the manner reserved for the lowest of society.
Notwithstanding his subsequent resurrection, this fact of history
must have been seen as a continuing source of embarrassment
as the movement grew. Whilst a century earlier, when the sect
was small and insignificant, Paul could have unashamedly and

---

1. *Dial,* pp143-5

defiantly proclaimed the cross as 'foolishness' to the Greeks and a 'stumblingblock' to the Jews (1 Corinthians 1:23) the thought of a world-wide religion being based on an executed criminal was daunting. As Justin says 'We are accused of madness; because, as they say, we assign the second place, after the immutable and eternal God, the Creator of all things, to a crucified man'.[1] If however it could be shown to the Roman world that the Christian leader was one of the gods, an emanation from the divine mind, the pre-existent creator, then Christianity would become more reputable.

Justin and the Holy Spirit

Although the position of the Son was being defined during this period, the role of the Holy Spirit was less to the fore. It was still regarded as the power of God in action, often being referred to as 'the prophetic Spirit', that is, the Spirit that effected divine inspiration. Sometimes the writers of this period fail to distinguish between the Logos and the Spirit, even at times using the terms interchangeably. There is no hint of a personal, co-equal member of a trinity in this extract from Justin:

> 'We are not atheists, worshipping as we do, the Maker of this universe, ...offering up to him prayers and thanks ... And that we with reason honour Jesus Christ our teacher of these things and born for this end, .. receiving him as the son of the true God, and holding him in the second place, and the prophetic Spirit in third rank'.[2]

Here Justin clearly distinguishes between the 'worship' rendered to the Father, and the 'honour' given to the Son. In third rank was the Holy Spirit, the inspirer of the prophetic scriptures, and to reverence these writings was to honour the 'prophetic Spirit' that spoke through them. The modern Trinity is nowhere expressed here; indeed, worship of the Father, Son

---

1. *Apol.* I p.51

2. Ibid.

and Holy Spirit on equal terms is expressly excluded. Evidently the doctrine as we know it today was not the belief of Justin or his Christian contemporaries.

THEOPHILUS OF ANTIOCH

Soon after Justin's martyrdom Theophilus became bishop of Antioch. He is noteworthy for being the first to use the word 'trias', trinity, in reference to the Deity. But Theophilus was still a believer in the supremacy of God, and the Son as a creation of God, being produced 'before all things' from the reason (logos) of the Father. In fact an examination of the passage in which 'trias' is used shows that Theophilus was not attempting to describe a trinitarian relationship. He is indulging in what for many of the 'Fathers' was a favourite pastime— attempting to find 'types' of Christianity in the Old Testament record. Speaking of the Genesis record of the creation of the sun, moon and stars he says:

'In like manner, also, the three days which were before the luminaries, are types of the *triad* of God, and his word, and his wisdom. And the fourth is the type of man, who needs light, that so there may be God, the Word, Wisdom, Man. Wherefore on the fourth day the lights were made'.[1]

No unbiased reader would ever conclude from this that Theophilus believed in and was referring to the Trinity in its conventional sense.

IRENAEUS

The writings of Irenaeus in the closing years of the second century marked a consolidation of the opinions that eventually gave rise to the Trinity. In some ways Irenaeus took Justin's arguments a little further. Because he felt that the Logos doctrine of Justin gave rise to the criticism that he was preaching two separate Gods, Irenaeus in an attempt to emphasise the monotheism of God insisted that the Logos was inseparable

---

1. Ad Autol., 1. ii, c. 15.

from the Father, just as light is inseparable from the sun. To quote Leitzmann on this: 'God was entirely *nous*, entirely logos, entirely operative spirit, and entirely light, and anyone who separated one of these from God would make him a composite being.'[1] The question was 'How could God beget a Son and remain only one God?'. Irenaeus could not find a logical answer, and so resorted to saying that such things were unknowable by humans and not revealed in Scripture. Isaiah 53:8 was quoted in support: 'Who shall declare his generation?' Thus it seems that Irenaeus was the first to introduce the idea of an unknowable 'mystery' into the debate about God.

But the subordination of the Son to the Father is still not in doubt: Irenaeus says 'the Father is above all, and is himself the head of Christ'.[2] Thus with many such allusions he leaves us in no doubt that the co-equality of the Son with the Father was not part of his teaching. Rusch comments here:

> 'For Irenaeus the Son is fully divine. ... Still he is clearly a second-century theologian, as his picture of the Trinity discloses. There is a single personage, the Father, the Godhead itself, with his Word (reason) and his Wisdom. Not only is monotheism reaffirmed, but the real, eternal distinctions in the Godhead are stressed.[3]

Irenaeus also more closely defines the Holy Spirit, making an exact distinction between it and the Logos..

THE THIRD CENTURY
CLEMENT OF ALEXANDRIA
Alexandria was one of the greatest cities in the world. For centuries it had been a seat of learning: the fame of its philosophers rivalling that of Athens and Rome. Here was the

---

1. Vol. II, p.210.

2. Contra Her. 1, v. c, 18, para 2

3. Rusch, W.G. *The Trinitarian Controversy* p.7. Fortress Press, Philadelphia, 1986

greatest library of the ancient world, reputedly containing over four hundred thousand volumes. It was almost inevitable therefore that in Alexandria the real interface between Greek and Christian ideology should occur. Towards the end of the second century a Christian theological school was established in the city, where 'Christian ideas were handled in a free and speculative fashion and worked out with the help of Greek philosophy'.[1] In the early days of the third century the school was presided over by Clement, a man of great learning in both Greek culture and philosophy, and in Christian thought and ethics. Clement's achievement was not to further develop Christian theology,[2] but to make it more respectable in the eyes of the outside world. Many have commented on this:

> 'The crucial achievement of Clement and Origen was to put over the Gospel in terms by which it could be understood by people familiar with the highest forms of Greek culture. They established once for all the respectability of the new faith'.[3]

> 'He was the first to bring all the culture of the Greeks and the speculations of Christian heretics to bear on the exposition of Christian truth.'[4]

In Clement's view Plato and the other Greek philosophers were inspired by the Logos, although not to the same extent as the Hebrew prophets, with the objective of making the Gentile world receptive to Christ. For example he states:

> 'Philosophy ... educated the Greek world as the law did the Hebrews to bring them to Christ. Philosophy therefore is a

---

1. *Encyclopaedia Britannica,* Art, 'Origen'

2. 'Clement gives us no theory of the relation of the logos to the Father or to the Holy Spirit, nor any doctrine in regard to the nature of Christ's humanity' - Leitzmann, Vol. II p.294.

3. Lion Handbook, *The History of Christianity,* p.77

4. Encyclopaedia Britannica, Art. 'Clement of Alexandria'

preparation, making ready the way for him who is being perfected in Christ'.[1]

It will be seen that this is a radical departure from New Testament Christianity which had a different view of the 'wisdom of this world':

'Where is the wise man? Where is the scribe? Where is the debater of this age? Has not God made foolish the wisdom of the world? For since, in the wisdom of God, the world *did not know God through wisdom*, it pleased God through the folly of what we preach to save those who believe' (1 Corinthians 1:20-21).

As far as Clement's theology was concerned, he followed what had become the traditional approach, being influenced by thinkers such as Plato. For example, after quoting part of Plato's second 'Epistle' he comments:

'For myself, I cannot understand the meaning of this text except as referring to the Holy Trinity: for the third is the Holy Spirit, and the second the Son, by whom "all things were made" according to the Father's will'.[2]

Thus Rusch is certainly correct when he says:

'Clement presents in a Platonic framework an image of the Trinity which he linked with the Christian triad of Father, Son and Holy Spirit (*Who is the Rich Man That is Saved?* 34.1). Understandably, Clement's trinity, although Christian in character, has a strong resemblance to the triad of Neoplatonism, the One, Mind and World Soul'.[3]

---

1. *Stromateis*, 6.6.

2. *Stromateis*, 5.14

3. Rusch, p.12

But it is necessary to stress once more that, in common with Justin, Clement still regarded Christ as a created being. As Lamson says:

> 'None of the Platonising Fathers before Origen have acknowledged the inferiority of the Son in more explicit terms than Clement. Photius, writing in the ninth century, besides charging him with making the Son "a creature", says that he used "other impious words full of blasphemy".'[1]

Thus Clement's views on Christ—already more developed and different from the earlier Fathers— were later regarded as blasphemous by a Church which had adopted the Trinitarian formula.

TERTULLIAN

Tertullian lived about the same time as Clement, but westward along the North African coast at Carthage. He was the first Christian of note who wrote in Latin; and brought into common use the basic terms that were so vehemently discussed in the Arian controversy a century or so later. He coined the expression *trinitas* to denote Father, Son and Holy Spirit, and also the concepts of *persona* and *substantia*, which later were expressed as the 'three persons in one substance'. This was in response to criticism that the Christians were either worshipping two separate Gods, the Father and the Son, thus exposing themselves to the charge of polytheism; or teaching that there was no difference at all between them, and therefore God Himself actually suffered on the cross. He considered that the one divine 'substance' was shared between two 'persons': thus God is at the same time one or two depending on how He is viewed. But despite these attempts at explanation the rank and file Christians at this time regarded these speculations of their scholastic leaders as something new. As Lamson again says:

---

1. p.150.

'That the whole "logos doctrine", as it was called, was by many regarded as an innovation, clearly appears. Neander in his "Lectures on Christian Dogmas" notices what he calls a "Unitarian monotheistic interest" as manifesting itself about the time of Origen, or a little earlier. He quotes Tertullian as saying that "ignorant people" were "alarmed at the names of the Trinity, and accuse us (that is, the philosophical Christians) of wishing to teach three Gods, while they would be worshippers of one God.'[1]

It is salutary to thus learn that the doctrine which is regarded today as the mainspring of Christianity was rejected by many when it was first defined.

But whilst advocating a sort of unity in the Godhead, Tertullian at the same time decidedly retained the ideas of Justin concerning the pre-existence and creation of the Son, and his subordination to his Father.

One opinion of Tertullian, however, had a most potent legacy. Because many rank and file Christians were comparatively poorly educated and needed short and simple answers to their questions, he felt it better to appeal to the Rules of Faith and the Creeds than to Scripture. In this way the tradition and authority of the Church began to be put on a par with revelation, leading fairly swiftly to the dominance of the Church authority; so that it even made binding pronouncements on how Scripture should be interpreted. So for the past 1600 years or so the position has been that as described by this 19th century cleric: 'My belief in the Trinity is based on the authority of the Church: no other authority is sufficient'.[2]

ORIGEN
Origen was without doubt the most influential Christian scholar of the third century. Born of a Christian family in

---

1. p. 224.

2. Rev. J. Hughes, quoted by White, p.67.

Alexandria—that place where, as mentioned earlier, 'Christian ideas were handled in a free and speculative fashion and worked out with the help of Greek philosophy'[1]—he was a diligent student both of Scripture and philosophy. Although many of his views were repudiated by his contemporaries, and even more by later generations, the sheer industry with which he set about recording the results of his studies has bequeathed to him a reputation unequalled among early Christian writers. We are not here concerned with his many fanciful opinions which were later rejected by his fellow Christians, but only with his contribution to the definition of the Christian doctrine of God.

The tide of opinion concerning the Godhead which commenced its flow with Justin and Ignatius was now flowing strongly, and men such as Clement and especially Origen needed only to channel it into more clearly defined directions. Abbot says of this time:

'It is certain that what is called the "development" of Church dogmas was now very rapidly proceeding. As to the influence of "philosophy" upon this growth of Church opinion, it may be distinctly traced throughout the second century. ... In Clement and Origen this tendency received open encouragement ... '[2]

In confirmation of the accuracy of the last statement one only needs to turn to almost any writer who describes Origen's contribution to the debate about God. It is striking that although Origen professed to rely only on Biblical writings for his knowledge of divine things, in no case can one find recorded any reasoned *Scriptural* arguments of his on the topic. Instead later writers consistently allude to *philosophy* as the source of his concepts. The following are just a few of many representative samples of such comments on Origen, commen-

---

1. *Encyclopaedia Britannica*, Art. 'Origen'

2. Footnote on p.189 of Lamson

346

cing with Jerome, who belonged to the next generation or so after him:

> 'In this work (Stromateis) he compared the teaching of Christians and philosophers with one another, and demonstrated all the principles of our religion from Plato, Aristotle, Numenios, and Cornutus'.[1]

> 'Origen was the first to enter into the genuine tradition of the Platonic school, and both his intake and his output fully reflect the Platonic heritage which was alive in his day, and which was of increasing influence'.[2]

> 'As a philosophical idealist, however, he transmutes the whole contents of the faith of the church into ideas which bear the mark of Neo-Platonism'.[3]

> 'Origen tried to express the Christian faith in terms of the prevailing Platonic philosophical ideas of his time'.[4]

> 'This voluminous author, bible scholar, and theologian moved beyond Clement in constructing a theological system that weds the church's threefold understanding of God to the categories of Middle Platonism. Origen's imaginative work represents one of the most significant episodes in the history of theology'.[5]

There seems little doubt, then, as to the source of Origen's ideas about God. With reference to the last quotation one could legitimately enquire why, if the Apostles had laid down the elements of a faith 'which was once for all delivered to the

1. Jerome, Epist. 70,4,3

2. Leitzmann, Vol. II, p. 298

3. ibid.

4. Lion Handbook, p.103

5. Rusch, p.13.

saints' (Jude 3), Origen and his contemporaries needed to produce '*imaginative* work' on the 'threefold understanding of God'.

Origen's contribution to the debate was an attempt to develop further the ideas on the 'begettal' of the Son. Up to now the belief had been that the Son had been created by the Father at some remote but distinct time. In some of his writings Origen suggests that the begettal was a continuous process:

> 'Thus human thought cannot apprehend how the unbegotten God becomes the Father of the only-begotten Son. For it is an eternal and ceaseless generation, as radiance is generated from light.'[1]

Here Origen propounds the concept of *eternal generation,* and thus laid the foundation of the current Trinitarian view. Rawlinson says of this:

> 'His doctrine of the Eternal Generation of the Son by the Father is the great contribution of Alexandrine Platonism to the Christian Creed'. [2]

Origen's concept of the *eternal generation* of the Son was the basis of the Arian controversy to which we will come shortly. The main dispute centred around the origin of the Son. Was he a created or uncreated being? The *eternal generation* aspect of Origen's belief was appealed to by those who believed the Son had always existed. On the other hand the Arians protested that Origen quite definitely supported their time-honoured idea that the Son was subordinate to the Father. And this is true. He says that the Son and Spirit 'are excelled by the Father, as much, or more, than they excel other beings';[3] and that "The Father,

---

1. Extracted from *De Principiis.* I.2.3-6

2. A.E.J.Rawlinson. *Essays on the Trinity and Incarnation,* p.250

3. Comment in Joan, t, xiii, 25

who sent him (Jesus), is alone good, and *greater* than he who was sent';[1] 'prayer should be offered to God alone, definitely not to the Son, who had the office of High Priest and mediator;[2] and that 'Greater is the power of the Father than that of the Son and the Holy Spirit; and greater that of the Son than that of the Holy Spirit'.[3]

How the Church resolved these opposing views will become evident when we consider the Council of Nicea and later events; but for the moment we note that both sides claimed support from Origen, and also that in the middle of the third century the position of the Holy Spirit was considered to be inferior to both the Father and the Son.

It is also worth recalling in passing that philosophers considered man to be composed of three entities—a 'soul' that was pre-existent, a 'mind' and a 'body': a three-in-one relationship. We have already seen that the Platonic concept of the world soul, of which human souls were a part, had infiltrated into Jewish and then Christian thought. This led to the analogy that because man was made in the image of God so the Divine essence also *had* to be manifested in three aspects. Among others, Origen leaned to this view, which probably contributed considerably to the inclusion of the Holy Spirit as the third member of the Godhead.

ARTEMON, BERYLLUS, AND PAUL OF SAMOSATA

Before leaving the time of Origen three other personalities can contribute a little to our unravelling of the ebb and flow of ideas in these formative years of Church doctrine. All three claimed that Jesus did not personally pre-exist prior to his birth, and alleged that in this they were retaining the original faith. At the beginning of the third century Artemon—with other

---

1. ibid. t. vi,23

2. De Orat. 15

3. *De Princip.* 1,i, c.3,5

shadowy figures known mainly from the allusions by Eusebius— seems to have declared that Christ was born of a virgin by the power of the Holy Spirit. Of these that historian writes:

> 'They affirm that all the ancients, and the very Apostles, received and taught the same things which they now assert: and that the preaching of the truth was preserved till the times of Victor, who, from Peter, was the thirteenth Bishop of Rome; but, from the times of Zephryrinus, the truth has been adulterated'.[1]

So even in the middle of the third century some were still insisting on what they claimed was the old faith. The inference that this original faith was being modified by some in the third century is therefore very strong. We also know little about Beryllus, bishop of Bostra in Arabia, except that he too seems to have taught that Christ had no personal pre-existence before his appearance on earth, though while on earth the divinity of the Father dwelt in him. However, we do know that Origen converted him to what was by then the orthodox views of the *pre-existent* Logos.

The views of the third writer, Paul of Samosata, in the second half of the third century, are a little more defined. He believed that the Son did not always exist as a person, but did exist from all time *only* in the foreknowledge of God. Lamson describes them thus:

> 'He held that there was in the divine nature only one *hypostasis* or person; that Christ was man by nature, yet was higher than other men, as conceived by the Holy Spirit. He first began to exist when born of Mary. The divine Logos united itself with him, and dwelt in him as in no other sent of God, but did not, properly speaking, incarnate himself in him; it had no personal subsistence. The divine

---

1. Eusebius, 5,28.

Reason itself, the Wisdom or Power of God, revealed itself
in him, as it had never revealed itself in any other prophet.
So great was the illumination he hence received, and so was
his nature exalted by means of it, that he could with
propriety be called the Son of God.[1]

Hanson confirms that for Paul 'the Son was Jesus Christ the
historical figure *without any pre-existent history at all*'.[2] So
Chadwick comments that 'Paul's doctrine is akin to the
primitive Jewish/Christian idea of the person of Christ'.[3] Here
again we seem to be hearing the echoes of the original, non-
trinitarian, beliefs about the nature of Christ.

The question needs to be faced here that if the pre-existence
of the Son as the divine Logos and creator of the world had
been from the beginning an integral part of the Christian
message, it would be most unlikely that in the middle of the
third century some leading Christians (for Paul of Samosata had
a large following) would be propounding a doctrine that would
apparently degrade the leader of their movement into a mere
man. It would have been detrimental, if not fatal to the
Christian cause of converting the world from paganism. All the
prejudices and hostility of the those who believed in the majesty
of the gods would have been aroused. But the fact that in such
circumstances the doctrine *was* preached, and gained sufficient
foothold for Church councils to be called to denounce it,[4] is
strong presumption that the beliefs they were advancing were
indeed ancient, if not original.

As we conclude our brief review of the third century we note

---

1. Priestly, p.256.

2. p.71 - italics ours

3. p.114

4. At Antioch, A.D. 269-272 (These were the councils that also condemned
the use of the word *homoousia*, 'consubstantial' to describe the relationship
between the Father and Son: which term became orthodox after the Council
of Nice!).

that during it the Church, using the instrument of philosophy, had made great advances in its thinking about the Son, whilst still accepting his subordination; but at the same time there were considerable groups who regarded this progress as denying the original beliefs of the Apostolic Church.

THE FOURTH CENTURY

As we have seen, the first three centuries had been a period of intense examination and speculation concerning the nature of the Christian God. Jewish and Christian Scriptures, a considerable amount of pagan philosophy, a desire to make Christianity respectable, and a generous pinch of human pride, obstinacy and lust for power, had all been thrown into the furnace of controversy in an attempt to forge a credible concept of God. The fourth century saw the mould cracked open and the rough and unpolished outlines of the final shape emerge.

Two very different writers comment on the background to the development of the Trinity during this period:

'By the beginning of the fourth century it seemed that, though fixity of theological terminology had not yet been secured, the lines of interpretation of the person of Jesus Christ had been safely and firmly laid, and so the *development of doctrine* might quickly proceed, keeping pace with enlarged experience and able to meet new conditions as they arose. The old religions and the old philosophies of the world had contributed to the process of interpretation what they could.'[1]

'Even now, but for the commanding characters of the champions who espoused each party, the Trinitarian controversy might have been limited to a few provinces, and become extinct in some years. But it arose, not merely under the banners of men endowed with those abilities

---

1. J.F.Bethune-Baker, p.155 (italics ours).

which commanded the multitude; it not merely called into action the energies of successive disputants, the masters of the intellectual attainments of the age,—it appeared at a critical period, when the rewards of success were more splendid, the penalty upon failure proportionately more severe. The contest was not merely for superiority over a few scattered and obscure communities, it was agitated on a larger theatre, that of the Roman world, the proselytes whom it disputed were sovereigns; it contended the supremacy of the human mind, which was now bending to the yoke of Christianity. It is but judging on the common principle of human nature to conclude, that the grandeur of the prize supported the ambition and inflamed the passion of the contending parties, that human motives of political power and aggrandisement mingled with the more spiritual influences of the love of truth, and zeal for the purity of religion.[1]

Such language, from historians with avowed Trinitarian sympathies, gives us little cause for confidence in the outcome of the discussions that centred around the definition of the Father/Son relationship during this period. Social pressures, philosophical arguments, personal prestige and political necessity took precedence over biblical truth.

This century also saw the establishment of Neoplatonism, which greatly influenced many of the decisions of the Church relating to the Godhead. As always, we say this on the basis of independent, often Trinitarian, authorities:

'Christian Neoplatonism ..... flourished from the fourth century onward. Its origins can be traced back to the second and third centuries AD. Clement and Origen of Alexandria understood Christian revelation in Platonic terms. Combining the teaching of Origen and Platinus, Christian Neoplatonists fashioned a distinct Neoplatonism.

---

1. Millman, Vol. II p.357

Culling from philosophy and from the Bible, they erected a Platonic interpretation that lasted through the Christian Middle Ages. Specifically based on a close reading of the Bible and Plato, their contributions to Neoplatonism's legacy were theological. The Trinitarian doctrines of Marius Victorinus and Augustine are based on Porphyry's interpretation of the unity of substance between the three divine hypostases.[1]

And of the Arian theology which caused so much dispute in this century we read:

'This (Arian) theology is a skillful and original blend of the biblical concern with a freely creating personal God and the philosophical concern with the preservation of the pure singularity of the primal monad. This latter theme was becoming increasingly important in the philosophy of the day, as Neoplatonism gradually took shape, blending Platonic language and cosmology with Aristotelian logic and elements from Pythagorean numerology. We hear of Alexandrine Christians who had interests in all these areas; and it was known that Plotinus, father of Neoplatonism, had studied under the same teacher as the great Origen.[2]

So, in this rather contentious environment, and on the basis of contribution by the old philosophies, the Church set out on its task of conquering the world; and the 'development' of its teaching on Christ was a crucial element in its armoury.

In the early years of this century Christianity suddenly found itself respectable. Constantine became Emperor and declared the once hated faith to be the official religion. But if he thereby hoped to consolidate and unify the empire under his hand he was soon rudely surprised. For with his ascent to the purple he also inherited the controversy about the nature of God that had

---

1. *Encyclopedia of Early Christianity,* Art. 'Neoplatonism'

2. Ibid, Art. 'Arianism'

been simmering for decades, and was now coming to the boil. In Alexandria bishop Alexander expressed views about the God/Christ relationship that were opposed by Arius, one of his presbyters. The resultant conflict threatened the peace and integrity of the empire and so, for the first time, a civil ruler in the person of the Emperor became involved in formulating Church dogma.

As we have already seen, up to this period all the 'Fathers' of the church had accepted the subordination of the Son to the Father.[1] This view continued to be held by Arius. In his 'Thalia', quoted by Athanasius, he expresses it thus: 'God was not always a Father, but there was a time when God was alone, and was not yet Father: the Son was not always ... the Word of God was made out of nothing, and once he was not : he was not before he was begotten'.[2] Wright summarises his views in language refreshingly free from the jargon of those times. "Arius claimed that the Father alone was really God; the Son was essentially different from the Father. He did not possess by nature or right any of the divine qualities of immortality, sovereignty, perfect wisdom, goodness and purity. He did not exist before he was begotten by the Father. The Father produced him as a creature. Yet as the creator of the rest of creation, the Son existed 'apart from time before all things'. Nevertheless he did not share in the being of God the Father

---

1. Lamson: "They occasionally make use of a phraseology, which, in the mouth of a modern Trinitarian, would imply a belief that the Son is of one numerical essence with the Father. But this they never thought of asserting. The most they meant to affirm was that the Son, as begotten of God, partook in some sort of the specific nature (that is, a divine), just as an individual of our race partakes of the same nature or essence with the parent from whom he sprung (that is, a human). At the same time they taught that he was relatively inferior to the Father from whom he was derived, and entitled to only inferior homage". p.284. Hanson: "There is no theologian in the Eastern or Western church before the outbreak of the Arian controversy, who does not in some sense regard the son as subordinate to the Father", p64. ."Many ... could not ... abandon completely a subordinationism that had been hallowed by long tradition", p274.

2. Orat. i. contra Arian, 5

and did not know him perfectly".[1] It is noteworthy, and exceptional, to find that Arius appealed to Scripture in defence of his claims—something comparatively rare in all the convoluted writings of those times. As Wright continues: 'He had a sharply logical mind and appealed to Biblical texts which apparently backed up his arguments—for example, John 17.3 ('the only true God'), 1 Timothy 6:16 ('alone possesses immortality'), Colossians 1:15 ('first-born of all creation') and Proverbs 8:22 (in the *Septuagint,* 'the Lord created me at the beginning of his work').[2]

All this was anathema to Alexander, and to Athanasius his successor as bishop of Alexandria. For them, making Christ a secondary divine being was to deny his divinity. If the Son was divine—as both Arius and Alexander believed he was—then he had to be divine in exactly the same sense as the Father. This necessitated his pre-existence with the Father from all time. To suggest that 'there was a time when he was not' was, in their view, to deny the very fundamentals of Christianity.

Finding life intolerable in Alexandria, Arius moved to the more liberal Palestine from where he wrote a letter to Alexander claiming that the Arians were only preaching the established traditional views. Alexander, meanwhile, was busy sending to all parts acrimonious[3] letters warning the bishops against Arius and his opinions. This war of words increased, with numerous letters exchanged by both sides. The effect on the Church was predictable. Contention filled the churches, factions developed, passions were inflamed, until the whole empire was affected.[4] 'They fought against each other', says

---

1. D.F. Wright, *The History of Christianity*, p.156. Lion.

2. ibid, p157

3. The Arians were "enemies of Christ", "apostates", "all preceding heresies appear in comparison innocent". Theodoret, Hist. 1.i.e.6.

4. Stanley reports that the controversy was 'carried to a pitch beyond any bounds which faith or wisdom could reasonably sanction'. *History of the Eastern Church*, Lect. II, p.61.

Theodoret, 'with their tongues instead of spears'.[1] Even the pagans were outraged by this behaviour, and their theatres echoed to the ridicule of the Christians.[2]

Looking at the dispute with the advantages of hindsight it appears that the ultimate losers—the Arians—had the more reasonable position. As Wiles says in a recent work:

'A very different perspective on Arianism, which has been put forward occasionally by rebel spirits in the past, is beginning to establish itself as the consensus view of modern scholars. ... Earlier Christians had not raised explicitly the precise question which was now the issue of contention between the two sides. Traditional ways of speaking about the divinity of the Son were ambivalent at best; on balance they stood somewhat nearer to that of the Arians than of the orthodox (i.e. his opponents). Either side could, and both sides did, claim with some plausibility that the witness of earlier tradition was in their own favour. But neither claim (particularly that of the orthodox) is as convincing or as decisive as they claimed it to be. *Both sides were innovating* in a way they were quite unprepared to admit. But on balance it was the Arian heretics who were the more conservative, the orthodox who were the more innovative'[3]

This confirms that later developments involved a *moving away* from the previously established position, not a reinforcing of it.

THE COUNCIL OF NICEA
Constantine, worried about the effect of this dispute on the peace of the empire, tried to smooth out the differences, and in a letter to Alexander asks him to restore harmony. But

---

1. Ibid

2. Eusebius, Vita Const., 1. ii. c. 61

3. M.Wiles. Chapter on 'Orthodoxy and Heresy' p.205 in *Early Christianity*, Ed. Hazlet. (italics ours)

Alexander was inflexible and Arius would not retract. In an attempt to end the controversy and to preserve the peace of his empire Constantine in the year 325 summoned a general Church council at Nicea, within easy reach of his residence at Nicomedia on the Bosphorus in modern Turkey. Probably over 300 (but some say 220) bishops attended, the vast majority being from the Eastern churches. Of these a few were committed Arians, a few supported Alexander, whilst the great majority had no particular loyalty to either view.[1]

Few particulars of the council survive, but those that are available are not such as give immense confidence in the outcome of the debate, crucial as it was to the history of the church—indeed a turning point of that history.[2] Eusebius the historian attended the Council in his capacity as the bishop of Caesarea, and from his *Life of Constantine*—undoubtedly a panegyric written as an obituary, but useful for some historical data—we can reconstruct some of the events. The Emperor, seated on a stool rather than a throne, presided over a debate which initially was characterised by not a little acrimony and personal abuse, and he did all he could to preserve peace and unity.[3] The representatives even sent to him written accusations about their colleagues. To his credit he collected all these and publicly burnt them unopened, telling the bishops that they must await the judgment of the One on high.

During the following discussion the 18 Arian supporters[4] presented a draft creed for consideration, but it was met with intense disapproval and the document even torn in pieces by their opponents. Eusebius of Caesarea, in an attempt at compromise, then submitted the Creed of his own church. This

---

1. See, e.g. *Encyclopaedia Britannica* Art. 'Nicea, Council of'

2. As Stanley says, it must be remembered that 'they (the Councils) were assemblies of fallible men, swayed by the good and evil influences to which all assemblies are exposed' - Lect. II p.70

3. Stanley op.cit. p120

4. Theod. i 6.

was approved by the Emperor, but was sufficiently non-controversial to be also accepted by the Arians. This was enough to present a fatal difficulty, for the opposition were determined to find a form of words that the Arians could *not* endorse. Much discussion ensued, when many terms to describe the God/Christ relationship were rejected. At last a letter from a prominent Arian was produced. In it the writer had stated that to say that the Son was of *one substance* or *consubstantial* (Gk. *homoousion*) with the Father was a proposition the Arians could not accept.

This was just what Alexander and his party wanted. If this term could be included the battle would be won! In the interests of peace and unanimity Constantine (no doubt after suitable representations from Alexander's party) suggested the inclusion into the Caesarean Creed the Alexandrine phrase 'of the substance (*homoousion*) of the Father'. Eventually this was approved—with a certain amount of reluctance by some, and from a variety of motives[1]—by almost all the Council, and so became an obligatory article of faith: all who believed otherwise suffering the condemnation of the Church. The Creed of Nicea, before it was later modified to form the more familiar Nicene Creed, read thus:

> We believe in one God, the Father Almighty, Maker of all things and invisible.

> And in one Lord Jesus Christ, the Son of God, begotten of the Father, only begotten, that is to say, of the substance of the Father, God of God, Light of Light, very God of very God, begotten not made, being of one substance with the

---

1. Many commentators on this Council have suggested that fear of offending the Emperor, or dread of the influential Bishop of Alexandria, or the fact that this final formula was sufficiently ambiguous to accommodate a wide variety of consciences, played a part in their agreement to support the Creed. Also in Encyc. Brit. Art. 'Nicea': 'We are compelled to the conclusion that ... the voting was no criterion of the inward convictions of the Council'; and Moeller: 'The majority of the Greek bishops only agreed against their wills, out of regard to the Emperor'. p.383.

Father, by whom all things were made, both things in heaven and things in earth—who for us men and for our salvation came down and was made flesh, and was made man, suffered, and rose again on the third day; went up into the heavens, and is to come again to judge the quick and the dead.

And in the Holy Ghost.

But those that say, "there was when He was not", and "before He was begotten He was not", or who profess that the Son of God is a different "person" or "substance", or that he is created, or changeable, or variable, are anathematised by the Catholic Church.

Thus Trinitarianism, largely as we know it today, became official Church doctrine. Despite the respect that later ages have accorded to this Council, it was very unsatisfactory in many particulars. By his overriding desire for peace and unity Constantine, probably unintentionally, had introduced a new doctrine into the Church. As one writer says of the clauses he inserted: 'That he appreciated the importance of these alterations, or realised that this revision was virtually the proclamation of a new doctrine, is scarcely probable'.[1] The Arians protested, quite rightly, against the introduction of the non-Scriptural *homoousion* in relation to Christ. And the majority saw in the insertion of this term into the new creed an accommodation to almost any interpretation.[2]

It is probably easier to understand the Greek word

---

1. *Encyclopaedia Britannica*, Art: 'Nicea'

2. Neander, vol. II, pp.377-378. Person says: 'As it stands, the *homoousios* can be read either as an affirmation of the divine unity or as an affirmation of the equal deity of the Son, and it is difficult in the light of theological discussions which took place prior to the Council to believe that the ambiguity was accidental'. Mode of Decision-Making, p.105

homoousia[1] if it is split into its components, *homo* and *ousia*. *Homo* means 'the same as', but *ousia* has a wide range of meaning. It can mean 'substance', or an 'entity' or 'person', or 'man' in a generic sense, or simple 'matter'. Ambiguity was built into the word. Kelly says of it: 'There are few words in Greek susceptible of so many and so confusing shades of meaning. .... The precise meaning of *ousia* varied with the philosophical context in which it occurred and the philosophical allegiance of the writer'.[2] In the works of the Neoplatonists the combined word *homoousia* is often used as a technical expression. By this term the Nicea Creed sought to teach that the *essence* of the Father and Son was identical, although their *personalities* were different. In this way they attempted to preserve the numerical unity of the Godhead, whilst admitting the plurality of the composition. But it must be remembered that essentially the Creed was not an attempt at an all-embracing definition of the Godhead, but a calculated anti-Arian document[3] designed to quash the idea that the Son was a created being and therefore inferior to the Father.[4] Incidentally, the word *homoousia* had previously been condemned by the Council of Antioch in 264 as being heretical; but times had changed!

AFTER THE COUNCIL OF NICEA
With Nicea Constantine's attempt to unite Christianity appeared to have succeeded. Because of the ambiguity in the application of the meaning of 'consubstantial' (*homoousia*) even Arians were able to demonstrate their orthodoxy and came back in

---

1. For a more detailed consideration of these terms see Appendix 2 to this chapter.

2. J.N.D.Kelly, *Early Christian Creeds,* p.243

3. "We have already seen that According to Anthanasius N (the Nicene formula) was constructed as a deliberately anti-Arian document. Indeed, we do not need Athanasius to tell us so. Its consciously anti-Arian tone is unmistakable", Hanson, p.164

4. 'The issue at Nicea was the Son's co-eternity with the Father, not the unity of the Godhead'. - Rusch, p.20

favour at court and were tolerated within the church. But it was very much a case of papering over the cracks, and it was not long before the weaknesses of the Creed of Nicea became apparent. Rusch comments on this period:

> 'At the Council the emperor himself had spoken, and no one in the emperor's lifetime moved against his creed. In a real sense the council was the product of the emperor. The Council of Nicea was invited by the emperor. Meetings and doctrinal discussions were in his hands. A new chapter in church and state relations had opened. The differing interpretations of what the council was teaching may have been an advantage initially, for with imperial pressure all but two bishops finally subscribed to the creed. But with the passing of time and the removal of Constantine from the scene, Nicea's lack of clarity became a weakness'.[1]

The next emperor, Constantius, intervened in the dispute, and, mainly for political reasons, tried to resolve the disagreement. He supported the Arians, and it was left to Athanasius, who had attended Nicea as a young deacon but was now bishop of Alexandria, to defend the Nicean faith.[2] Gradually the Arians lost ground, although their beliefs persisted in some quarters for another three centuries. Later at the Council of Constantinople in the year 381 Basil of Caesarea, Gregory of Nazianzus and Gregory of Nyssa— known as the 'Cappadocian Fathers', devised a formula which reconciled most of the objections. At the same time more prominence was given to the deity of the Holy Spirit. As the anathemas (against those that say "there was when He was not") appended in 325 at the end of the Creed of Nicea no longer applied they were removed, giving the basis of the present Nicene Creed. As Rusch again says: 'At Constantinople a coherent doctrine of God ... was achieved. Refinements and nuances of thought were yet to occur, but the trinitarian

---

1. p.20

2. Chadwick, pp.141-151 gives a good detailed account of this period.

controversy had ended'.[1]

It just remained to make the belief universal. This was done, not by widespread discussion within the Christian community at large; not even by an appeal by the Church leaders for the flock to rally behind them; but by Imperial decree. Gibbon records that the Emperor Theodosius, immediately after his baptism, on 28th February 380, issued an edict compelling all his subjects to believe in the Trinity on pain of severe penalty:

> 'It is our pleasure that all the nations which are governed by our clemency and moderation should steadfastly adhere to the religion which was taught by St Peter to the Romans .... According to the discipline of the apostles, and the doctrine of the Gospel, let us believe the sole deity of the Father, the Son, and the Holy Ghost, under an equal majesty and a pious Trinity. We authorise the followers of this doctrine to assume the title of Catholic Christians; and we do judge that all others are extravagant madmen, we brand them with the infamous name of Heretics, and declare that their conventicles shall no longer usurp the respectable appellation of churches. Besides the condemnation of Divine justice, they must expect to suffer the severe penalties which our authority, guided by heavenly wisdom, shall think proper to inflict upon them'.[2]

Here for the first time a civil ruler lays down the conditions for Christian orthodoxy and threatens the use of the power of the state against all who do not agree. A far cry from the original simplicity and democracy of the early Church! And Theodosius was as good as his word. A stream of further edicts against those he termed heretics issued from the imperial throne during the next fifteen years. Gibbon says that these were directed especially against 'those who rejected the doctrine of

---

1. p.24.

2. *Decline and Fall*, ch. 27.

the Trinity'[1] and consisted of heavy fines, exclusion from office, closing of meeting places with any building or ground used by them for worship being forfeited to the state, and if none of these prompted the return of the wanderers to the fold, the capital penalty was enacted. It was Theodosius who first instigated official *Inquisitors of the Faith*—a term that later struck terror into the hearts of many a devout believer. It is as well that the earlier 'Fathers' of the Church had passed away, for their beliefs would have easily qualified them for these penalties. But such was the price of 'progress'!

THE TRINITY IN THE WEST

The Eastern Church had been the main arena of the conflict over the relationship between God and Christ over the preceding centuries. The West had only sent a few delegates to the Council of Nicea. The Latin speaking Tertullian had already made a contribution to this debate, but it was left to Augustine of Hippo in N. Africa to champion the doctrine in the West. He was influenced by Neoplatonism, especially the Christian Neoplatonist Victorinus who lived in Rome. Using these resources he produced his treatise *On the Trinity* in which he 'brought Western trinitarian thought to new heights of theological reflection'.[2]

The Athanasian Creed

For most Christians, in the West at least, the one creed that defines the Trinity is the Athanasian Creed. With its formation, alongside the already establish Apostles' and Nicene creeds, the three major creeds of the Western Church were now in place. For full impact it is here given in its entirety:

> 'Whosoever will be saved: before all things it is necessary that he hold the Catholick Faith.
> Which Faith except every one do keep whole and undefiled: without doubt he shall perish everlastingly.

---

1. *Decline and Fall*, ch. 27.

2. Rusch, p.25

And the Catholick Faith is this: That we worship one God in Trinity, and Trinity in Unity;

Neither confounding the Persons: nor dividing the Substance.

For there is one Person of the Father, another of the Son: and another of the Holy Ghost.

But the Godhead of the Father, of the Son, and of the Holy Ghost, is all one: the Glory equal, the Majesty co-eternal.

Such as the Father is, such is the Son: and such is the Holy Ghost.

The Father uncreate, the Son uncreate: and the Holy Ghost uncreate.

The Father incomprehensible, the Son incomprehensible, and the Holy Ghost incomprehensible.

The Father eternal, the Son eternal: the Holy Ghost eternal.

And yet there are not three eternals: but one eternal.

As also there are not three incomprehensibles, nor three uncreated: but one uncreated, and one incomprehensible.

So likewise the Father is Almighty, the Son Almighty: and the Holy Ghost Almighty.

And yet there are not three Almighties: but one Almighty.

So the Father is God, the Son is God: and the Holy Ghost is God.

And yet they are not three Gods: but one God.

So likewise the Father is Lord, the Son Lord: and the Holy Ghost Lord.

And yet not three Lords: but one Lord.

For like as we are compelled by the Christian verity to acknowledge every Person by himself to be God and Lord:

So we are forbidden by the Catholick Religion to say: There be three Gods, or three Lords.

The Father is made of none: neither created, nor begotten.

The Son is of the Father alone: not made, nor created, but begotten.

The Holy Ghost is of the Father and of the Son: neither made, nor created, nor begotten, but proceeding.

So there is one Father, not three Fathers; one Son, not three Sons; one Holy Ghost, not three Holy Ghosts.

And in this Trinity none is afore, or after other: none is greater, or less than another:

But the whole three Persons are co-eternal together: and co-equal.

So that in all things, as it is aforesaid; the Unity in Trinity, and the Trinity in Unity is to be worshipped.

He therefore that will be saved: must thus think of the Trinity.

Furthermore, it is necessary to everlasting salvation: that he also believe rightly in the Incarnation of our Lord Jesus Christ.

For the right Faith is, that we believe and confess: that our Lord Jesus Christ, the Son of God, is God and Man;

God, of the Substance of the Father, begotten before the worlds: and Man, of the Substance of his Mother, born in the world;

Perfect God, and perfect Man: of a reasonable soul and human flesh subsisting;

Equal to the Father, as touching his Godhead: and inferior to the Father, as touching his Manhood.

Who although He be God and Man: yet he is not two, but one Christ;

One; not by conversion of the Godhead into flesh: but by taking of the Manhood into God;

One altogether; not by confusion of Substance: but by unity of Person.

For as the reasonable soul and flesh is one man: so God and Man is one Christ;

Who suffered for our salvation:

Descended into hell',

Rose again the third day from the dead.

He ascended into heaven, he sitteth on the right hand of the Father, God Almighty:

From whence he shall come to judge the quick and the dead.

At whose coming all men shall rise again with their bodies: and shall give account for their own works.

And they that have done good shall go into life everlasting: and they that have done evil into everlasting fire.

This is the Catholick Faith: which except a man believe faithfully, he cannot be saved'

Because of the name of the creed it is commonly assumed that it is the work of Athanasius, bishop of Alexandria (c298-373), who so vehemently opposed Arianism, and thus it expresses comparatively early Christian teaching. This is not so. The creed is unknown in the Eastern Church, to which Athanasius belonged. No mention of it occurs until the sixth century, and some of these writings are of doubtful authenticity; and it did not come into general use until after the seventh century. Its author remains anonymous. It did not, like the Nicene creed, arise from a Church council, nor was it, as far as is known, a response to a particular situation that had developed.

One could hardly have a better example of how the simple Apostolic faith had been elaborated. Twelve simple words is all that the 'Apostles creed needed to express the original beliefs about God. The Athanasian creed uses 372. Similarly 21 words define the original belief about Jesus, whilst 157 are required later.

But whatever might be justifiably said about its contents in comparison with the simple teaching of Scripture and the primitive faith of the earliest Christians as revealed in the 'Apostles' creed, its *dogmatism* stands out prominently. The abstruse speculations of philosophy blended with religion have now become *compulsory beliefs* without which salvation is impossible: 'Whosoever will be saved .. it *is necessary* that he hold the Catholick Faith' ... 'He that will be saved, *must* thus think ... ' 'This is the Catholick Faith: which *except a man believe faithfully, he cannot be saved*'. The trend first noticed in Tertullian has now matured. The Church has become greater than Scripture, and allegiance to the Church and its officers is the criterion for divine acceptance. Ambrose (339-397) reflected this attitude when he said 'Nothing can be found in this world more exalted than priests or more sublime than bishops'. As one more modern clerical writer puts it:

'In one sense, then, the Athanasian creed marks a climax. It puts the claim of dogma amazingly high. Though it has not forgotten that Christ is to "judge ... all men ... according to their own works", orthodoxy is "before all things necessary". ... One understands the motives at work; but it is not with God that "we have to do", still less with conscience, but with—the Church. There is no shadow of excuse in the theory for dissent from Church teaching. Ignorance is encouraged; bad mistakes are excused; but *submission* is exacted to the uttermost.[1]

Thus the net of domination of the Church over the minds of its members was drawn tighter.

THE DEITY OF THE HOLY SPIRIT

The history of the development of the doctrine of the deity of the Holy Spirit must make difficult reading for those who contend that the Trinity as believed today was an original article of the Christian Faith. For the first three centuries minds were so concentrated on the position of the Son that the place of the Holy Spirit in the alleged trinity was almost ignored. And this was not because, as some claim, that the deity of the Holy Spirit was 'taken for granted'. The early Rules of Faith and the Old Roman creed down to the more elaborate Nicea creed contain nothing that in any sense would indicate separate personality of the Holy Spirit or its equality with God. It was regarded as subordinate to God, and usually thought of only as the power of God. In both creeds is the simple assertion "I believe in the Holy Spirit", which defines or explains nothing. Had the Fathers believed that the Holy Spirit was a person co-equal and consubstantial with the Father, why did they not say so? The omission is the more striking when we remember that at Nicea the consubstantiality of the Son was the subject of debate, and the creed formulated to express their findings. Why exclude the Spirit from the same discussion if it too was so intimately involved?

We have already noted (p. 339) that Justin about the year 150

---

1. R.Mackintosh, in *Encyclopaedia Britannica,* Art, Dogmatic Theology

placed the 'Prophetic Spirit in third rank'. That this view was
the consistent one is shown by many references from the early
Fathers, from whom we learn that the lower rank of the Holy
Spirit was asserted well into the fifth century. Bishop Huet
confesses that 'so late as the time of Basil' (late 4th century)
'and still later, the Catholics dared not openly acknowledge the
divinity of the Spirit'.[1] And Neander writes of this same Basil
that though he 'wished to teach the divinity of the Holy Spirit in
his church, he only ventured to introduce it gradually'.[2]
Another of the 'Cappadocian Fathers', Gregory of Nazianzus,
who was one of the earliest advocates of the divinity of the
Holy Spirit, expresses the uncertainty of the Church in his day
on the matter. Writing about the year 380 he said 'Some of our
theologians regard the Spirit simply as a mode of divine
operation: others, as a creature (i.e. creation) of God; others as
God himself; others, again, say that they know not which of
these opinions to accept, from their reverence for Holy Writ,
which says nothing upon it'.[3] These facts are completely
inexplicable if it is supposed that the doctrine of the Trinity was
the original belief of the Church. As Hanson says:

> "When we examine the creeds and confessions of faith
> which were so plentifully produced between the years 325
> and 360, we gain the overwhelming impression that no
> school of thought during that period was particularly
> interested in the Holy Spirit".[4]

How then did the position change to make the Holy Spirit a
third and co-equal member of the Trinity? It seems, at first at
least, not to have been the result of a positive decision: rather
the deity of the Holy Spirit came in on the back of the decision
to give the Son complete equality with the Father. The

---

1. Origiana, 1. ii. c. 2.

2. *History of Christian Dogmas*, pp.303-5

3. Ibid

4. Hanson, p.741

following extract summarises the process:

> 'During the ante-Nicene period there is no settled "Doctrine of the Holy Spirit": thought on the subject is fluid and unformed. At the Council of Nicea (325) it is significant that whilst the Father and the Son receive careful and elaborate definition, there is but bare mention of the Holy Spirit in third place without any definition at all. But when the *homoousia* (identity of nature with the Father) of the Son had been successfully asserted in the Arian controversy, the results were transferred, without any corresponding discussion, to the Holy Spirit, as the third *hypostasis* of the Godhead (Synod of Alexandria, 362).[1]

Thus the Holy Spirit, almost by default as it were, became 'God the Holy Spirit'. Later Athanasius pressed for official recognition of the deity of the Holy Spirit:

> 'Another achievement of Athanasius was to bring the Holy Spirit into the centre of reflection and to insist on his full divinity'[2]

THE COUNCIL OF CONSTANTINOPLE

The formal creeds soon acknowledged the change. The Council of Constantinople (381), was attended by only 150 bishops, but they were "carefully chosen from areas which would be friendly to Meletius, who was its president".[3] Following the initial leadership of Gregory and the other Cappadocians, this council produced the almost final version of the Nicene creed, which elaborated the mention of the Holy Spirit. Instead of a brief reference to its existence, the Spirit was now 'the Lord, and Giver of life, Who proceedeth from the Father through the Son, Who with the Father and Son together is worshipped and

---

1. *Encyclopaedia Britannica,* Art: Holy Spirit

2. *Encycopedia of Early Christianity,* Art: Trinity

3. Hanson, p806

glorified, Who spake by the prophets'. It is significant that this insertion did not gain immediate recognition by many of the churches. Hanson comments that it was a development 'made in the teeth of the witness of Scripture'[1], and Du Pin says that 'This creed was not at first received by all churches, and there were some that would add nothing to the Nicene Creed. For this cause it was, perhaps, that no other creed but that of Nicea was read in the Council of Ephesus (the third general council, A.D. 431); and there it was forbidden to make use of any other'.[2] But gradually the new views were accepted, and the next few decades saw the Holy Spirit, which previously had been regarded as subordinate to the Father, now becoming a co-equal Being, part of the Eternal Trinity. This new view filtered quickly through the Christian world. One fifth-century writer records that the monks of Antioch abandoned the usual chant of 'Glory be to the Father, *through* the Son, *in* the Holy Spirit', and replaced it with 'Glory be to the Father, and the Son, and to the Holy Spirit', as is familiar to many worshippers today.[3]

Historians have not been kind to the Council of Constantinople, at which the tri-unity and equality of Father, Son and Holy Spirit was finally accepted. Speaking of the decree on the equal Deity of the Holy Spirit, Gibbon says:

'The sober evidence of history will not allow much weight to the personal authority of the Fathers of Constantinople. In an age when ecclesiastics had scandalously degenerated from the model of apostolic purity, the most worthless and corrupt were always the most eager to frequent and disturb the episcopal assemblies. The conflict and fermentation of so many opposite interests and tempers inflamed the bishops: and their ruling passions were, the love of gold

---

1. p.875

2. Hist. Eccles., Vol. II, p. 272

3. Reported by Philostorgius, Hist, 1. iii, c, 13.

and the love of dispute'.[1]

Gibbon goes on to say that this description was not the report of an infidel anxious to denigrate Christians, but the assessment of one of the actual participants in the Council. As an example of the partisan spirit of that synod one can cite the case of Gregory of Nazianzus, who was chosen president on the death of Meletius, but had to step down because of the factional politics of the delegates. Of this Hanson records:

"Gregory's tenure of the presidency of the council cannot have endured long, though it was enough to render him disgusted with such assemblies for the rest of his life. This is how he describes the response of the council to his arguments on behalf of appointing Paulinus (as president):
'I finished my speech; but they squawked in every direction, a flock of jackdaws combining together, a rabble of adolescents, a gang of youths, a whirlwind raising dust under the pressure of air currents, people to whom nobody who was mature either in the fear of God or in years would pay any attention, they splutter confused stuff or like wasps rush directly at what is in front of their faces'.
Even this is not one of his most ferocious utterances about councils."[2]

The council then elected an unbaptised layman to take charge of the proceedings, after rapidly ordaining him as a bishop. It was against such a background that decisions on what proved to be the faith of the Church for the next 1600 years was reached! Again the Emperor issued an edict making the findings of the Council of Constantinople binding on all:

"We now order that all churches are to be handed over to the bishops who profess Father, Son and Holy spirit of a

---

1. Decline and Fall, ch. 27.

2. Hanson, p809

single majesty, of the same glory, of one splendour, who
establish no difference by sacrilegious separation, but the
order of the Trinity by recognising the persons and uniting
the Godhead ... Anyone who refuses to communicate with
these (bishops) is declared to be an heretic and is to be
refused office in the church".[1]

This brief description of the Council of Constantinople gives
an insight into the final formation of the doctrine of the Trinity
that few of its present day adherents are aware of. It does not
make happy reading or give the reader much confidence in the
outcome of the deliberations. Yet the whole doctrinal
foundation of the present church was laid in councils such as
these—councils to which history has accorded a sanctity and
veneration that is scarcely deserved.

Another feature of the development of the doctrine of the
Trinity that should not be overlooked is the involvement of the
Emperor in the formulation and enforcement of the new beliefs.
We have already seen that the Council of Nicea was convened
by Constantine, and all later progress was carefully watched
and controlled by his successors. In the end the result of the
deliberations reflected his decisions.

'If we ask the question, what was considered to be the
ultimate authority in doctrine during the period ... there can
only be one answer. The will of the Emperor was the final
authority. When Constantius is represented as saying
brusquely to the pro-Nicenes at Milan who alleged that he
was transgressing ecclesiastical law, "But what I wish, that
must be regarded as the canon" he summarises a situation
which did in fact prevail over most of this time'.[2]

Although in practice the Emperor could not enforce his will
on a majority that did not agree with him, the involvement of

---

1. Theodosius: *Episcopi tradi*, July 381

2. Hanson, p849

civil rulers in the determination of Christian doctrine allegedly essential for salvation would have been anathema to earlier generations, especially to original Christians.

Whilst it is not strictly relevant to our study, it may be of interest to note that it was ideas about the Holy Spirit which contributed to the separation of the Greek and Latin Churches. The orthodox view in the East was that the Spirit proceeded *from* the Father *through* the Son. But in the Third Council of Toledo, in Spain, in the year 589, the Holy Spirit was regarded as proceeding from *both* the Father and the Son. This 'double procession of the Spirit' although not at first accepted by all in the Western Church, eventually was a major cause of the rift that to this day separates the Roman Catholic Church from the Greek Orthodox Church.

THE LATER CENTURIES

The fifth century saw a consolidation of the new doctrines concerning God. In noting this Mosheim goes on to describe how the original simple Christian faith was now actually derided:

'In the controversies which in this century agitated nearly all Christendom, many points of theology were more fully explained and more accurately defined, than they had been before. Thus it was with the doctrine of *Christ*, his person and natures ... For that *devout and venerable simplicity of the first ages of the church*, which made men believe when God speaks, and obey when he commands, was thought by the chief doctors of this age to be *only fit for clowns.*'[1]

In his record of the next century Mosheim is even more severe, saying that 'the barriers of ancient simplicity and truth being once torn up, there was a constant progress for the

---

1. Eccles. Hist. Book II, Cent v., ch.3 (italics ours).

worse'.[1] It is therefore difficult to disagree with the verdict of Macaulay when he commented: 'In the fifth century Christianity had conquered paganism, and paganism had conquered Christianity. The Church was now victorious—and corrupt'.[2] During the next few centuries the controversy over the Trinity subsided and the doctrine soon became an unchallenged dogma of both the Eastern and Western Churches. With the spread of Christianity into areas where Greek and Latin were not commonly used, and the consequent unavailability of the Biblical records to those people, and especially with the increased power and dominance of the Church, any doubts about the doctrine did not surface or were strangled at birth.

But with the onset of the Reformation and the invention of printing there were opportunities for established beliefs to be questioned once more. In Germany, the Low Countries, Switzerland and Poland little communities of Bible-loving Christians sprang up. In almost every case the first orthodox doctrine that they discarded was that of the Trinity. Sadly, in those days the spirit of Theodosius still held sway, and many of those protesters paid for their boldness with their lives.[3]

With the advent of the eighteenth century the power of the European civil and religious authorities to punish those they deemed heretics had passed away. England had reached that stage somewhat earlier. With the removal of such sanctions the anti-trinitarian move gathered pace. Primitive Baptists and Quakers were included in those who dissented from the orthodox faith—not to speak of the Unitarian Church which had a substantial following in the late eighteenth and nineteenth centuries, and still is of considerable size, especially in the United States. (Unfortunately this latter organisation has

---

1. Eccles. Hist. Book II, Cent vi, Ch. 3

2. Quoted by Stannus, p.7.

3. For a full treatment of this topic see A.Eyre: *The Protesters*, and *Brethren in Christ*.

abandoned its original biblical belief that Jesus was born by the power of the Holy Spirit acting on Mary for the view that Christ had a human father). The words of William Penn, the founder of the Quaker movement, illustrates these non-conformist views about the Trinity:[1]

'Before I conclude this head, it is requisite that I should inform thee, reader, concerning the origin of the Trinitarian doctrine: Thou mayest assure thyself, it is not from the Scriptures, nor reason, since so expressly repugnant; although all broachers of their own inventions strongly endeavour to reconcile them with the holy record. Know then, my friend, it was born about three hundred years after the ancient gospel was declared; it was conceived in ignorance, brought forth and maintained by cruelty.[2]

In recent times the doctrine of the Incarnation and the Trinity has again come under the theological spotlight. A group of scholars under the editorship of John Hick published *The Myth of God Incarnate* which questioned many of the basic assumptions underlying the Trinity and its relevance for the Christian world of the post-20th century.

SUMMARY

It now remains for us to bring together the salient features in the development of the Doctrine of the Trinity. We have seen that it was not present in the earliest church, but was formed as a gradual development over the subsequent 400 or so years. It cannot be stressed too strongly that the battle that was finally resolved at the councils of Nicea and Constantinople was not simply between the adherents of a primitive orthodox faith and the protagonists of a heresy. If it was as simple as that the

---

1. Other present-day sects that do not accept the Trinity include the Jehovah's Witnesses, who teach the pre-existence of Jesus but not his equality with the Father. Among other sects the Christadelphians come nearest to the original beliefs.

2. Quoted by Stannus, p.7

demarcation lines of the conflict would have always been clear. Rather the battle was over the development of *a completely new doctrine,* of which the final details were emerging. Hanson's comment emphasises this:

'It is not a story of embattled and persecuted orthodoxy maintaining a long and finally successful struggle against insidious heresy. It should be perfectly clear that at the outset nobody had a single clear answer to the question raised, an answer which had been known in the church and always recognised as true, one which was consistently maintained throughout the whole controversy. ... It was only very slowly, as a result of debate and consideration and the re-thinking of previous ideas, that the doctrine which was later to be promulgated as orthodoxy arose.[1]

In an earlier work the same writer stresses the identical point:

'In order to understand the doctrine of the Trinity it is necessary to understand that the doctrine is a *development, and why it developed* .... It is a waste of time to attempt to read Trinitarian doctrine directly off the pages of the New Testament. The doctrine is an interpretation and development of the witness of the New Testament, not a direct transcription of its words ...'

Hanson then explains how Christianity, once it had outgrown Jewish roots, needed to be able to define its concept of God to the intellectuals of the Graeco-Roman culture. In the following paragraph he sums up the process that the present chapter has attempted to describe. His words should be seriously pondered by those who believe that the doctrine of the Trinity is a basic part of the original Christian message—and they are words that suggest that the divine prediction that forms the title of this chapter is not inaccurate.

---

1. Hanson, p 870

'The answer to this inevitable pressure towards a coherent Christian theology was given by the Church through a process of theological exploration which lasted at least three hundred years. This process has often been represented by theologians in grandiloquent terms as a majestic pondering or an unerring homing towards the truth or an heroic preservation of the faith against the malignant attacks of heresy. In fact it was a *process of trial and error (almost of hit and miss), in which the error was by no means all confined to the orthodox.* In the process of discovering the best way of stating the Christian doctrine of God, theologians like Justin Martyr, Irenaeus and Tertullian, who were in their day regarded as pillars of orthodoxy, held some doctrines which would have been regarded as rankly heretical two centuries later. The process did not give the impression of developing in a straight line of clear and consistent orthodoxy, infallibly guided by some previous instinct for truth, but rather of a history of search in different directions to solve immediate problems, of a pendulum swinging from one extreme to another, of vicissitude and uncertainty and disagreement and revision and reassessment, of new fashions clashing with old loyalties, resulting in a gradual general advance, like the history of any other humane discipline. Science, literary and artistic criticism and historical research advance by a process of trial and error. So does theological development. *It would be foolish to regard the doctrine of the Holy Trinity as having been achieved in any other way.*[1]

So the Trinity is admitted by all to be a new doctrine, not present in the early church, and not even believed by the early Christian Fathers. It owes its origin and its respectability not to the Bible, but to the fumbling of the Church towards a coherent doctrine of God. That Church then used its own authority to impose this new belief on all its adherents as a condition of

---

1. Hanson, *Reasonable Belief - A Survey of the Christian Faith,* pp171-172. Pub: OUP, 1980, Italics ours.

salvation. Mackintosh comments on this with some irony:

'The adoption of a non-Biblical phrase at Nicea constituted a landmark in the growth of dogma; it (the Trinity) is *true,* since the Church—the universal Church speaking by its Bishops— says so; though the Bible does not! ... We have a formula, but what does the formula contain? No child of the Church dare seek to answer.'[1]

Finally, let Rusch sum up:

'Judgments on the development and final formation of the doctrine of the Trinity vary. For some it is the high point of theological and intellectual achievement that preserved the uniqueness of Christianity and allowed it to enter, and finally win, the Graeco-Roman world. *Others have seen the developments traced in this volume as a capitulation of the biblical revelation to a foreign system from which Christianity has still not yet escaped.*'[2]

As but two of the 'others' to whom Rusch refers, the present authors give his latter assessment a hearty 'Amen'.

WHAT THIS CHAPTER HAS SHOWN
In this chapter we have briefly traced the development of the doctrine of the Trinity from the times of the Early Fathers. We have noted the gradual importation of Greek philosophical concepts and language into Christian writing. We have seen how belief in the personal pre-existence of Jesus gradually became established. We have seen that slowly the length of this alleged pre-existence increased from just prior to the Creation to way back into infinite time. We have seen that the previous universal belief in the subordination of the Son to the Father was by degrees changed to one of absolute equality. We have seen that although in this debate the position of the Holy Spirit

---

1. *Encyclopaedia Britannica,* Art. Dogma

2. Rusch, *The Trinitarian Controversy,* p.27 Italics ours

was almost disregarded at first, it was later included to give the Spirit co-equal deity with the Son and the Father. We have seen how the various Councils, some of which were unrepresentative and ill-run, debated this matter and emerged with findings to become binding on all from that time on. And finally we have seen that for the first time the civil power of the Emperor was invoked to compel acceptance of the new doctrine on pain of severe sanctions.

We have also discovered how that due to the priority of Church authority over the teaching the Bible, coupled with the inaccessibility of the Bible to most people, the new doctrine of the Trinity remained unchallenged for over a thousand years until the Reformation. But once the Bible was available in the mother tongue of its readers, one of the first of the established doctrines to be challenged was the doctrine of the Trinity—a challenge that has continued down to the present day.

EPILOGUE

Was the vicar right .... ?

The vicar in our Prologue obviously had strong views on the doctrine of the Trinity. Having heard the evidence, can you share his point of view? Had he accepted the doctrine just because it was part of the long-established position of the Church, or had he deduced it from his own personal study? Would he have taken the same line if he had known that:

> Many of his fellow Trinitarians have accepted that the Trinity is not a Bible doctrine:
>
> the Apostolic church did not teach it; nor did their immediate successors, the 'Apostolic Fathers':
>
> the doctrine of the Trinity is really a product of the 4th century, and was formulated only after considerable opposition at a series of sometimes unrepresentative and poorly run church councils, and established as official church policy by edict of the Roman Emperor:
>
> and that most of the biblical passages commonly used to support the doctrine of the Trinity only appear to do so if they are read with the Trinity already in mind. Taking the passages in their context, and with regard to the intentions of the writers and the understanding of the original readers, no such meaning was intended?

This present volume adduces what we hope to be compelling evidence that the "faith which was once for all (time) delivered to the saints"[1] knew nothing of the doctrine of the Trinity: that it was rather "a capitulation of the biblical revelation to a foreign system from which Christianity has not yet escaped"[2].

It is the authors' prayer that their labours will help some to escape the 'foreign system', and come to recognise and love the 'only true God, and Jesus Christ whom He has sent' and so at last receive the eternal life that will be freely given to those who truly know him[3].

---

1. Jude 3

2. Rusch, W.G.: *The Trinitarian Controversy*, p.27

3. John 17:3

APPENDIX 1 TO CHAPTER 8

THE DEVELOPMENT OF THE TRINITY SUMMARISED

Date

40-90   God a Unity and also the God of Jesus. Jesus great but subordinate.

Jesus pre-existed only in the mind and purpose of God.

All doctrine Bible based.

Deviations in doctrine predicted.

90-120   Early 'Rules of Faith' and Creeds have no trinitarian allusions.

Ebionites and Nazarenes fled from Jerusalem, taking primitive views about Christ.

The 'Apostolic Fathers' regarded God as supreme, Jesus subordinate.

120-150   'Christ' and 'God' used interchangeably by Ignatius, and first references to Christ's personal pre-existence.

150-200   Justin Martyr, the first 'Christian philosopher', and Irenaeus taught that Christ was a pre-existent God, but still subordinate to the Father.

200-300   Clement of Alexandria consciously used Greek philosophy to define Christian beliefs about God and Christ. The relationship of Father, Son and Holy Spirit developed on a Platonic framework.

Tertullian used 'trinitas' to denote the Father, Son and Holy Spirit relationship.

Origen propounded the idea of the 'eternal generation' of the Son, thus paving the way for the Arian controversy about whether the Son was a created being. Meanwhile Paul of Samosata insisted that Jesus was a man who had no previous personal existence.

300-325   The long held belief that Christ was created and was subordinate to the Father was finally and successfully challenged in the Arian controversy. The basis of the present trinitarian doctrine worked out at the Council of Nicea.

381   The Arian dispute finally settled at the Council of Constantinople in favour of what had now become orthodox views. The hitherto unexamined position of the Holy Spirit settled by its inclusion in the co-equal trinity. Emperor Theodosius enforces compliance.

500-600   The Athanasian Creed formulated by an unknown author, and eventually accepted as the official basis for salvation.

c1500   As a result of translations of the Bible into the common languages many individuals and protestant groups renounce the doctrine as unscriptural.

APPENDIX 2 TO CHAPTER 8

On the meaning and use of crucial words in the Trinitarian dispute

For the reader who wishes to enquire more deeply into the arguments used during the discussions on the Arian controversy an insight into the meanings of some of the words used is essential.[1]

hypostasis

This basically means 'anything set under', a 'support' (i.e. the legs of an animal or the base of a statue) and is metaphorically used to describe 'ground of hope', and thus 'confidence'; also 'subsistence, reality, substance, nature, essence'.[2] It occurs five times in Scripture where it is translated 'confidence' (2 Corinthians 9:4; 11:17; Hebrews 3:14), 'substance' (Hebrews 11:1,A.V.), and the 'nature' (A.V.'person') of God (Hebrews 1:3).

ousia

This has the fundamental meaning of 'that which is one's own, one's property, state, condition'; metaphorically the 'being, substance, essence' of a thing.

It can readily be seen that in their metaphorical use *hypostasis* and *ousia* are virtually interchangeable, and they were considered to be such prior to the Arian controversy. The problem was that *ousia* could mean either a particular being or a common essence. Similarly *hypostasis* had this dual meaning, but the idea of a particular entity was more prominent. In the anathemas of the Creed of Nicea *ousia* and *hypostasis* were

---

1. For a detailed consideration of this topic the reader is directed to Hanson, ch.7, from which this summary is taken.

2. This and following definitions from Liddell and Scott, Greek-English Lexicon

used as synonyms.

homo and *homoi*

These are prefixes denoting similarity: *homo* meaning 'the same as', whilst *homoi* means 'like' or 'similar to'.

A lot of the discussion in the fourth century was directed to a fine tuning of the meaning of these words. The Arians were happy to combine 'homoi' and 'ousia' to form *homoi-ousia*, meaning 'of like substance'. By this they alleged that the Son was like the Father, in the sense that any son has the same nature as his father, without being entirely identical to him. This was also the general view of all the bishops prior to Nicea. At that Council, however, the Alexandrine party insisted on *homo-ousia*, (the 'consubstantial' of the Nicea Creed) indicating identity in *every respect,* or 'identity of essence'. *Homo-ousia* was a word sometimes found in earlier Classical and Christian writers, but not in the sense of identity, nor equality. Nor was it found in Scripture.

Whilst the inclusion of this word did not please the hard-line Arians, the majority at the Council, because of the inherent ambiguity in the word *ousia*, were prepared to read their own views into it and so sign the document with a relatively clear conscience. Eusebius the historian, a firm supporter of Arius, agreed to sign on this basis, and his letter back to his church at Caesarea explaining and justifying his change of heart makes interesting reading, and confirms that the Creed of Nicea could have been 'all things to all men'.[1]

In the post-Nicene period, however, this ambiguity proved to

---

1. 'To the very last hour I was firm in my resistance to such formulae as were different from mine. But I did not quarrel about accepting what was not displeasing to me, as soon as the meaning of the words was made clear to me and when it seemed to agree with the beliefs professed by me in the creed which I had introduced'—concluding lines of his Letter to the Church at Caesarea.

be a drawback to the unity which the emperors and some of the bishops so much desired. Despite Nicea the Arians seemed to be winning the day, and the Trinitarians were on the defensive. So the emperor Constantius proposed a simpler creed with broad and imprecise definitions using Scriptural terms, to which he hoped all could agree. Reluctant to go back on Nicea, this proposal was rejected by the Church and much effort was given to trying to reinterpret the use of the crucial words. This was particularly the work of the 'Cappadocian Fathers', Basil and the two Gregories. They arrived at a distinction between the words which, although it was a distinction probably not present originally, enabled them to reconcile both sides. They showed that it was possible to interpret *homoi-ousios to patri* ('like the Father') in the light of *homo-ousios to patri* ('of the same substance as the Father'). The difference between *ousia* and *hypostasis*, they claimed, is as between the universal and the particular. Thus it was possible for God to exist simultaneously in one *ousia* but three *hypostases*; that is, One Substance but Three Persons. In this way a middle path was found between those who complained that the Church was teaching three Gods (three *hypostases*, or three separate beings with different natures), thus denying the unity of God; and those who were holding that there was no distinction at all between the Father and the Son (the Monarchians, or Sabellians). By the Cappadocians' definition the difference between *homoi-ousios* and *homo-ousios* shrank to negligible proportions. At the Council of Constantinople in 381 the desired unanimity was secured, and the parts of the Nicea Creed condemning the 'homoiousians' were deleted, no longer being considered necessary. Thus, as one writer observes: 'The Nicene Fathers led the way by converting what was before a scholastic study into an article of the Catholic Faith ..... which was then forced upon the Oriental Church'.[1]

---

1. Quoted by Lamson, p.340.

APPENDIX 3 TO CHAPTER 8

BOOKS CONSULTED IN THIS STUDY OF THE HISTORY OF THE TRINITY

BETHUNE-BAKER, J,F. An Introduction to the Early History of Christian Doctrine. Methuen. 5th Ed., 1933.

BIGG Cholse, D.D. Professor of Ecclesiastical History. 'The Christian Platonists of Alexandria, (The Bampton Lectures of the Year 1886). Oxford 1913.

BLUNT, J.J., D.D. The Right use of the Early Fathers. Murray, London,1869.

BLUNT, J.J., The History of the Christian Church During the First Three Centuries. Murray, London, 2nd Ed., 1857.

BURTON, Edward, D.D. Lecture upon the Ecclesiastical History of the First Three Centuries. Oxford, 1845.

CHADWICK, H. The Early Church. (Vol 1 of the Pelican History of the Church). Hodder and Stoughton, 1968.

DAILLE, J. On the Right Use of the Fathers. Pub. Bohn, London. 1843.

DUNN, J.D.G. Christology in the Making. 2nd. Ed. SCM Press Ltd, London, 1989.

ENCYCLOPAEDIA BRITANNICA, 14th Ed.

ENCYCLOPEDIA OF EARLY CHRISTIANITY, Editor Everett Fergusson. St. James's Press, Chicago and London, 1990. Arts.: 'Trinity'; 'Neoplatonism'; 'Arianism'.

ENCYCLOPEDIA OF RELIGION, MacMillillan, London and New York, 1987. Article: 'Trinity'

EUSEBIUS. The History of the Christian Church, Penguin Classics Edn. 1988.

EYRE, Alan. The Protesters. Pub. The Christadelphian, 1985.
Brethren in Christ. Pub: Christadelphian Study Service, Australia

GIBBON,E. The Decline and Fall of the Roman Empire.

GOODSPEED, E.J. The Apostolic Fathers, An American Translation. Pub: Independent Press, London. 1950

HANSON, R.P.C. The Search for the Christian Doctrine of God. T & T Clark, Edinburgh, 1989

HAZLET, I. Editor. Early Christianity, Origins and Evolution. SPCK,London, 1991.

LAMSON, A., D.D. The Church of the First Three Centuries. British and Foreign Unitarian Association, London, 1875.

LIETZMANN, Hans. A History of the Early Church. Lutterworth Press, London, 1961.

LION HANDBOOK, The History of Christianity, Ed. T. Dowley. Lion Publishing 1977.

MOSHEIM, J.L., D.D. Ecclesiastical History. Translated by Murdock and Soames, Edited by Stubbs, London,1863. (3 Vols.)

MILLMAN, H. H. Dean of St. Paul's. History of Christianity, A New and Revised Edition, 3 Vols. London, 1863.

MOELLER, W. History of the Christian Church. Swan Sonnenschein & Co. Ltd, London, 1898.

PAINE, Levi Leonard. Professor of Ecclesiastical History at Bangor Theological Seminary. 'A Critical History of the Evolution of Trinitarianism'. Boston and New York, 1900.

PRIESTLY, Joseph. A History of the Corruptions of Christianity. (To which are appended Considerations in Evidence that the Apostolic and Primitive Church was Unitarian). The British and foreign Unitarian

Association, London, 1871

RUSCH, William G. The Trinitarian Controversy. Fortress Press, Philadelphia, 1980.

STANLEY, A.P. History of the Eastern Church. Pub. John Murray, London, 1884

STANNUS Hugh, H. A History of the Doctrine of the Trinity in the Early Church. 1882. London, Christian Life Publishing Co. 281 Strand, London.

WHITE, P.E. The Doctrine of the Trinity. F. Walker, 2nd Ed., 1937.

Index of Scriptural References

391

Index of Scriptural references

Index of Scriptural references

72:1-8, 74
78:38-39, 44
78:40-41, 89
82:1-2, 59
82:6, 59, 74, 175, 196
83:18, 25, 57
86:10, 25
86:12, 56
86:15, 48
89:1,2 45
89:6, 63, 59
89:14, 45
89:26-27, 221
89:28, 45
89:33, 45
90:1-2, 33
92:2, 45
93:2, 33
97:5, 56
97:7, 63
97:9, 63
97:12, 48
98:3, 45
99:2, 63
100:5, 45
102:5-22, 293
102:12, 48
102:24-27, 33
102:25-27, 294
103:8, 48
103:20, 163
103:20-21, 39
104:4, 35
104:29-30, 84
104:30, 245
106:48, 33
110:1, 197
111:4, 48
112:4, 48
116:5, 48
119:105, 141
119:137, 43

119:160, 305
130:3-4, 44
135:13, 48
139:1-4, 37
139:7, 38
143:7,10, 111
145:8, 48
146:4, 84, 273
147:10-11, 259
147:15-18, 244

Proverbs
1:23, 104
3:19, 245
6:23, 141
8:1, 246
8:12, 246
8:22, 356
8:22ff, 246
30:5-6, 137
30:10, 56

Ecclesiastes
1:4, 288, 294
9:5, 273

Isaiah
1:10, 9
2:2-4, 53
3:7, 46
4:1, 52
6:1, 63, 65
6:3, 303
6:5, 65
6:8-9, 192
7:14, 217
8:18, 177
8:19-20, 12
9:6, 59, 111, 195, 221
9:6-7, 74, 151, 174
10:21, 174
11:1-4, 74

11:2, 110, 117
11:2-3, 86
11:11-16, 49
13:13, 294
19:14, 85
26:8, 48
30:27, 50
31:3, 35, 305
32:15, 104
33:14, 40
34:4, 294
40:13, 92
40:28, 33
41:4, 53, 304
42:1, 86, 183
42:5, 86
42:8, 57
43:10, 33
43:10-11, 25
43:13, 227
44:3, 104
44:6, 25, 33
44:8, 16, 26
44:9-20, 42
45:5, 26
45:6, 26
45:18, 26
45:21, 26, 261, 269
45:22, 26
45:22-24, 51
46:10, 37, 162
46:8-10, 222
46:9, 26
46:9-11, 227
47:7, 46
51:9, 222
53:10, 176
55:3, 284
55:10-11, 244
57:15, 33, 63
60:9, 49
61:1, 60, 183

393

Index of Scriptural references

394

Index of Scriptural references

395

Index of Scriptural references

Index of Scriptural references

Index of Scriptural references

Index of Scriptural references

Index of Subjects

Index of Subjects

Index of Subjects

Index of Subjects